INTRODUCTION TO CANADIAN INSURANCE LAW

THIRD EDITION

Craig Brown
Andrew Mercer

Introduction to Canadian Insurance Law, Third Edition
© LexisNexis Canada Inc. 2013
November 2013

Library and Archives Canada Cataloguing in Publication

Brown, Craig, 1949-, author
     Introduction to Canadian insurance law / Craig Brown
and Andrew Mercer. — Third edition.

Includes index.
ISBN 978-0-433-47531-6 (pbk.)

     1. Insurance law—Canada. I. Mercer, Andrew, 1984-, author II. Title.

KE1149.B77 2013   346.71'086   C2013-906896-1
KF1164.B77 2013

Published by LexisNexis Canada, a member of the LexisNexis Group
LexisNexis Canada Inc.
123 Commerce Valley Dr. E., Suite 700
Markham, Ontario
L3T 7W8

Customer Service
Telephone: (905) 479-2665 • Fax: (905) 479-2826
Toll-Free Phone: 1-800-668-6481 • Toll-Free Fax: 1-800-461-3275
Email: customerservice@lexisnexis.ca
Web Site: www.lexisnexis.ca

Printed and bound in Canada.

About the Authors

Craig Brown, Professor of Law at Western University, Canada and Counsel to the law firm Thomas Gold Pettingill, is one of the most well-respected authors in the insurance law field. He is the author of *Insurance Law in Canada, No Fault Automobile Insurance in Canada* and the *Encyclopedia of Insurance Law (Canada)*. He has served as an arbitrator in insurance disputes and advised government, the insurance industry and members of the legal profession on matters of insurance law.

Andrew Mercer is a lawyer at Thomas Gold Pettingill LLP, a litigation boutique in Toronto, Ontario. His practice involves providing opinions and representing clients in insurance coverage disputes and commercial matters. In his insurance coverage practice, he represents both insurers and policyholders.

Preface

This book is designed for those who require a general acquaintance with the principles of insurance law as applied in Canada. It should assist students by proving a framework for managing the detail contained in treatises, casebooks and primary sources. It should also help those engaged in insurance-related fields — such as brokers, actuaries and adjusters — whose work, although not primarily legal, is pursued against a background of legislation, regulations and adjudication. As explained in Chapter 1, this book is not a textbook. Rather, it is a road map for navigating the massive detail of the law.

In this edition, in addition to updates necessitated by new cases and legislation, we have included a new chapter dealing with the rudiments of several classes of insurance explaining how the legal framework differs for each of them. This is intended to further the goal of making the general thrust of insurance law accessible to readers not previously acquainted with it.

We wish to thank again Randy Bundus of Insurance Bureau of Canada for permission to use their glossary of insurance terms which has been modified for use in the book.

Craig Brown
Andrew Mercer
July 2013

Table of Contents

Table of Cases

Chapter 1

The Nature of Insurance Law

INTRODUCTION

Apart from Chapters 16 and 17, this book is about solving legal problems that have to do with insurance contracts. These are the problems (or perhaps questions is a better word), whose answers determine the rights and obligations of people making claims against insurance companies and the rights and obligations of companies in responding to those claims.

Insurance law in the broad sense encompasses more than this. It includes licensing and other forms of regulation of insurance companies and brokers and agents. It includes rules pertaining to government programs like workers' compensation, employment insurance and public health insurance. In Chapter 16, readers are introduced to schemes by which governments in Canada regulate insurance companies, and the regulation of brokers and agents is discussed in Chapter 7. In Chapter 17 we describe some classes of insurance and their distinguishing features from a legal point of view. But, for the most part, our focus is the law relating to the contracts insurers make with their customers.

Note too that, while our subject is the solving of problems, it is not the intention here to present more than a few actual solutions. This is not a textbook.[1] This book is more concerned with asking the right questions than providing the answers. The answers themselves are to be found in the statutes, in the law reports, in the databases, in the digests, in the annotations, in the encyclopaedias, and in the textbooks. There you will find the details of relevant statutes, thousands of decided cases and, possibly, detailed analysis. But navigating all that information requires a road map. That is what this book is: a framework for the systematic approach to insurance law problems. It is based on the conviction of its authors that proper organization of a problem goes more than half way to its solution.

---

[1] For a textbook, see C. Brown & Donnelly, *Insurance Law in Canada*, looseleaf (Toronto: Thomson Carswell).

THE NATURE OF INSURANCE

In order to make sense of insurance law it is necessary first to understand some basic things about insurance itself. One of the objects of insurance law is to make sure that insurance functions as it is supposed to; to ensure a proper balance between insurers' maintaining sufficient financial viability to stay in business and the meeting of their customers' reasonable expectations. So what then is insurance and how is it supposed to function?

Insurance is a mechanism for spreading the risk of loss. Houses burn down. Jewellery is stolen. Ships sink. Courts order people to pay damages. People who face the possibility of occurrences such as these can team up with others in the same position. They can contribute to a fund from which money will be available to pay for losses when they occur. Each contribution, or "premium", is much less than the potential loss the contributor faces. This is possible because the losses covered by the system are random losses. Among a relatively large number of people facing similar risks, only a relative few (whose identity is unknown at the outset) will actually suffer loss. The contributions of the many pay for the losses of the few.

Life insurance is also based on the random occurrence of events but in a slightly different way. Although everyone whose life is insured is certain to die, the deaths are still random in their timing. The premiums for insuring a life are calculated on the basis of its expected duration. Whether an individual life exceeds this expectation or falls short of it is fortuitous. At any point in time, the premiums of the many, together with the income they earn when invested, should cover the cost of claims arising from the relatively few deaths occurring around that time.

The sharing of risk, whether it be the risk of property loss, incurring liability for damages, or premature death, can be arranged, broadly speaking, in one of two ways. The group of individuals can enter into a multilateral agreement wherein each agrees to contribute, along with the others, to make good the loss suffered by any member of the group. While an intermediary may be used, his or her role is merely to coordinate. Part, or even all, of the premium may not be payable until the insurance period has ended, when the volume of loss is known. This is referred to as "mutual" or "reciprocal" insurance. It was the form of early marine insurance (a favourite meeting place for negotiating such matters was a coffee house called "Lloyd's") and is still used today, particularly in agricultural insurance.

The other form by which insurance is arranged is where the intermediary, rather than merely coordinate the mutual promises to contribute to losses, undertakes himself, herself or itself (in the case of a corporation) to pay the losses. The risks faced by each of the contributors are transferred to the professional underwriter who accepts them in exchange for the premium usually paid in advance. These days this is by far the most common form by which insurance is arranged. Except for the syndicates of individual underwriters who operate under the auspices of modern-day Lloyd's, most underwriters are corporations. When we refer to insurance contracts, mostly we mean contracts between underwriters and their customers whereby the former have accepted risks in exchange for premiums.

THE NATURE OF INSURANCE LAW

The essential characteristic of insurance — that it is about the transfer of risk of random loss — distinguishes insurance contracts from other kinds of contracts. It also explains why the law of insurance contracts differs from the law of contracts generally. General contract law applies to insurance transactions. For example, the customer's offer to buy insurance must be accepted by the insurer, or the insurer's agent, before it is binding. But insurance law involves more.

The body of law found in both statutes and case law that applies distinctively to insurance contracts can be explained by reference to five underlying principles. These are utmost good faith, fortuity, indemnity, consumer protection and compensation.

Utmost Good Faith

Although legislation in recent years has given protection to consumers of goods and services in a variety of ways, the traditional rule, "let the buyer beware", still has considerable application. Founded in the theory of free market economics, this rule maximizes economic freedom. If a person wants information relevant to the deal into which he or she is entering, that person bears the burden of asking for it. In the absence of specific questions, which must be answered truthfully, the other party has no obligation to volunteer any information. You need not disclose that the used television you are selling tends frequently to scramble the picture. If the buyer did not ask about that, the buyer cannot seek later to scrap the deal on the ground that you failed to mention the defect.

But it is different with insurance contracts. Given that insurance involves the transfer of risk, courts have long decreed that the parties to insurance contracts do not deal at arm's length. It is reasoned that the nature of risk in any given case is so open-ended that it would be impossible for the insurer, who is being asked to accept the risk, to contemplate in advance all the factors that might relate to it. The customer is therefore bound by a duty of utmost good faith in negotiating the contract to disclose all matters relevant to the risk whether or not the insurer has asked about them. This rule was developed at a time when ship owners and cargo consigners were arranging to underwrite each other's voyages over coffee at Lloyd's. The only source of information about a voyage and its risks was the person who was going to undertake it. It was reasonable to require that person to be completely frank. Today's more sophisticated underwriters perhaps do not need such protection. Indeed, as we shall see, legislation has modified the rule for some classes of insurance.[2] Nonetheless, more than a remnant of the old rule remains.

---

[2] See Chapter 5.

A duty of utmost good faith also rests with insurers. An insurer is not permitted to take advantage of a customer's innocent non-disclosure if the insurer has entered into the contract knowing of the non-disclosure; that is, accepting the premium while expecting never to have to pay out even if loss occurs.[3] Another example of an insurer's duty to act in good faith arises at the claims stage. It is bad faith for an insurer to take advantage of its customer's physical, emotional or financial vulnerability by unreasonably delaying or contesting a claim.[4] This has a particular application in liability insurance. Liability insurers reserve to themselves the authority to defend and settle claims made against the insured person, claims which may result in the insurer having to pay the damages. Despite this authority, an insurer may not decline an offer of settlement of damages without acting in good faith by taking into account the interests of the insured person.[5]

Fortuity

As we have seen, insurance only works if the losses it covers occur randomly; if they are fortuitous. The assumptions on which insurance is based are undermined if successful claims arise out of loss which is not fortuitous. To address this, the rules pertaining to the interpretation of insurance contracts include two presumptions. Unless the words are very clear that the contrary is intended, contracts are presumed not to provide cover for loss that is certain to occur, such as normal wear and tear.[6] It is also presumed that there is no cover for loss that is deliberately caused by a person who will benefit from the insurance. Accordingly, murderers cannot recover under insurance on the life of their victims and arsonists who burn down their own houses cannot collect fire insurance.[7]

Indemnity

Most insurance other than life insurance is indemnity insurance. This is insurance whose objective is to provide for financial loss flowing from misfortune such as damage to property, the incurring of liability to pay damages or personal injury. The arrangement is that the financial loss will be made good by the insurer. But the principle of indemnity requires that no more than the loss actually sustained be paid. A claimant is not permitted to profit from the

---

3   See *e.g., Banque Keyser Ullman SA v. Skandia (UK) Insurance Co.* (1987), 2 W.L.R. 1300.

4   *Whiten v. Pilot Insurance Co.*, [2002] S.C.J. No. 19, 2002 SCC 18 (S.C.C.). See also Chapter 12.

5   *Dillon v. Guardian Insurance of Canada*, [1983] O.J. No. 2534, 2 C.C.L.I. 227 (Ont. H.C.J.). See also Chapter 12.

6   *British and Foreign Marine Insurance Co. v. Gaunt*, [1921] 2 A.C. 41 (H.L.). Note, however, that there may well be cover for the unexpected consequences of wear and tear: see *Consolidated Bathurst Export Ltd. v. Mutual Boiler and Machinery Insurance Co.*, [1979] S.C.J. No. 133, [1980] 1 S.C.R. 888 (S.C.C.). This rule does not, of course, apply to life insurance. Death, after all, is certain to occur. It is its timing that is fortuitous.

7   This issue often arises in the form of a dispute about the meaning of the word "accident", or the word "intentional". See Chapter 9.

situation by receiving more from the insurer than was lost. To allow profit in this sense is thought to be wasteful, and to encourage people, if not actually to engineer loss so as to profit from it, at least to take less care than they otherwise might. This is sometimes called "moral hazard" and its avoidance is the main objective of the indemnity principle.[8]

Several rules of insurance law give effect to this principle. A person who suffers loss which is insured is prevented from keeping both the insurance money and the proceeds of some other claim which that person might have, say against another insurer, a negligent neighbour or a professional guilty of malpractice, in relation to the same loss. If there are claims against more than one insurer, there can be recovery in total only for the amount of loss.[9] Where there is a claim against someone who is not an insurer, as well as an insurer, the insurer is "subrogated" to the other claim, meaning it can be used to reimburse the insurer rather than over-compensating the claimant.[10] The rules about salvage preclude a claimant's being paid insurance money for a total loss of property while keeping the property for its scrap value.[11] When a claim is made, the customer must prove both that loss occurred and how much was lost.[12] It is implicit in this requirement that the loss was suffered by the claimant and not by someone else. In other words she or he has to demonstrate an "insurable interest" in what was lost.[13]

Consumer Protection

In one way or another, much of the law regarding insurance contracts has as an objective the protection of customers. In some instances this is indirect. The rules mentioned previously that have to do mainly with preserving the financial viability of insurers, those upholding the principles of fortuity and randomness for example, serve to further the interests of consumers insofar as they protect the integrity of insurance funds, helping to ensure their availability for legitimate claims.

But much of the content of insurance law is designed directly to protect consumers. This is true of some rules of interpretation of contracts that direct courts to give effect to "reasonable expectations" or to resolve ambiguities in favour of the insured person. This is because insurers are usually more sophisticated than their customers in understanding the business and drafting contracts. In the past, some unscrupulous insurers have taken advantage of this, foisting on unsuspecting buyers terms seriously diminishing the value of the coverage if not rendering it completely worthless. Now insurance contracts in Canada are subject to extensive regulation. For example, fire insurance and accident and

---

8   Another objective is the prevention of gambling. If people were permitted to "insure" other people's property, it would be tantamount to betting on whether that property would be damaged.
9   See Chapter 14.
10 See Chapter 13.
11 *Ibid.*
12 See Chapter 11.
13 See Chapter 6.

sickness insurance contracts must contain certain clauses laid down in legislation.[14] These clauses cannot be modified to the prejudice of the customer. The terms of auto insurance contracts are controlled almost entirely by the government, either by legislative mandate of clauses or by a process whereby wordings must be approved before use.[15]

Other aspects of the contractual process are also subject to regulation. Here are two examples. For most types of insurance an insurer may not insist on payment of the premium before a policy it has delivered to a customer takes effect.[16] An insurer may not refuse to pay out on a loss on the grounds of misrepresentation unless the facts misrepresented are relevant to the insured risk, even if there is a term in the contract appearing to allow it to do so.[17]

Compensation

Much of the law relating to automobile insurance has to do with ensuring the availability of money to compensate the victims of accidents. Originally auto insurance was made up of purely private arrangements; voluntary contracts between insurers and customers to provide certain protection in the event of motor vehicle accidents. Over the years this system of private contracts has been adopted and modified by legislatures as an instrument of public policy.

In every province some form of auto insurance is compulsory. In some, like Quebec and Ontario, the emphasis is on insurance which provides benefits to the person named in the insurance contract and members of his or her family in the event of personal injury or death. In others, like Alberta and New Brunswick, the chief requirement is insurance that will pay the damages suffered by anyone injured or killed as a result of the fault of someone insured under the contract, although the compulsory package includes some first-party benefits as well.

Even insurance designed to pay damages for which an insured person is liable is viewed less as protection for the person who bought the insurance than as providing benefits for injury victims. Legislation gives a person injured in a car accident a direct claim against the insurer of the person who caused the accident. Such a claim succeeds despite any default, such as late payment of premiums or failure to give timely notice of the accident, on the part of the insured person.[18] Other terms of the legislation provide for compensation for the injured person in the event the driver at fault is uninsured or cannot be identified.[19]

For other types of insurance the concern for compensation is less emphatic. But, nonetheless, it is there. The idea of indemnity, mentioned above, is not only the negative concept restricting a claimant's financial recovery, it is also a

---

[14] See *e.g.*, Ontario *Insurance Act*, R.S.O. 1990, c. I.8, ss. 148, 300.
[15] *Ibid.*, s. 227.
[16] *Ibid.*, s. 134.
[17] *Ibid.*, s. 124.
[18] See *e.g.*, New Brunswick *Insurance Act*, R.S.N.B. 1973, c. I-12, s. 250.
[19] *Ibid.*, s. 255.

positive notion. By definition, indemnity is about the making good of losses. Subrogation, for example, described above as a mechanism for ensuring claimants do not profit from insurance, does not arise until an insurer has made good the loss or at least undertaken to do so. And those rules that can be put down to consumer protection are really about giving those who buy insurance reasonable treatment when it comes to providing for loss.

Life insurance, although not indemnity insurance, also has a compensation rationale. A fundamental rule of life insurance law is that no person can insure the life of another without an insurable interest in that life. The historical reason for this rule was the elimination of gambling on the date of death of a famous person, a practice apparently popular in the 18th century. A gambling contract can be drawn in terms similar to an insurance contract which, after all, turns on speculation. Legislation was introduced to distinguish real insurance from disguised gambling. The distinguishing feature of insurance proper was a relationship between the person buying the insurance and the person whose life was insured such that the former could be said to suffer a loss if the latter died, a loss for which some form of compensation was appropriate.

Note that different rationales of insurance law have arisen at different times. At a point in time a prevalent risk has generated the need for insurance of a certain type. In turn that insurance has sometimes required a legal framework to curb abuse or, better, to pursue public policy goals. The viability of early marine insurance turned on full disclosure of the risk. This led to the development of the utmost good faith principle. Increasing urbanization and industrialization created risks which gave rise to fire insurance, workers' compensation and liability insurance. Rules were developed by courts and legislatures to protect consumers of insurance, while at the same time enabling insurers to remain solvent so as to have the funds to pay consumers' reasonable claims. In the 21st century this process has accelerated with the technology revolution. The point is that, to be fully understood, the rules of insurance law need to be seen in context, particularly in a historical context.

SUMMARY

Insurance law differs from other areas of commercial law because insurance is about the transfer of the risk of fortuitous loss. Its goal is to strike a proper balance in protecting both the financial viability of insurers and the legitimate interests of their customers. Accordingly, insurance law is based on the principles of:

- utmost good faith;
- fortuity;
- indemnity;
- consumer protection; and
- compensation.

Chapter 2

How Legal Issues Arise in Insurance

INTRODUCTION

The key stage in approaching any problem involving issues of insurance law is the identification of what precisely those issues are. Once the right questions are asked, work can begin on finding the appropriate legal answers. An insurance contract creates obligations for both the insurer and the customer. When there is a dispute about whether one of the parties has failed to live up to his or her side of the bargain, the law provides a means for resolving it. This may entail a court action. But, whatever the process, it involves posing and answering certain questions. These are the issues.

Not all disputes about unmet obligations involve legal issues. Consider, for example, the customer's principal obligation: to pay premiums. Whether or not premiums have been paid is a matter on which the parties might disagree. While it is a disagreement that might need a court to sort it out, it is a question of fact rather than law.

In contrast, take the case where the customer has paid the premium to a broker rather than to the insurer. Let us assume this is a fact about which there is no dispute. But there may be a dispute about whether paying premiums to a broker satisfies the obligation to pay the insurer. This is a question of law. In other words, in this context, the question "has the customer met his or her obligation to pay premiums?" can only be answered by resorting to the relevant law.

DETERMINATION OF AN INSURER'S OBLIGATION TO PAY

The insurer's main obligation is to pay the appropriate amount of money or, for property damage, otherwise make good the loss when a valid claim is made. If there is a disagreement about the validity of the claim, it may involve a dispute about facts, the law or both. Assuming the facts are agreed upon, whether a claim is valid as a matter of law may turn on one or more of many issues.

Perhaps the chief legal principle applicable here is that people must live up to the contracts into which they enter. Therefore the fundamental question, or legal issue, is whether the facts demonstrate that a contract was made at all. If it was, an issue almost as fundamental is: what did it provide? This raises questions of interpretation for which the law provides guidelines.

Even where there is a contract and no problem with respect to its interpretation, there may still be a dispute as to whether the insurer has to pay out. The insurer may claim to be excused from its obligation because the customer has failed to meet one of his or her obligations. In addition to paying premiums, the customer must disclose all information relevant to the insurance when the contract is negotiated. There are usually also numerous other conditions which have to be met, such as keeping the insurer informed about relevant changes in circumstances and complying with requirements of time and form when it comes to making claims. Failure to meet these conditions may mean loss of the insurance contract's protection. Thus, a legal issue may be whether the customer has satisfied the conditions on which a valid claim must be based.

But the terms of a contract an insurer relies upon to deny coverage may be inconsistent with the requirements of legislation. Insurers are not permitted to use contract terms that are inconsistent with legislation.[1] Added to this, there may be case law, binding judicial precedent, which must also be taken into account. This shows how legal issues can become complex. Not only is it necessary to ask whether a condition has been satisfied, it is also necessary to ask whether the condition itself is permitted. There are questions of interpretation of the contract, questions of interpretation of legislation that governs the contract and questions of interpretation of the case law bearing upon the issue as well.

Questions about the validity of claims make up the bulk of disputes which arise and call for resolution by resort to insurance law. But there are other matters too. In some limited circumstances people outside the contractual relationship may have claims under the policy. There are rules of insurance law that resolve them. After an insurer has paid a claim, it may be entitled to reimbursement, wholly or partially, from another insurer or some other person. Insurance law determines when such rights arise.

IDENTIFYING POTENTIAL ISSUES

A useful method of issue-spotting is to review the facts of a problem against a checklist of the possible legal issues that might arise. The items on this list must necessarily be general for the most part. New issues and sub-issues are continually being created by new forms of words used in contracts, new legislation, and new arguments raised about old questions by ingenious lawyers. How this list is arranged is entirely arbitrary. But there should be some logic to it. The goal is to avoid missing some issue or, less importantly, to avoid unnecessary duplication of inquiry.

One way to provide a methodical review of possible issues is to arrange them in order, corresponding more or less to the chronology of the life of an insurance contract under which a claim is made. The checklist can be divided into sub-parts corresponding to: (1) issues relating to events preceding the making of

---

[1]   See *e.g.*, Ontario *Insurance Act*, R.S.O. 1990, c. I.8, s. 126.

the contract; (2) issues relating to the contents of the contract; and (3) issues relating to events arising after loss has occurred.

A list built along these lines looks like this:

1. *Pre-contractual Issues*

    •   Did the customer have the kind of interest in the thing or person insured which the law recognizes as an "insurable interest"?[2]
    •   What are the parties required to disclose to each other when negotiating the contract, and did they meet this requirement?
    •   What are the legal implications of the role played by a broker in arranging the contract? For example:

        •   did the broker have authority to commit the insurer?
        •   what if the broker received true and complete information from the customer but transmitted false or incomplete information to the insurer?
        •   what are the circumstances that cause the broker to be liable to either party and did they arise in this case?

2. *Issues Relating to the Contract*

    •   Was the contract in force at the relevant time?

        •   had it been formed?
        •   had it been renewed?
        •   had it come to an end?

    •   What did the contract provide?

        •   what do the words used mean?
        •   was the loss caused by one of the perils specified in the coverage?[3]
        •   was the loss fortuitous?
        •   is the loss excluded?
        •   what are the conditions of maintaining coverage, and have they been met?

---

[2] As we shall see in Chapter 6, this is a pre-contractual question only for non-indemnity insurance. For indemnity insurance, it is only relevant at the time of loss. To be strictly precise, insurable interest should appear at a different place on the checklist depending on the type of insurance. But given the purpose of the checklist, to promote efficient canvassing of issues, it does not really matter where it is placed, as long as it is there somewhere.

[3] Although this is a matter that can only be determined after loss, it nonetheless relates to the terms of the contract as concluded. In most cases, every issue, whether it relates to the contents of the contract, or the negotiations, comes up only after loss has occurred and a claim lodged. Again, it does not really matter where on the list an item appears, as long as it is there and its placement makes sense to the user.

3.   *Issues Relating to the Claims/Settlement Process*

- What are the obligations of the insured for providing notice and proof of loss and otherwise cooperating in the disposal of the claim, and have they been met?
- Are there grounds for excusing defects in the claim?
  - do the criteria for obtaining relief from forfeiture exist?
  - has the insurer waived, or is it estopped from raising, the defect as an answer to the claim?
- Has the insurer dealt with the claim in a manner consistent with the duty of good faith owed the insured?
- Does the case involve liability insurance?
  - must the insurer pay for the defence of the action by the third party against the insured?
  - has the insured met his or her obligations regarding dealings with the third party?
- If the claim has been settled, in what circumstances may it be reopened, and do any of those circumstances exist in this case?
- What are the options for dispute resolution?
  - are arbitration and/or appraisal required or available? If so, what are the conditions, procedure, *etc.*?
  - have the pre-conditions been met for litigation? Is it too late?

- Does the insurer have any subrogation rights?
- Does the insurer have any salvage rights?
- Are there multiple insurers? If so, what rules apply to determine each one's liability?
- Do any persons, not party to the contract of insurance, have rights against the insurer? For example:
  - beneficiaries
  - assignees
  - judgment creditors
  - unnamed insureds?

Chapter 3

Where to Find Insurance Law

INTRODUCTION

In the previous Chapter we considered the questions of law that can come up in relation to insurance contracts. Now the focus shifts to the answers. Not specific answers but the sources to be consulted for finding them.[1] There are five types of material that might contain answers to the legal questions posed by a particular set of facts. These are: legislation, regulations, judicial decisions (case law), insurance contracts themselves and agreements among insurers.

LEGISLATION

Federal versus Provincial Jurisdiction

The federal parliament and the provincial legislatures are empowered by the Canadian Constitution[2] to enact laws within their respective spheres of jurisdiction. In the field of insurance federal powers relate mainly to the incorporation, winding up, licensing and related regulation of insurance companies.[3] It is the provinces which have jurisdiction over the law pertaining to most insurance contracts.[4] This means that the law discussed in this book is almost entirely subject to provincial control. The fact that some of that law has evolved over

---

[1] To lawyers the term "source of law" has two slightly different meanings. It might be used to denote an institution authorized by the constitution to create or pronounce law. In this sense Parliament is a source of law; so is a judge. The alternative use of the term refers to the *products* of those institutions. Thus a statute enacted by Parliament or a regulation promulgated pursuant to authority delegated by Parliament is a "source" of law. These are material which you can consult in order to discover the rules that make up the law. The same is true of the reasoned decisions issued by judges.

[2] *Constitution Act, 1982*, being Schedule B of the *Canada Act 1982* (U.K.), 1982, c. 11.

[3] Federal legislation also governs marine insurance contracts. See *Marine Insurance Act*, S.C. 1993, c. 22.

[4] *Citizens Insurance Co. v. Parsons* (1881), 7 App. Cas. 96 (P.C.). Canada's *Constitution Act, 1867* (U.K.), 30 & 31 Vict., c. 3, makes no specific mention of "insurance". The *Parsons* case established that provincial jurisdiction with respect to insurance contracts arises under its general powers over "property and civil rights" and does not encroach upon the federal "trade and commerce" power.

time through the decisions of judges in Canada and elsewhere does not affect this. The legislature of a province is free at any time to abolish or modify any aspect of contract law applying there.

Provincial Insurance Acts

All the provinces and territories of Canada have used this power to shape insurance contract law extensively. Each has legislation dealing with most aspects of insurance contracts made within its boundaries. Apart from that concerning auto insurance, which varies widely, the legislation is similar in most provinces. In Quebec, because of the distinct language and legal tradition, the statute is structured differently, but for the most part the rules themselves are broadly similar to those elsewhere.

The provincial statutes[5] deal both with the form and content of contracts. They include rules about disclosure and misrepresentation in negotiations, entry into force, the contents of policies, notice and proof of loss, valuation of loss, salvage, subrogation, contribution among multiple insurers, third party rights and termination of contracts. For some classes of contracts they even mandate some of the terms. There is a high probability that part, if not all, of the solution to a legal problem relating to an insurance contract will be found in a statute.

The Framework of Provincial Insurance Statutes

Finding one's way around the insurance acts in most provinces is complicated by the fact that they provide not one set of rules, but several. For the purpose of regulating contracts, insurance has been divided into several classes, each of which has different rules. For example, the question of what the obligations of the customer are regarding disclosure of information during negotiations may be responded to differently according to the class of insurance. Different classes exist because provincial insurance statutes are the product of piecemeal tinkering. At one time there were problems with fire insurance, so legislation was passed to deal with them. At another time the focus was life insurance, or auto insurance, and so on.[6]

---

[5] In most provinces the principal statute is called the *Insurance Act*. See *e.g.*, Ontario *Insurance Act*, R.S.O. 1990, c. I.8. In Quebec the relevant provisions are part of the *Civil Code of Québec*, S.Q. 1991, c. 64 (Art. 2389 *ff*). In Newfoundland there are several statutes, each dealing with a distinct class of insurance; see *e.g.*, *Fire Insurance Act*, R.S.N. 1990, c. F-10. Four provinces, British Columbia, Manitoba, Quebec and Saskatchewan, also have statutes applicable to their respective government-run auto insurance schemes.

[6] Most additions or changes to the legislation have been the product of the annual conferences of insurance regulators from across the country. The agenda of such a meeting includes whatever is topical at the time. The regulators draft a solution which is then recommended to respective governments. In this way accident and sickness legislation appeared in 1921, fire insurance and life insurance in 1925, and automobile insurance in 1932. This is not to say that legislation did not exist before. But these meetings provided a major impetus for legislation and are the reason that much of it is uniform among most provinces and territories.

Those classes given separate treatment in this way are fire, life, automobile, accident and sickness, livestock (in all but Alberta, British Columbia, Newfoundland and Nova Scotia), weather (in Alberta, Manitoba, New Brunswick, Prince Edward Island and Saskatchewan) and marine insurance. There are other provisions devoted to insurance contracts generally. These apply to classes of insurance not otherwise covered and augment the material relating to some of the specified classes.

Rules enacted for marine insurance usually take the form of a separate act. There is a federal statute[7] (enacted because of some uncertainty about constitutional jurisdiction in the field) and parallel legislation in British Columbia,[8] Manitoba,[9] New Brunswick[10] and Ontario.[11] In Nova Scotia[12] and Quebec,[13] it is part, albeit a separate part, of the general body of insurance contract legislation. In Alberta, Prince Edward Island and the Yukon Territory, marine insurance is not treated as a distinct class in the provincial legislation but is presumably covered by the federal Act which is also the case for Newfoundland.[14]

For the other classes the typical pattern is to deal with them as discrete parts of the same act. For example, in Ontario's Act,[15] fire insurance is the subject of Part 4, life insurance Part 5, auto insurance Part 6 and accident and sickness Part 7. Part 3 relates to contracts generally except marine, life and accident and sickness insurance contracts. In Newfoundland, the corresponding groupings are contained in separate statutes.[16] In Alberta and British Columbia there is no longer a separate part devoted to fire insurance since it is rare these days for insurance to cover only the risk of fire. In these provinces what was formally applicable only to fire insurance has now been absorbed into the part dealing with insurance contracts generally.[17]

Quebec's legislation is organized in a way different from all other jurisdictions in Canada. Material concerning insurance contracts is included in the *Civil Code of Québec*.[18] It is structured according to a broad distinction between marine insurance and non-marine insurance. Marine insurance rules are similar to those contained in the Marine Insurance Acts of other provinces. Non-marine insurance is subdivided into "insurance of persons" dealing with "the life health

---

[7] See *Marine Insurance Act*, S.C. 1993, c. 22.

[8] *Insurance (Marine) Act*, R.S.B.C. 1996, c. 230.

[9] *Marine Insurance Act*, R.S.M. 1987, c. M40.

[10] *Marine Insurance Act*, R.S.N.B. 1973, c. M-1.

[11] *Marine Insurance Act*, R.S.O. 1990, c. M.2.

[12] R.S.N.S. 1989, c. 231, Part IX.

[13] *Civil Code of Québec*, S.Q. 1991, c. 64, Arts. 2505-2628.

[14] In Newfoundland and the Northwest Territories, not only is there no separate marine insurance legislation, the general insurance legislation expressly states that it does not apply to marine insurance.

[15] R.S.O. 1990, c. I.8.

[16] For example, *Insurance Contracts Act*, R.S.N.L. 1990, c. I-12.

[17] Alberta *Insurance Act*, R.S.A. 2000, c I-3, Part 5; British Columbia *Insurance Act*, R.S.B.C. 2012, c. 1, Part 2.

[18] *Civil Code of Québec*, S.Q. 1991, c. 64, Arts. 2389*ff.*

and physical integrity of the insured"[19] and "damage insurance" which includes property insurance and liability insurance.[20] Some of the articles under property insurance are devoted exclusively to fire insurance.[21]

Another respect in which Quebec's legislative pattern is different is in the treatment of auto insurance. That is the subject of a separate statute mainly because basic auto insurance is sold by a government administered monopoly.[22] Government schemes, governed by separate legislation, also operate in British Columbia,[23] Manitoba[24] and Saskatchewan.[25]

Identifying the Appropriate Legislation

Clearly then, solving a legal problem relating to an insurance contract requires not only reference to legislation, or reference to the right piece of legislation, but the right part of that legislation. A vital question, early in the process is: what class (in terms of the statutory framework) of insurance are we dealing with?

It might seem that this would not be problematic; that the appropriate classification would be self-evident. After all, fire insurance, car insurance and life insurance are all conceptually distinct. But, for several reasons, there can indeed be problems. Some classes are identified by peril, such as fire. Others are designated by subject matter, like automobile. What part of the legislation applies to a problem involving a car which has been destroyed by fire? When someone is killed in an accident, and the event is covered by insurance, is it life insurance or accident insurance? Another difficulty is that it is common these days for insurance on property to cover loss not just from fire but also from numerous other perils such as theft or vandalism. Is such a contract governed by several different sets of statutory rules depending upon what happens to the property, or does just one set of rules apply? If so, which set?

The answers to questions like this are found partly in the legislation itself and partly in case law. In Quebec the structure of the legislation itself all but eliminates the problem because the classes are defined in such a way that overlap is almost impossible. In the other provinces and territories it is the structure of the legislation which has created the problem. Therefore, additional provisions are necessary merely to guide the reader through that structure. Some of these define terms like "life insurance".[26] Others are "application" sections. One is included near the beginning of each part stating to what it applies.

---

[19] *Ibid.*, Arts. 2391-2392.

[20] *Ibid.*, Art. 2396.

[21] *Ibid.*, Arts. 2485-2486.

[22] Quebec *Automobile Insurance Act*, R.S.Q. 1977, c. A-25.

[23] *Insurance (Motor Vehicle) Act*, R.S.B.C. 1996, c. 231.

[24] Manitoba *Public Insurance Corporation Act*, R.S.M. 1987, c. P215.

[25] *Automobile Accident Insurance Act*, R.S.S. 1978, c. A35.

[26] See *e.g.*, Ontario *Insurance Act*, R.S.O. 1990, c. I.8, s. 1:

"Life insurance" means an undertaking by an insurer to pay insurance money,

   (a)   on death,

   (b)   on the happening of an event or contingency dependent upon human life,

   (c)   at a fixed or determinable future time, or

Here is an illustration of how these provisions work. Consider the example of a ship's cargo which is lost in a fire while the ship is at sea. Assume the loss is covered by a contract of insurance. Assume as well that there is a question about salvage rights. On the face of it, this might be a question of marine insurance, or it might be one of fire insurance. The problem is we find that marine insurance and fire insurance legislation have different rules about salvage. Therefore, in order to answer the legal question, it is necessary first to determine the appropriate classification. The Marine Insurance Acts declare themselves to apply to insurance which covers losses, principally to a ship or its cargo, occurring on a "voyage or marine adventure at sea or on an inland waterway, during delays incidental thereto, or during transit otherwise than by water incidental to a voyage or marine adventure."[27] That seems to fit our example but it does not eliminate all uncertainty. Might not this also be fire insurance? We have now to check the fire insurance provisions. We find help both in the definition of "fire insurance"[28] (a contract is not fire insurance if the cover against loss by fire is merely incidental to other coverage) and in the application section in the fire insurance part. The latter tells us that the fire insurance legislation does not apply, even though the peril of fire is covered, whenever the contract falls within the class of marine insurance.[29]

Statutory definitions and application sections like these solve most classification problems.[30] Our example of insurance coverage for a car destroyed by fire would be easily settled. The case would be governed by the rules dealing with auto insurance unless the insurance was restricted to damage occurring on designated premises or the vehicle (like a farm vehicle) was not required to be registered for use on the road.[31]

The answer is less clear when insurance on other types of property is involved. This is because it is usual for contracts to insure property against multiple perils including fire. Houses and their contents are insured against flood, theft, fire and so on. The fire insurance part provides that it is to apply to insurance against loss or damage arising from the peril of fire except: (a) insurance falling within certain other classes of insurance; or (b) where the peril of fire is an incidental peril to the coverage provided.[32] It would seem from this

---

(d) for a term dependent on human life, and ... includes,

(e) accidental death insurance but not accident insurance,

(f) disability insurance, and

(g) ... an annuity ...

Disability insurance is defined separately and refers to cover attached to life insurance. Insurance against disability not included in a life insurance contract is not governed by life insurance legislation.

Note too that insurance providing cover in the event of an accident is "accident insurance" not "life insurance", unless there is cover for non-accidental death too.

[27] See *e.g.*, Ontario *Insurance Act, ibid.*, ss. 2–4.

[28] See *ibid.*, s. 1.

[29] See *ibid.*, s. 143.

[30] See *ibid.*, s. 143 (fire), s. 226 (auto), s. 291 (accident and sickness), ss. 32, 33 (livestock), ss. 334–36 (weather).

[31] *Ibid.*, s. 226.

[32] *Ibid.*, s. 143.

that it must be decided, in a particular case, whether fire is merely an incidental part of the coverage.[33] However, it has now been decided by the Supreme Court of Canada that the legislation dealing with fire insurance does not apply to modern multi-peril policies even where one of the perils insured against is fire.[34]

Thus, it would appear, the fire part of an Insurance Act applies only to policies restricted to fire loss coverage. However, in limited circumstances, a single contract may still be governed by more than one part of the legislation. A contract which is primarily fire insurance (and governed by the fire part of the legislation) may nonetheless provide what the legislation refers to as "extended" cover against riot, civil commotion, war or invasion. Such extended cover is not subject to the fire insurance legislation[35] but falls under that part of the legislation dealing with insurance contracts generally.

REGULATIONS

Provincial insurance legislation invariably empowers the government to make detailed regulations without further recourse to the legislature. The only requirement is that the regulations are within the scope of the authority provided by the statute. Typical of regulations bearing upon insurance contracts are those containing details of mandatory auto no-fault insurance[36] and uninsured motorist cover.[37] They provide all the terms of those types of contracts except for the amount of premium.

CASE LAW

All of the provinces and territories of Canada, except Quebec, derive their legal systems from England. The foundation of English law is the Common Law, a system which evolved case by case over the centuries. That tradition has been continued in Canada. Pronouncements of law by judges in giving reasons for decisions in individual cases constitute primary authorities. The strength of this authority varies with the court. Judgments of the Supreme Court of Canada must be followed by all other Canadian courts when deciding similar cases. Courts are bound in this sense by the decisions of all higher courts in their hierarchy. For example, the British Columbia Supreme Court must follow precedents set

---

[33] *Chiasson v. Century Insurance Co. of Canada*, [1978] N.B.J. No. 65, 21 N.B.R. (2d) 192 (N.B.C.A.); *Slijepcevic v. State Farm Fire & Casualty Co.*, [1979] O.J. No. 4427, 26 O.R. (2d) 566 (Ont. C.A.).

[34] *KP Pacific Holdings Ltd. v. Guardian Insurance Co. of Canada*, [2003] S.C.J. No. 24, 2003 SCC 25 (S.C.C.); *Churchland v. Gore Mutual Insurance Co.*, [2003] S.C.J. No. 25, 2003 SCC 26 (S.C.C.).

[35] See *e.g.*, Ontario *Insurance Act*, R.S.O. 1990, c. I.8, s. 144.

[36] See *e.g.*, *Automobile Accident Insurance Benefits Regulations*, Alta. Reg. 352/72; *Statutory Accident Benefits Schedule*, O. Reg. 776/93.

[37] *Uninsured Automobile Coverage*, R.R.O. 1990, Reg. 676.

by the British Columbia Court of Appeal. Decisions of courts in other provinces or foreign jurisdictions are also frequently referred to by Canadian courts at all levels. Such decisions are not technically binding but may be highly persuasive depending upon the country of origin and rank of the court whose judgment is being considered. Judgments of the House of Lords and the Court of Appeal of England are usual afforded great weight in Canada. Those of Australia, New Zealand and, increasingly in insurance cases, the United States are also treated as persuasive.

In insurance law cases, courts resort to the decisions of other courts in earlier cases to discover: (1) how legislation has been interpreted; (2) how typical contract language has been interpreted; or (3) law that has been developed entirely by the courts. Historically, court-developed law can be traced to three sources, those bodies of English Law known as Equity, Common Law and the Law Merchant, but, for practical purposes, they have merged into a single category, usually called Common Law.

It is important to note that a rule found in case law may be modified or even abolished by legislation. Therefore caution must be exercised when reading a judicial precedent lest it has been subsequently displaced by statute. The point is doubly important in connection with foreign precedents for it is frequently the case that other countries have less or different legislation. For example, in solving a problem about a customer's duty of disclosure during negotiations for a fire or auto insurance in Ontario, English cases are of little use because the Ontario *Insurance Act* has significantly modified the common law in that area.

THE TERMS OF THE CONTRACT

An obvious place to look for the rights and obligations of the parties to an insurance contract is the written evidence of the contract itself; that is, the policy. Strictly speaking, a policy is not a source of "law" but it can be as important as statutes or cases in defining an insurance entitlement. That is because, despite extensive law on most aspects of insurance, there is still room for the contracting process. In other words, subject to some limits, parties can make their own rules. Indeed, there are even times when party-made rules may differ from those laid down by case law or even legislation. For example, case law has established that an insurer is entitled to exercise subrogation rights only when the claimant has been fully indemnified. But it is permissible, and common, for policies to grant an insurer these rights when only partial payment has been made.[38] Similarly, the statutory rule that a claimant's criminal conduct does not automatically invalidate the claim may be reversed by the terms of the contract.[39]

---

[38] See Chapter 13.

[39] See *e.g.*, Ontario *Insurance Act*, R.S.O. 1990, c. I.8, s. 118.

INDUSTRY AGREEMENTS

Occasionally insurers, in agreements concluded collectively with other members of the industry, commit themselves in ways which affect their position when it comes to dealing with claimants. In this sense such agreements may be regarded as sources of answers to legal questions arising out of contracts between insurers and their customers.

Two industry agreements which fall into this category are the "Agreement Respecting Standardization of Claim Forms and Practices, and Guidelines for the Settlement of Claims" which, among other things, commits insurers to waiving their strict rights to written notice and proof of loss in cases of small claims, and the "Agreement of Guiding Principles with Respect to Overlapping Coverages Relating to Property Insurance" which determines the amount recoverable from each insurer in certain cases of multiple insurance. These are multilateral arrangements devised under the auspices of the Insurance Bureau of Canada.

CROSS-BORDER ISSUES

Because insurance is a matter of provincial jurisdiction, sometimes legislated rules of insurance law may vary from province to province. There are differences, as well, in the law between provinces and other countries such as the United States. This can be significant if a person enters into an insurance contract in one jurisdiction and suffers loss, arguably covered by the contract, in another jurisdiction. In the event of a dispute about coverage, issues may arise as to where the dispute should be litigated and which law should apply.

A court in a province will hear a case if it is satisfied it has a "real and substantial" connection with the case bearing in mind where the parties reside, where the facts occurred, where the witnesses live and so forth.[40] On accepting jurisdiction over a case, a court will not necessarily apply the law applicable to its territory. It will apply the law that the parties intended to apply. If that is not clear, it will apply the system of law with which the contract has its closest and most real connection.[41] For insurance other than life insurance, *e.g.*, accident and sickness insurance and marine insurance, most provinces have legislation providing that its law applies to insurance contracts made there, or covering property situated there or insured persons resident there.[42]

Automobile insurance gives rise to particular cross-border problems because of the contiguous nature of North American jurisdictions and the propensity for

---

[40] See *e.g.*, *M.J. Jones Inc. v. Kingsway General Insurance Co.*, [2004] O.J. No. 1087, 185 O.A.C. 113 (Ont. C.A.).

[41] *Imperial Life Assurance Co. of Canada v. Colmenares*, [1967] S.C.J. No. 30, [1967] S.C.R. 443 (S.C.C.).

[42] See *e.g.*, Ontario *Insurance Act*, R.S.O. 1990, c. I.8, s. 123. *Cf. Civil Code of Québec*, S.Q. 1991, c. 64, Art. 3119. For provisions relating to life and accident and sickness insurance, see *e.g.*, Ontario *Insurance Act*, ss. 173, 292 respectively.

people to travel by car. These problems are addressed by a complex mix of legislation, regulations, case law and agreements between insurance regulators. For example, where an insured person carries the minimum amount of third-party liability coverage permitted in his or her home province and incurs liability in excess of that in another province with a higher minimum, legislation in most provinces provides that the higher amount applies.[43] A similar rule applies to no-fault personal injury benefits in that a person suffering injury in a province other than that where he or she lives is entitled to the higher of the benefit levels in his or her policy or those required in the province where the accident happened.[44]

So-called no-fault regimes differ from province to province in another respect. There is considerable variation in the extent to which the right to sue an at-fault driver is curtailed. In Manitoba and Quebec the right is completely abolished. In other provinces, such as Newfoundland and British Columbia, the right to sue remains intact although damages recoverable are reduced by the amount of no-fault benefits available. In Ontario, a person may sue only if his or her injuries meet a threshold of severity. In Saskatchewan motorists choose between no-fault cover and cover that allows them to sue and be sued. Occasionally an injured person brings a suit in one province with respect to injuries suffered in an accident that occurred in another. In general the rule is that the law of the place where the accident happens applies,[45] except where that would result in injustice.[46]

SUMMARY

The rules governing disputes about insurance contracts are found in:

- statutes and regulations (mainly provincial);
- cases previously decided by courts;
- the terms of contracts; and
- industry agreements.

These include rules to resolve dispute involving cross-border issues.

---

[43] See *e.g.*, Ontario *Insurance Act*, R.S.O. 1990, c. I.8, ss. 45(1), 252.
[44] This arises from the reciprocity provisions (see *ibid.*) and/or an agreement between governments or undertakings filed by insurers in other jurisdictions.
[45] *Tolofson v. Jensen*, [1994] S.C.J. No. 110, [1994] 3 S.C.R. 1022 (S.C.C.).
[46] *Lau v. Li*, [2001] O.J. No. 1389, 26 C.C.L.I. (3d) 94 (Ont. S.C.J.).

Chapter 4

Making and Ending an Insurance Contract

A critical issue for someone claiming under an insurance contract is whether, at the relevant time, there was indeed a contract in force. It is a complete answer to a claim if the insurer can show that no obligations were undertaken or, if they were, they have expired. It is therefore important to know when and how a contract is created, when and how it ceases to be, and the circumstances by which it is renewed.

MAKING A CONTRACT

Offer, Acceptance and Consideration

A contract is based on agreement. This is established by one party offering terms to another who accepts those terms. They cannot be at cross purposes or equivocal. They must be of one mind. But this is not all. To be enforceable by a court, an agreement must involve an exchange of promises to give something of value. It is not a contract in the legal sense if a woman offers to rake leaves for her neighbour and he merely "accepts" her kind offer; that is, if her promise is merely gratuitous. He must promise to give something in return, like money, or doing her laundry, or refraining from cutting down a tree. This is called "consideration".

And so it is with insurance contracts. Except in the case of a renewal, it is usually the customer who makes the offer. This is so even where the insurer has solicited the business and provided the form on which the particulars of the proposed insurance are set out. So, if an insurer's representative said to a prospective customer, "would you like to buy some insurance for $X per year?" and the customer responded, "yes", a contract would not normally have been established at that point. The context of the conversation and the process that would then commence would demonstrate that the representative was really saying, "If you would like insurance on these terms, make a proposal to that effect to the insurer."

The reason an insurer prefers to operate this way is that time is needed to assess the risk that will be undertaken if a contract is made. It may be that the representative is empowered to accept the proposal on the spot, but this is usually only on a temporary basis. So the customer proposes and, as far as long-term contracts are concerned, the insurer accepts or rejects it. If it is accepted, the contract is created when that acceptance is put in the mail or otherwise communicated to the customer.

As with other types of contracts, it is necessary that the insurer accepts terms as offered. If the "acceptance" contains new terms it is not an acceptance at all, but rather a counter-offer. There is no contract until the customer accepts the revised terms.

However, it would be misleading to suggest that all the terms of insurance contracts are established in this way. Policies, which are the written evidence of insurance contracts, are invariably lengthy documents containing many terms.[1] Sometimes entire sections of a policy are included only because they form part of an all-or-nothing package, not because they were requested or even contemplated by the customer when the offer was made. Yet they still constitute part of the coverage purchased. Even the requested coverage is circumscribed by details, such as the time limits for notifying the insurer of loss and matters to be included in the proof of that loss, which are seldom in the mind of customers when contracts are formed. But it is not suggested that they are any less part of the contract because of that.

Some contract terms are imposed by law. For example, accident and sickness insurance contracts include mandatory statutory conditions. No-fault auto insurance contracts are almost entirely mandated by legislation or regulation. The only thing insurer and customer need to agree on is the type of contract. Indeed even that is hardly the product of free choice, at least on the customer's part, since auto insurance is compulsory for all owners of motor vehicles. Nonetheless the product of the process is a contract of insurance.

What then must be agreed upon for a contract to be created? It has been held that, at a minimum, there must be agreement about the definition of the risk, the duration of the risk, the premium and the amount of insurance.[2] The definition of the risk includes the subject matter of the insurance (for example, the property, person or liability covered) and the perils against which there is coverage (for example, fire, accident, *etc.*). The duration is defined by the starting and terminating dates of the period for which the insurance is in effect. The premium is the amount of money the customer agrees to pay for the insurance. The amount of insurance may be a specific sum or described in general terms. A life is usually insured for a specific amount while property, which may be either partially damaged or totally lost, is typically insured for the "actual cash value" of the loss or the "cost of replacement", subject to a limit.

It is possible, of course, that other matters are included among those actually discussed and failure to agree on them may mean that no contract is concluded. But absent that, agreement on the four basic terms is sufficient to establish a contract.[3]

---

[1]   See Chapter 8.

[2]   *Davidson v. Global General Insurance Co. and Ocean Accident & Guarantee Corp.*, [1964] O.J. No. 680, [1965] 1 O.R. 505 (Ont. H.C.J.).

[3]   There are times when a contract arises even when all four of these essential terms are not present. Temporary coverage is often effective instantaneously, say upon the purchase of a new car. The insurance may be agreed so as to be effective immediately even though the premium has not

Payment of the Premium

As stated, the customer's main obligation under the contract is to pay the premium. But except for life insurance, the contract comes into force, in the sense that both parties are bound to obligations, before the premium is actually paid. Remember the requirement for the creation of contractual obligations is that each party merely promise to carry out those obligations. Unless otherwise agreed, one party's obligation is not deferred until the other party's obligation is carried out. In the context of insurance, this means that the insurer may still have to pay a claim even though the premium is yet to be paid.

At one time it was the practice of insurers to include as a term of a contract the condition that no claim need be met unless the premium was paid before the loss occurred. But this had several adverse effects. First, it was often unfair because, despite the fact that the policy stated that the contract was to run from a particular date and the premiums would be measured to reflect that, the actual period of coverage would not commence until the later time when payment of the premium was received. Second, there would be uncertainty about when the premium was received and therefore when coverage commenced. Third, there was inconvenience because there are many situations in which it is necessary for the coverage to have effect instantly before it is possible for the physical delivery of the premium.

For these reasons it has been provided by statute that, where a policy has been delivered, the contract is as binding as if the premium has been paid.[4] This does not apply to life insurance.[5] Thus, apart from life insurance, delivery of the policy amounts to acceptance of the customer's offer and a contract is born at that point. If there is a loss, the customer may claim under the contract and sue if not satisfied. If the premium is unpaid, the insurer may sue for it or deduct the amount owing from any insurance payable to the customer.[6]

But two things should be noted about acceptance by delivery of a policy. First, acceptance of an offer may be signified in ways other than delivery of a policy. Indeed a contract of insurance may not be in writing at all. For example, an oral contract is a common form of interim arrangement concluded by a broker. In such cases the contract is formed entirely by the spoken word. Second, an insurer cannot unilaterally create a contract and impose on a customer the obligation to pay a premium merely by issuing a policy. That

---

been settled. Similarly, a homeowner's contract may come into being even though the customer has not specified all the perils against which the insurance actually provides protection or which are excluded.

[4] See *e.g.*, Ontario *Insurance Act*, R.S.O. 1990, c. I.8, ss. 134, 303. See also *Civil Code of Québec*, S.Q. 1991, c. 64, Arts. 2425-2426.

[5] See, Ontario *Insurance Act*, *ibid.*, s. 180 regarding life insurance. Unless the policy provides otherwise, a contract of life insurance does not come into effect until there has been both delivery of the policy and payment of the premium.

[6] But this does not apply to money payable to a third party such as a mortgagee. *McMynn v. Lombard General Insurance Co.*, [2004] O.J. No. 1755, 70 O.R. (3d) 534 (Ont. C.A.).

action must be in response to an offer by the customer and be in the same terms as that offer.[7]

RENEWALS

Depending on the type of insurance, "renewal" can mean one of two things. A term life insurance contract, for example, may provide for its own renewal. The customer merely has to indicate that he or she wishes the contract to be extended in time, subject perhaps to a varied premium, this having been contemplated as a possibility at the outset and addressed in the policy. Automobile insurance, property insurance or liability insurance, on the other hand, is usually issued for a specific period of time with a stated expiry date. The "renewal" of a contract of this type is really the substitution of a new one rather than an extension of the old one. Whereas a renewable life insurance contract merely requires the unilateral action of the customer for it to be extended, an automobile insurance contract's renewal requires fresh agreement by both parties.

In this latter situation it is typically the insurer who makes the offer and the customer who accepts. The offer comes in the form of a letter or renewal notice setting out the proposed terms of the new contract. Often these terms are the same as for the previous contract, although there may be a new premium depending perhaps on the customer's claims record.

This letter invites the customer to accept before a specified date. It may be the date of expiry of the old contract but it is not uncommon for the insurer to give a "grace period" extending the time in which acceptance and/or payment may be made. If the customer responds positively before the deadline, a new contract comes into being. If there is no response from the customer, the insurer cannot, on its own, create a new contract merely by sending out renewal documents in whatever form. It has been suggested that if an insurer sends out a document which is in the form of a "policy", then it has delivered a policy and, pursuant to the statute,[8] the contract takes effect even though no premium has been paid.[9] This is anomalous. An insurer cannot impose an obligation on a customer to pay premiums when the customer has not agreed.[10] It seems inconsistent for a customer to be able to claim when he or she has not accepted the obligation to pay the premium.[11] But it is true that, even if there has been no acceptance of the insurer's offer to renew,[12] a claim arising out of loss which

---

[7]   This is of particular significance when it comes to the renewal of insurance contracts. See the next section, Renewals.

[8]   See *e.g.*, Ontario *Insurance Act*, R.S.O. 1990, c. I.8, ss. 134, 303. See also *Civil Code of Québec*, S.Q. 1991, c. 64, Arts. 2425-2426.

[9]   *Patterson v. Gallant*, [1994] S.C.J. No. 111, 26 C.C.L.I. (2d) 165 (S.C.C.).

[10] *Stevenson & Hunt Insurance Agencies Ltd. v. MacDonald*, [1978] O.J. No. 3433, 87 D.L.R. (3d) 603 (Ont. Prov. Ct.).

[11] See *Leslie v. Pitts Insurance Co.*, [1970] O.J. No. 450, [1970] I.L.R. 1-355 (Ont. H.C.J.).

[12] The rule applicable to contracts generally, that silence does not signify acceptance of an offer (even if the offer says something like, "if I do not hear from you by Tuesday, I'll assume you

occurs during the grace period is covered by the insurance. But in these circumstances, the granting of a grace period is a voluntary extension of the old contract rather than the creation of a new one.

Where the law requires an insurer to issue a policy in particular terms, that requirement is satisfied in the case of a renewal by issuing a "receipt" referring to the original policy.[13]

TERMINATION

An insurance contract can be brought to an end because the date or event specified in the contract for its expiry has come to pass. As we have seen homeowner's and auto insurance is usually written for a set period, say six months or a year. When the designated date arrives the contract is at an end subject possibly to an extension or grace period. A "renewal" replaces it with a new contract. Life insurance may be written for a set period (if so it is called term insurance). It may be renewable in the sense that the original contract is extended for subsequent periods at the instigation of the customer. Alternatively life insurance may be of the whole-of-life variety, in which case it exists (assuming premium payments are kept up) until the person whose life is insured dies.[14]

Other types of insurance may also be designed to terminate on the occurrence of a particular event. Marine insurance, for example, is commonly written to extend for the duration of a voyage or until cargo reaches a specified destination. Crop insurance may expire with the harvest; construction insurance on the completion of the project. Because the date of arrival at a destination or of a harvest or of the completion of a building cannot be known in advance with certainty, it is the event rather than its date that is specified in the policy.

A contract of insurance may also be ended by the parties entering into a new contract by which they agree to terminate the contract of insurance. So, if the insurer decides that it wants out of a contract, it can ask the customer to agree in return for repayment of at least some of the premium. If the customer agrees, then the contract ends.[15] Note that the contract to end the contract of insurance is marked by an exchange of value. The insurer gets excused from carrying the risk and the customer gets his or her money back.

If the contract (or legislation) allows it, a contract of insurance may also be terminated by one of the parties following the appropriate procedure for the unilateral withdrawal from the contract. In Quebec either party may terminate a contract, unless it is transport insurance. The customer may do so by giving the insurer written notice which takes effect as soon as the insurer receives it. If the insurer initiates the termination, the contract ends 15 days after the customer

---

accept") applies here. But the exception to the rule also applies. Silence can amount to acceptance if the parties have established a long-standing practice to that effect.

[13] See *e.g.*, Ontario *Insurance Act*, R.S.O. 1990, c. I.8, ss. 124(3), 145, 148.

[14] Of course, term life insurance also comes to an end if the person whose life is insured dies before the end of the term.

[15] *Ellis v. London-Canada Insurance Co.*, [1954] S.C.J. No. 1, [1954] S.C.R. 28 (S.C.C.).

receives notice of it.[16] In other provinces broadly similar rules apply to fire, auto and accident and sickness insurance.[17]

Unilateral termination by an insurer of an automobile insurance contract is restricted under compulsory auto insurance legislation. Because it is a criminal offence for the owner of a motor vehicle to allow it to be operated without insurance, such insurance may not be cancelled arbitrarily. Insurers are permitted to cancel only if premiums are not paid, the customer has given false information in applying for the insurance, or there has been a material change in the risk, such as modification of the vehicle for racing.[18]

Sometimes insurance contracts give protection to people not party to them, such as a lender of money to insured persons when the loan is secured against the insured property.[19] In Quebec, these people are entitled to notice of termination in the same manner as the insured people themselves.[20] Elsewhere the same rule applies to contracts of fire insurance.[21]

SUMMARY

A threshold question attending any insurance claim is, was there, at the relevant time, a contract of insurance in force? To answer this question it is necessary to ascertain whether a contract was created (by agreement to mutually acceptable terms involving coverage in exchange for a premium) and whether that arrangement was still in existence (in that it had not come to an end or had not been renewed) at the time of the loss.

---

[16] *Civil Code of Québec*, S.Q. 1991, c. 64, Art. 2477.

[17] See *e.g.*, Ontario *Insurance Act*, R.S.O. 1990, c. I.8, s. 148, statutory condition 5, s. 300, statutory condition 6; *Statutory Conditions – Automobile Insurance*, O. Reg. 777/93, statutory condition 11. The requirements imposed on an insurer must be strictly observed. See *e.g.*, *Transportation Lease Systems Inc. v. Guarantee Co. of North America*, [2003] O.J. No. 5237, [2004] I.L.R. 1-4260 (Ont. S.C.J.). In contrast, the notice to terminate given by the customer need not be given in writing. See *Stevenson & Hunt Insurance Agencies Ltd. v. MacDonald*, [1978] O.J. No. 3433, 87 D.L.R. (3d) 603 (Ont. Prov. Ct.).

[18] See *e.g.*, *Compulsory Automobile Insurance Act*, R.S.O. 1990, c. C.25, s. 12.

[19] See Chapter 15.

[20] *Civil Code of Québec*, S.Q. 1991, c. 64, Art. 2478.

[21] See *e.g.*, Ontario *Insurance Act*, R.S.O. 1990, c. I.8, s. 147.

Chapter 5

Non-Disclosure and Misrepresentation

INTRODUCTION

In Chapter 1 we saw that contracts of insurance are contracts of utmost good faith. In consequence, special rules apply to them. Chief among these is the rule that, in negotiating the contract, the parties must fully and accurately disclose to each other everything relevant.[1] One must not draw the other into a contract by withholding information which, if known, might cause a change of mind. This distinguishes insurance contracts from most other types of contracts which allow the parties to keep silent on any matter, however relevant to the transaction, unless asked about it.

The greater part of the burden of this obligation to disclose falls on the customer. In buying insurance he or she is transferring the risk of particular loss to the insurer. The insurer will usually only accept that risk if it judges the likelihood of loss occurring to be relatively low. Even if it agrees to underwrite the risk, the amount of the premium will vary with the likelihood of loss occurring. It is therefore important to the insurer that it not be misled about factors on which the likelihood of loss may turn. For example, an insurer being asked to accept the risk that a house will burn down will be interested in the materials from which it is built, activities conducted in it, the existence of smoke detectors, its proximity to a fire station, the state of the wiring and so on. But some of these facts are known only to the customer. If they are not disclosed, the insurer may not discover the truth until after loss has happened. That is why the customer has a duty to disclose all relevant matters as well as to respond truthfully to any questions asked.

This general rule about disclosure dates from the infancy of modern insurance when underwriters were relatively unsophisticated. Indeed insurance was often a transaction among merchants agreeing to cover each other's losses. Not only did those accepting the risk have no knowledge of much that was relevant to that risk, they had no means of finding out about it. Over the years this has changed and, as we shall see, the rules about disclosure have changed too. Nonetheless, the present-day rules can only be properly understood against this historical backdrop.

---

[1] For disclosure requirements in making claims, see Chapter 10.

THE RULES DEVELOPED BY COURTS

Many of the disclosure rules that apply in Canada today have been legislated. But for the most part, the legislation has modified rather than replaced the case law which has evolved over the centuries in England, Canada and elsewhere. It is therefore necessary to start with a description of the rules developed in thousands of decided cases.

A person applying for insurance must disclose all matters within his or her personal knowledge that are vital to determining the nature and extent of the risk.[2] The duty applies even in the absence of questions from the insurer.[3] It is irrelevant whether the failure to disclose is deliberate or inadvertent.

When information is disclosed, it must be full and accurate. Thus, in addition to the duty to disclose, there is the duty, common to all contracts, not to misrepresent either directly or by partial omission.[4] Accuracy is required only in respect of matters relevant to the insurance. However, case law did not prevent an insurer from extending the duty, by the terms of the contract, to include facts not necessarily relevant. A practice developed whereby insurers demanded that customers warrant the accuracy of all representations which were stated to be the "basis of the contract". Any inaccuracy, however trivial or irrelevant to the risk, entitled the insurer to deny coverage under the contract on the ground that the customer was in breach of a warranty.[5] The duty applies only to facts past and present, not to opinion or speculation about the future.[6]

The test for determining if a fact is relevant (or "material") is an objective one in the sense that the fact must be such that a prudent insurer would take it into account in either deciding whether to accept the risk or in setting the premium.[7] However, the test also has a subjective element. If a particular insurer would not have acted any differently had it known the non-disclosed fact, even if other "prudent" insurers would, it may not rely on the customer's non-disclosure of the fact as a reason for turning down a claim.[8] But an insurer's

---

[2]   For most writers the seminal case is *Carter v. Boehm* (1766), 3 Burr. 1905, 97 E.R. 1162 (K.B.). Often information is imparted to the insurer only indirectly, the customer's dealings being mostly with a broker or agent. For the role played by intermediaries in connection with the customer's duty of disclosure, see Chapter 7.

[3]   *W.H. Stuart Mutuals Ltd. v. London Guarantee Insurance Co.*, [2004] O.J. No. 5156, 16 C.C.L.I. (4th) 192 (Ont. C.A.).

[4]   *Bell Pole Co. v. Commonwealth Insurance Co.*, [2003] B.C.J. No. 8, 10 B.C.L.R. (4th) 90 (B.C.C.A.).

[5]   For most types of insurance this practice has been effectively outlawed. See below.

[6]   However, policies often contain a clause requiring that the customer report changes relevant to the risk as they arise. See *e.g.*, Ontario *Insurance Act*, R.S.O. 1990, c. I.8, s. 148, statutory condition 4.

[7]   *Mutual Life Insurance Co. New York v. Ontairo Metal Products Co.*, [1925] A.C. 344 (P.C.). *Civil Code of Québec*, S.Q. 1991, c. 64, Art. 4466.

[8]   *Pan Atlantic Insurance Co. v. Pine Top Insurance Co.*, [1994] 2 Lloyd's Rep. 427 (H.L.). See also *Great Northern Insurance Co. v. Whitney*, [1918] S.C.J. No. 58, 57 S.C.R. 543 (S.C.C.). Conversely, an insurer which is unique in deeming a particular matter relevant cannot rely on non-disclosure relating to that matter as a reason for declaring a contract void. However, evidence of an insurer's practice in this regard may be sufficient to establish the industry norm if it

failure to ask about a matter does not necessarily mean it does not consider it to be relevant.[9]

An applicant for insurance must disclose information he or she actually has or ought reasonably to know. The information must be personal in that it is not readily available to the insurer other than from the applicant. The insurer is presumed to know about matters in the public domain such as a war going on in a location to be visited by an insured ship. The applicant must disclose the location but need not mention the war.[10]

It is in this sense that the insurer has a duty concerning disclosure in negotiations. The insurer must exercise good faith in finding out from public sources matters notorious in regard to the risk it is being asked to accept. In this it must meet the standard to be expected of the reasonable insurer. It is contrary to good faith for an insurer to accept premiums from a customer when it knows or should know that there is information relevant to the risk which the customer has not related. If the customer has disclosed facts which would induce a reasonable insurer to follow up by seeking further detail, the insurer cannot complain about the absence of detail or nuance which it could have reasonably discovered for itself.[11]

The consequence of non-disclosure or misrepresentation by the customer is loss of coverage because the insurer is entitled to render the contract "void".[12] This may be altered by the terms of the contract to provide, for example, for an adjustment of the amount of insurance and/or premiums in the light of the true facts.

A MODERN APPLICATION

Coronation Insurance Co. v. Taku Air Transport Ltd.[13] is a case decided by the Supreme Court of Canada in 1992. It arose out of an airplane crash. The air carrier sought indemnification from its insurance company. The insurer refused to pay alleging that the customer had failed to disclose its bad accident record and misrepresented the seating capacity of the plane (the air carrier had said it was four when it was really five) when applying for the insurance.

The court decided that the misrepresentation of the seating capacity was relevant to the insurance and therefore disqualified the claim. On the other hand,

---

is not challenged by the insured. See *Henwood v. Prudential Insurance Co. of America*, [1967]
S.C.J. No. 66, [1967] S.C.R. 720 (S.C.C.).

9

However, some recent cases have undermined the strictness of this approach by holding that an insurer may only raise the defence of non-disclosure if it has told the insured what it considers to be material. See *e.g.*, *Sagl v. Cosburn, Griffiths & Brandham Insurance Brokers Ltd.*, [2009] O.J. No. 1879, 2009 ONCA 388 (Ont. C.A.), leave to appeal refused [2009] S.C.C.A. No. 303 (S.C.C.); *Thomas v. Aviva Insurance Co.*, [2011] N.B.J. No. 371, 2 C.C.L.I. (5th) 1 (N.B.C.A.).

10 See *Carter v. Boehm* (1766), 3 Burr. 1905, 97 E.R. 1162 (K.B.).

11 *Ipapo Estate v. Citadel Life Insurance Co.*, [1989] M.J. No. 123, 37 C.C.L.I. 259 (Man. C.A.).

12 The misrepresented or undisclosed facts do not have to be connected to the cause of the loss. See *Thomson v. Maritime Life Assurance Co.* (2003), 5 C.C.L.I. (3d) 211 (Alta. Q.B.).

13 [1991] S.C.J. No. 96, 4 C.C.L.I. (2d) 115 (S.C.C.).

it was different with the failure to mention the accident record. While relevant to the risk, air accident records are in the public domain and an insurer involved in writing aviation coverage should know about them. Times have changed since the 1760s. Insurers are expected to know more now. In other words, matters exclusively within the customer's personal knowledge are fewer than they once were.[14]

HOW LEGISLATION HAS MODIFIED THE RULES

In the *Taku Air Transport* case the court applied essentially the same rules as its English ancestor applied in 1766. For some classes of insurance, however, Canadian legislation has changed those rules significantly.

As described in Chapter 1, provincial insurance statutes treat various classes of contracts differently in respect of several issues. One such issue is non-disclosure and misrepresentation. For present purposes the Quebec legislation has two classes: marine insurance and non-marine insurance. The statutes in the other provinces and territories have up to eight: fire, automobile, life, accident and sickness, weather, livestock and marine insurance, as well as a catch-all class for all other types.

Unspecified Classes of Insurance

The rules that apply to non-disclosure and misrepresentation in relation to types of insurance not specifically designated (non-marine insurance in Quebec and the types covered by the catch-all provisions in other provinces and territories) are similar to the rules described above as having been developed by the courts. The most significant way in which legislation has modified these rules is by the elimination of warranties of the truth of all facts. The legislation makes it clear that an insurer may only raise non-disclosure or misrepresentation by the customer if the discrepancy concerns a matter relevant to the insurance.[15] Whether a matter is relevant is a matter of objective fact and may not be decreed so merely by a term of the contract.

In Quebec there is a further difference in respect of property and liability insurance. Where the non-disclosure or misrepresentation is innocent, the contract is not automatically rendered void. Unless it is established that the insurer would have rejected the risk entirely had it known the true facts, it

---

[14] See also *Canadian Indemnity Insurance Co. v. Canadian Johns Manville Co.*, [1990] S.C.J. No. 82, [1990] 2 S.C.R. 549 (S.C.C.), where the court held that health risks associated with asbestos were sufficiently well known as to be beyond the personal knowledge of an asbestos manufacturer. The insurer could therefore not deny coverage because the manufacturer had not informed it of the risks of its product.

[15] See *e.g.*, Ontario *Insurance Act*, R.S.O. 1990, c. I.8, s. 124 (4), (5) and *Civil Code of Québec*, S.Q. 1991, c. 64, Arts. 2408-2413.

remains "liable towards the insurer for such proportion of the indemnity as the premium he collected bears to the premium he should have collected".[16]

Fire Insurance

In all provinces, except Quebec, the duty of disclosure applicable to fire insurance is provided by statute in the form of a "statutory condition".[17] This means that the legislation sets out a clause that is automatically part of every contract and which must be printed, without change, in every policy. The clause provides as follows:

> If a person falsely describes the property to the prejudice of the insurer, or misrepresents or fraudulently omits to communicate any circumstance that is material to be made known to the insurer in order to enable it to judge of the risk to be undertaken, the contract is void as to any property in relation to which the misrepresentation or omission is material.[18]

Note the ways in which this clause is different from the rules which evolved through case law. First, an insurer may rely on this clause only in cases where the information is material. Because the statutory condition may not be varied in any way, an insurer may not add a term to the contract making non-material inaccuracies a ground for denying coverage (that is, a "warranty"). Second, the clause makes a distinction between omissions and representations. An omission will void the contract only if the omission is fraudulent. For misrepresentations, the customer's intent is irrelevant. For an omission to be regarded as fraudulent the insurer must prove that the customer was aware of the facts that ought to have been disclosed and knew, subjectively, that those facts were relevant to the insurance.[19]

The third difference is the effect of the customer's delinquency. The entire contract is not rendered voidable, rather, the contract is void (from the outset, not merely when the insurer decrees it to be) only insofar as it covers property to which the non-disclosure or misrepresentation relates. The consequence of the contract being declared void as opposed to voidable is that a customer innocent of fraud is entitled to reimbursement of his or her premiums because the risk was never transferred.[20]

A point should be made about the phrase "any circumstance" that appears in the statutory condition. This does not widen the case law rule that only matters within the customer's personal knowledge and only facts rather than opinion

---

[16] *Civil Code of Québec, ibid.*, Art. 2411.

[17] In Alberta and British Columbia fire insurance is no longer a separate category for purposes of legislation relating to insurance contracts. However, the statutory conditions formerly applicable to fire insurance now apply to all property and liability insurance. See Alberta *Insurance Act*, R.S.A. 2000, c. I-3, s. 540; British Columbia *Insurance Act*, R.S.B.C. 2012, c. 1, s. 29.

[18] See *e.g.*, Ontario *Insurance Act*, R.S.O. 1990, c. I.8, s. 148, statutory condition 1.

[19] *Taylor v. London Assurance Corp.*, [1934] O.J. No. 244, [1934] 2 D.L.R. 657 at 663 (Ont. C.A.), revd [1935] S.C.J. No. 13, [1935] S.C.R. 422 (S.C.C.).

[20] *Imperial Bank v. Royal Insurance Co.*, [1906] O.J. No. 89, 12 O.L.R. 519 (Ont. H.C.).

count. Indeed, facts that must be disclosed fall into two categories; those concerning the state of the property, and those having to do with the financial status and honesty of the customer. There is no duty to disclose other information even if it is material in the sense that the insurer would take it into account.[21]

Another departure from the common law is reflected in another statutory condition that obliges customers to notify insurers of any ongoing changes in circumstances which are material to the risk.[22]

Automobile Insurance

In all provinces and territories the customer's duty of disclosure in applying for automobile insurance has been narrowed by statute.

In Quebec, the *Automobile Insurance Act* (a statute separate from the *Civil Code of Québec* which deals with other types of insurance contracts) provides that:

> The insurer shall not demand that the contract be void *ab initio* unless the insured has misrepresented or deceitfully concealed any fact known to him likely to materially influence a reasonable insurer in the decision to cover the risk.[23]

This is similar to the rule that applies in other provinces to fire insurance in that only matters relevant ("material") to the insurance count and in that non-disclosure must be fraudulent before an insurer can raise it as a reason for denying coverage.

In jurisdictions other than Quebec, the duty of disclosure is confined to two categories: particulars of the automobile to be insured and facts requested on the application form. If the customer gives false particulars of the automobile, thereby misleading the insurer to the extent that it writes insurance when it otherwise would have refused it or charged a higher premium, any claim by the customer is invalid. The same result ensues if the customer "knowingly misrepresents or fails to disclose in the application any fact required to be stated therein".[24]

An insurer may reject a claim on the basis of a statement attributed to the customer only if either: (1) it is contained in an application signed by the customer; or (2) it is in an unsigned application but is proven by the insurer to have been made by the customer. Further, the application form must be approved by the appropriate provincial authority — the Superintendent or

---

[21] *Cunningham v. Security Mutual Casualty Co.*, [1979] N.B.J. No. 315, [1980] I.L.R. 1-1178 (N.B.C.A.).

[22] See *e.g.*, Ontario *Insurance Act*, R.S.O. 1990, c. I.8, s. 148, statutory condition 4.

[23] R.S.Q. 1977, c. A-25, s. 92.

[24] See *e.g.*, Ontario *Insurance Act*, R.S.O. 1990, c. I.8, s. 233(1)*(ii)*. British Columbia, Manitoba and Saskatchewan each have a separate statute dealing specifically with auto insurance. These statutes adopt the same approach to the duty of disclosure. See *e.g.*, *Manitoba Public Insurance Corporation Act*, R.S.M. 1987, c. P215, s. 37.

Commissioner of Insurance — before it may be used at all.[25] In this way, buyers of insurance are protected against inappropriate or irrelevant inquiries.

A customer's failure to comply with the duty to disclose does not necessarily excuse the insurer from all obligations. Where a person is injured by the insured customer and claims under the third-party liability section of the policy, the insurer has to pay the claim (up to $200,000) despite any misrepresentation or failure to disclose on the part of the customer in his or her dealings with the insurer.[26] Similarly, insurers may have to pay no-fault personal injury benefits, for example, to passengers in the insured vehicle or to pedestrians hit by it, even though the customer is guilty of non-disclosure or misrepresentation.[27]

As with fire insurance, a statutory condition requires customers to notify insurers of material changes in the risk during the life of the contract.[28]

Life Insurance and Accident and Sickness Insurance

Life insurance or accident and sickness insurance may be purchased by a person against his or her own death, illness or injury or against the death, illness or injury of someone else with whom he or she has a family or financial connection.[29] When it comes to disclosure, a duty is imposed on the customer buying the insurance, not only on the customer's behalf, but also on behalf of the person(s) whose life or well-being is to be insured.[30]

In all written statements, including the application, and in any medical examination, these persons must disclose everything they know that is relevant to the insurance.[31] The test of relevance is that applied by the reasonable insurer. Some things, such as the insured person's medical history, age and occupation easily satisfy this test. Other things may be regarded as relevant by some, but not all, insurers. If a particular insurer shows it considers a fact to be relevant, the objective, reasonable insurer test will be satisfied unless the insured can show otherwise.[32]

---

[25] See *e.g.*, Ontario *Insurance Act*, R.S.O. 1990, c. I.8, s. 227.

[26] See *ibid.*, s. 258.

[27] See *ibid.*, s. 233(2). See also *Statutory Accident Benefits Schedule*, O. Reg. 776/93, s. 58 (3).

[28] See *e.g.*, *Statutory Conditions — Automobile Insurance*, O. Reg. 777/93, Sch. 1, statutory condition 1.

[29] See Chapter 6.

[30] Insurance in these classes is often sold on a "group" basis. By working for a particular employer or by belonging to a particular organization, an individual qualifies to sign up for a group insurance plan. Because of the numbers involved, insurers often calculate that the number of high risk individuals will likely be matched by low risk ones. In these circumstances it is uneconomical to expend resources investigating the insurability of each individual. Accordingly, for group insurance, there is no duty of disclosure unless evidence of insurability is specifically requested by the insurer. See *e.g.*, Ontario *Insurance Act*, R.S.O. 1990, c. I.8, ss. 184(3), 308(3).

[31] See *e.g.*, Ontario *Insurance Act*, *ibid.*, ss. 183, 308.

[32] *Henwood v. Prudential Insurance Co. of America*, [1967] S.C.J. No. 66, [1967] S.C.R. 720 (S.C.C.). Note, however, that if an individual insurer does not regard the matter as material, it cannot raise the customer's failure to disclose it. See *Pan Atlantic Insurance Co. v. Pine Top Insurance Co.*, [1994] 2 Lloyd's Rep. 427 (H.L.). See also *Great Northern Insurance Co. v.*

Misstatement of age does not nullify the contract. For life insurance, the benefits payable under the contract are adjusted to reflect the true age given the premiums actually paid.[33] Under accident and sickness insurance, the insurer may choose either to adjust the benefits or maintain the original level of benefits and adjust the premium.[34] In group insurance the consequences of misstatement of age are governed by the contract.[35]

The insurer may only use non-disclosure or misrepresentation to nullify the coverage within two years from the date the contract came into effect (or was reinstated if the coverage had lapsed) unless there was fraud.[36]

If a customer fails to comply with the duty to disclose in life or accident and sickness insurance, the insurer (if it discovers the discrepancy within the two-year period) is entitled to declare the contract void. For group insurance, the coverage can be terminated only for the person guilty of the misstatement or non-disclosure.[37] If the insurer learns about a breach of the duty to disclose and does nothing about it, it may not be entitled to raise the matter to its advantage again.[38]

Marine Insurance

There is a federal Marine Insurance Act and several provinces have specific marine insurance statutes. In most of them the duty of disclosure is a codified but largely unmodified version of the rules that have evolved through the courts.[39] Thus marine insurance is the only type of insurance in which the customer may be bound to warrant the accuracy of facts even if not relevant to the risk.[40]

One slight variation from case law is the rule that a misrepresentation relating to expectations or belief, as opposed to existing fact, can give the insurer the right to repudiate the contract if the misrepresentation is made in bad faith.[41] Bad faith need not be present when existing facts are misrepresented or withheld. In this respect the innocence of the customer is no excuse. But the

---

Whitney, [1918] S.C.J. No. 58, 57 S.C.R. 543 (S.C.C.). Conversely, an insurer which is unique in deeming a particular matter relevant cannot rely on non-disclosure relating to that matter as a reason for declaring a contract void. However, evidence of an insurer's practice in this regard may be sufficient to establish the industry norm if it is not challenged by the insured. See *Henwood v. Prudential Insurance Co. of America*.

[33] See *e.g.*, Ontario *Insurance Act*, R.S.O. 1990, c. I.8, s. 184. *Civil Code of Québec*, S.Q. 1991, c. 64, Art. 2420.

[34] See *e.g.*, Ontario *Insurance Act*, *ibid.*, s. 312; *Civil Code of Québec*, *ibid.*, Art. 2420.

[35] See *e.g.*, Ontario *Insurance Act*, *ibid.*, s. 312(2).

[36] See *e.g.*, Ontario *Insurance Act*, *ibid.*, ss. 184(2), 309.

[37] *Civil Code of Québec*, S.Q. 1991, c. 64, Art. 2423.

[38] See the discussion of "waiver" and "estoppel" in Chapter 11.

[39] See *e.g.*, Ontario *Marine Insurance Act*, R.S.O. 1990, c. M.2, s. 18 *ff.*

[40] This is not so in Quebec. The duty to disclose in marine insurance is confined to matters relevant to the insurance. See *Civil Code of Québec*, S.Q. 1991, c. 64, Art. 2546.

[41] See *e.g.*, Ontario *Marine Insurance Act*, R.S.O. 1990, c. M.2, s. 21.

customer satisfies the obligation to disclose facts so long as he or she provides enough information to alert the insurer to a situation in general terms.[42]

DISCLOSING NEW CIRCUMSTANCES

The obligations we have considered in this chapter so far relate to the disclosure of relevant facts during the negotiation of an insurance contract. It should be noted further that insurance policies commonly contain terms imposing an obligation to disclose changes in circumstances that are material to the risk and that happen while the contract is in force. Indeed, for automobile and fire insurance, such terms are mandated by legislation.[43]

For automobile insurance, examples of new facts that must be disclosed are sale of the vehicle, a lien, other insurance on the vehicle, modifications that put the vehicle into a higher premium category and a significant change in the use of the vehicle.[44] For fire insurance, examples are storage of inflammable substances, alterations that increase the risk of loss or its extent if it happens, or changes in the way a building is occupied in a way the insured person ought to know increases the risk.[45]

The consequence of failing to report a material change is that the insurance contract ceases to have effect. However, for fire insurance, legislation[46] protects a customer from this consequence if a court would regard it as unjust or unreasonable. For example, in *Marche v. Halifax Insurance Co.*,[47] the insured customers failed to report that they had left the insured premises unoccupied for longer than was allowed under the policy. But it was reoccupied before the fire happened. While the vacancy increased the risk, the reoccupation reduced it again. The Supreme Court of Canada held that it would be unjust to deny coverage in these circumstances.

---

[42] *Central Native Fishermen's Co-operative v. Commonwealth Insurance Co.*, [1979] I.L.R. 1-1091 (B.C.S.C.).

[43] See *e.g.*, *Statutory Conditions – Automobile Insurance*, O. Reg. 777/93, statutory condition 1 and Ontario *Insurance Act*, R.S.O. 1990, c. I.8, s. 148, statutory condition 4. Note that in Alberta and British Columbia, these statutory conditions apply to all property insurance. In Alberta and British Columbia fire insurance is no longer a separate category for purposes of legislation relating to insurance contracts. However, the statutory conditions formerly applicable to fire insurance now apply to all property and liability insurance. See Alberta *Insurance Act*, R.S.A. 2000, c. I-3, s. 540; British Columbia *Insurance Act*, R.S.B.C. 2012, c. 1, s. 29.

[44] See *e.g.*, *Kerr v. Canada Mercantile Insurance Co.* (1960), 67 Man. R. 124 (Man. C.A.); *Thompson v. Allianz Insurance Co.* (1998), 8 C.C.L.I. (3d) 280 (Alta. C.A.).

[45] See generally, *Scott v. Canadian Mercantile Insurance Co.*, [1965] O.J. No. 957, [1965] 2 O.R. 66 (Ont. H.C.J.).

[46] See *e.g.*, Ontario *Insurance Act*, R.S.O. 1990, c. I.8, s. 151.

[47] [2005] S.C.J. No. 7, [2005] 1 S.C.R. 47 (S.C.C.).

A WORD ABOUT DISCRIMINATION

The reason the law invests insurers with the right to certain information from people applying for insurance is to allow them (insurers) to make choices. Some people are better risks, and therefore more attractive as customers, than others. But factors that distinguish good risks from bad ones, determined by insurers' collective experience, are often factors that, in other contexts, are prohibited grounds of discrimination. Human rights codes ban businesses from discriminating in hiring and in doing business on the basis of, among other things, disability, age, marital status and sex. Yet these are the bases on which, for some types of insurance, experience shows the good risks may be distinguished from the bad.

For this reason, human rights legislation typically provides an exemption for insurers following standard insurance practices as long as they do so in good faith, and is restricted to specified factors such as age and health.[48] But the matter is more controversial in auto insurance where objections have been raised to the use of age, sex and marital status as relevant factors in setting premiums. The Supreme Court of Canada has upheld the use of age and sex as reasonable.[49] But occasionally the political judgment has been different resulting in a legislated ban on the practice.[50]

For present purposes, the point in all this is that, where an insurer is precluded by statute from distinguishing between risks on a particular factual basis (*e.g.*, religion), a customer's failure to provide information related to that fact cannot nullify the contract. Even if insurers' collective experience told them that adherents to a particular religion were greater risks,[51] they could not use that information as a ground for refusing coverage to those people. In other words, insurers are precluded from regarding such a fact as relevant to the risk. But unless precluded by statute, insurers are permitted to practise discrimination.

SUMMARY

In applying for insurance, a customer must disclose to the insurer all facts within his or her personal knowledge which are material to the risk. The precise requirements are modified by statute for fire, automobile, accident and sickness, life and marine insurance.

---

[48] See *e.g.*, Ontario *Human Rights Code*, R.S.O. 1990, c. H.19, s. 22 (as am. S.O. 2001, c. 32, s. 27(5)). Insurance statutes also reinforce the notion that discrimination should be fair. See Ontario *Insurance Act*, R.S.O. 1990, c. I.8, s. 438.

[49] *Zurich Insurance Co. v. Ontario (Human Rights Commission)*, [1992] S.C.J. No. 63, 93 D.L.R. (4th) 346 (S.C.C.).

[50] See *e.g.*, British Columbia's *Insurance (Motor Vehicle) Act*, R.S.B.C. 1996, c. 231, s. 50.

[51] Jehovah's Witnesses might be shown to pose an increased risk of accidental death because of their aversion to blood transfusions.

Chapter 6

The Need to Have an Interest in the Subject Matter

RATIONALE

An insurance claim will fail if the insurer can show that the person who bought the insurance (the "insured") lacked the appropriate connection to the subject matter of that insurance.[1] In property insurance, the subject matter is the thing the loss of or damage to which will trigger the entitlement to insurance money. In life or accident and sickness insurance, the subject matter is the person whose illness, injury or death will give rise to the claim.

The rationale for the requirement of this connection, or "insurable interest" as it is called, varies slightly depending on whether one is referring to indemnity insurance or non-indemnity insurance. Recall[2] that indemnity insurance provides payment in the event of proven financial loss consequent upon, say, property damage or personal injury. Non-indemnity insurance, most notably life insurance, involves payment upon the occurrence of a specified event whether or not it entails financial loss.

Indemnity insurance is, not surprisingly, governed by the indemnity principle. In Chapter 1 we saw that this principle holds that a person claiming under an indemnity contract should recover only that which he or she has actually lost and no more. Without rules giving effect to this principle there would, it is feared, be undue "moral hazard". The prospect of receiving more from an insurer than was lost is an incentive to engineer loss, or at least to be less careful in avoiding it. Apart from being wasteful, this would clearly be dangerous to people and property.

This is why a person claiming under an indemnity insurance contract must prove not only the occurrence of an insured event (such as a fire, an accident, *etc.*), but also that he or she suffered financial loss as a result. Proof of loss includes proof of its value. When confronted with this proof the insurer must pay the amount of loss but no more. Similarly, a claimant may not use the fact

---

[1] As we shall see in Chapter 15, the person making the claim may not be the person who purchased the insurance. The latter is sometimes called the "insured" even if it turns out that the person has no enforceable rights under the contract. In this Chapter, we are concerned with the connection between the insured and the subject matter.

[2] See Chapter 1.

that he or she has several sources of compensation to double up on the amount recovered. Sums available from other insurers or from lawsuits against those who caused the loss are taken into account in determining the amount of insurance recoverable.

Perhaps even more fundamental, so fundamental in fact that it hardly needs to be said, is the rule that if a person has suffered no loss at all that person has no claim at all.[3] A person may not claim when a neighbour's house burns down. It is the neighbour who has directly suffered the loss. No interest other than the neighbour's has been adversely affected. If a person could insure a neighbour's house and collect insurance when it burnt down, that person would be in a position to profit because the money would become available without the person first suffering any loss. In these circumstances, the temptation to help bring about the event which triggered the payment might be too much for some to resist. Hence the requirement that, to claim successfully under an indemnity insurance contract, one must show an insurable interest in the subject matter at the time loss occurred.

It is trite to say that the indemnity principle does not apply to non-indemnity insurance such as life insurance. There, it is not necessary for a claimant to show financial loss arising from the insured event. An independently wealthy person is not disqualified from receiving $5,000 from a spouse's life insurance policy just because that person suffered no financial loss upon the spouse's death. Nor is there any objection to full recovery under several policies. Because it is not the point of a life insurance contract to provide an indemnity, there is no concern about over-indemnification.

But the absence of a need to show prior financial loss heightens rather than lessens the concern about people profiting from insurance. Life insurance commonly involves one person (*e.g.*, A) insuring the life of another (*e.g.*, B). If B dies, A collects. Because there is no requirement that A show that financial loss has been caused to him or her by B's death, there is, it would seem, a reason for A to desire B's death. Perhaps there is even an incentive for A to conspire to bring about that death. This is one of the reasons that a person may not insure the life of just anyone. One is restricted to insuring one's own life and those in whose lives a person is deemed by the law to have an insurable interest.

There is another reason. It has to do with the similarity between insurance and gambling. Gambling has traditionally been viewed as socially undesirable. Except where governments have authorized and regulated specific forms of it, gambling is usually the subject of a blanket ban. Gaming contracts are illegal and unenforceable.[4] In the early days of life insurance in England, it was turned to use as disguised gambling. A popular subject of wager was the exact date of death of a prominent person known to be seriously ill. A straight bet was illegal. But a contract of "insurance" on the unfortunate person's life was another

---

[3]   As we shall see in Chapter 15, there may be circumstances in which a third party may claim. An example is a person to whom the insured person's rights of recovery under the insurance contract have been assigned. But, even here, if the insured person can show no loss, there is no right of recovery so the third party has no claim.

[4]   See *e.g.*, Ontario *Gaming Control Act, 1992*, S.O. 1992, c. 24.

matter. One bettor, the "insured" would pay a "premium". The other, giving odds, would be the "insurer" providing "insurance" against the subject's dying before a specified date. The insurer would keep the premium if the subject was still alive on the agreed date. If death had occurred by then, the insured would collect the "insurance" money.

Banning all insurance was not the solution. But because it seemed inappropriate in the case of genuine bereavement to demand that a claimant show personal financial loss, indemnity could not be used as the distinguishing, legitimizing feature. So other connecting factors, mostly based on family relationship, were substituted. These factors were based on the assumption that, when a close relative dies, the family suffers a loss, even if that loss cannot be measured in economic terms. It was also assumed that, in most cases, the incentive of financial gain was more than offset by familial affection so that the temptation to aid in the demise of the person whose life was insured was minimized.

DETERMINING WHETHER INSURABLE INTEREST EXISTS

Indemnity Insurance

The test for an insurable interest in the subject matter of indemnity insurance is whether the person who bought the insurance would, with reasonably measurable certainty, benefit from the continued existence of that subject matter or be prejudiced by its loss or destruction.[5] This "factual expectation" test has been adopted in Canada in preference to a more technical, legalistic test based on property or contractual rights in the subject matter.[6] This has its most significant impact in cases involving insurance taken out by shareholders in a corporation on property owned by the corporation. Under the old rule, the lack of ownership or other right in the property (incorporation creates a separate legal entity capable of owning property and incurring debts) meant a shareholder could not succeed in an insurance claim even if he or she was the sole shareholder. The same was true for a person who tried to claim on insurance he or she took out on the property of someone who owed him or her money unless the property in question had been put up as security for the debt.[7] Now the more flexible factual expectation test allows recovery in at least some of these cases.

In cases not involving shareholders, it is usually unimportant whether a factual expectation test or a property right test is used. Under either test, titleholders (including trustees, executors and administrators) have an insurable interest in the property they own; both vendors and purchasers of land have an insurable interest in that land between the date of contract and the date of closing;

---

5   *Lucena v. Craufurd* (1806), 127 E.R. 630 (H.L.).

6   *Kosmopoulos v. Constitution Insurance Co.*, [1987] S.C.J. No. 2, [1987] I.L.R. 1-2147 (S.C.C.).
    See also *Civil Code of Québec*, S.Q. 1991, c. 64, Art. 2481.

7   *Guarantee Co. of North America v. Aqua-Land Exploration Ltd.*, [1965] S.C.J. No. 65, [1966] S.C.R. 133 (S.C.C.).

liquidators have an insurable interest in the property of bankrupts; tenants have an insurable interest in leased property; lienholders and mortgagees have an insurable interest in the property over which the charge is held; and bailees have an insurable interest in property in their possession.

A special case arises where the insured customer is in possession of stolen property. If he or she knows or ought reasonably to know that the goods are stolen, the customer has no insurable interest. But if the goods have been acquired innocently, the possessor has an insurable interest until the true owner comes forward.[8]

In marine insurance, an insurable interest is an interest in a marine adventure. This includes direct property rights in the ship or cargo, the interest of crew members in their wages, the interests of shareholders in risks undertaken by the corporation, and the interests of general creditors.[9]

The risk insured in a liability insurance contract — liability to third parties — is itself an interest. Occasionally, claims against automobile liability insurance contracts have failed because the claimant was held to have had no insurable interest in the car. In these cases the person in whose name the car was registered and who took out the insurance was not the true owner, the arrangement being a scheme to trick the insurer into charging lower premiums.[10]

Non-indemnity Insurance

The test for insurable interest in non-indemnity insurance is a more or less arbitrary one laid down by statute.[11] A person has an insurable interest in his or her own life and well-being, that of his or her spouse, child or grandchild, any person on whom he or she is dependent, even partially, for support or education, an employee, any person in whose duration of life the insured has a financial interest and any person who consents to his or her life being insured. Note that, although financial loss need not be proved when a claim is made, the relationship between the person buying the insurance and the person whose life is insured is such that, should the latter die, the former is likely to have suffered financial loss. This addresses the concern about misplaced incentives as does a further provision which allows insurance to be placed on the life of someone who consents to it. The list of "approved" relationships distinguishes insurance transactions from those that amount to wagering.

---

[8] *Assaad v. Economical Mutual Insurance Group*, [2002] O.J. No. 2356, 43 C.C.L.I. (3d) 40 (Ont. C.A.).

[9] See *e.g.*, Ontario *Marine Insurance Act*, R.S.O. 1990, c. M.2, s. 5*ff.*

[10] See *e.g.*, *Wolfe v. Oliver*, [1974] N.S.J. No. 184, [1975] I.L.R. 1-644 (N.S.C.A.).

[11] See *e.g.*, Ontario *Insurance Act*, R.S.O. 1990, c. I.8, ss. 178, 1799 (life insurance) and ss. 305, 306 (accident and sickness insurance). *Civil Code of Québec*, S.Q. 1991, c. 64, Arts. 2418, 2419.

THE TIME WHEN THE INTEREST MUST EXIST

By definition, an indemnity insurance contract is not a wager. Its terms provide for insurance money to be paid only in the event of loss. The person who bought the insurance cannot "win" in the sense that, if a particular event happens, he or she will come out ahead. The person can only collect if he or she first loses the equivalent amount. Therefore, an indemnity insurance contract is not tainted with illegality from the start since its terms envisage loss as a condition of payment. However, should a claim arise, it is still necessary to ensure that the claimant does not "win" by receiving payment without having suffered a loss. Accordingly, it is at the time of the loss that the existence of an insurable interest is relevant for indemnity insurance.[12]

In contrast, because at least part of the concern with non-indemnity insurance is to make sure it is not really gaming in disguise, the crucial time to determine the existence of an insurable interest is the time at which the contract is made. If the contract is not supported by an insurable interest, it will not be insurance but a wager and therefore illegal. It is void from the start.

INSURING OTHER INTERESTS

We have seen how the rules about insurable interest respond to the concern that unscrupulous people might be tempted to destroy property belonging to others if they could profit from that through insurance. This has led to the general principle that people may not collect insurance in respect of property in which they have no interest. But in some situations, it is appropriate to allow one person to take out insurance in his or her own name, not only for personal benefit, but also for the benefit of others. Examples are: one member of a partnership insuring property belonging to all partners; a family member insuring property belonging to other members of the family; and a landlord insuring the interests of both himself or herself and the tenant.

The rule here is that it is permissible to insure the interest of another, and to collect the insurance when that interest is harmed, if the following conditions are satisfied: (1) the person taking out the insurance must have intended to insure interests other than his or her own; (2) the terms of the contract must permit it; and (3) the person taking out the insurance must have some interest in the insured property personally.[13] To the extent that the existence of other interests is relevant to the insurance, these must be disclosed to the insurer.[14]

---

[12] See *e.g.*, *Daishowa-Marubeni Ltd. v. Toshiba Int'l Corp.*, [2003] A.J. No. 1189, 5 C.C.L.I. (4th) 11 (Alta. C.A.). Note, however, that the policy may contain a term excluding or limiting coverage with respect to property acquired after the policy came into effect. See *e.g.*, *Rose Corp. v. American Home Insurance Co.*, [2004] O.J. No. 379, 7 C.C.L.I. (4th) 9 (Ont. C.A.).

[13] *Keefer v. Phoenix Insurance Co. of Hartford*, [1901] S.C.J. No. 6, 31 S.C.R. 144 (S.C.C.).

[14] See, generally, Chapter 5. See *e.g.*, Ontario *Insurance Act*, R.S.O. 1990, c. I.8, s. 148. For fire insurance this obligation to disclose is underscored by statutory condition 2: Unless otherwise specifically stated in the contract, the insurer is not liable for the loss or damage to property

SUMMARY

If it is suspected that there may be an impediment to a successful claim because the person who bought the insurance lacked the requisite insurable interest, these are the steps to be followed to test that suspicion:

1. Determine whether the contract is an indemnity or a non-indemnity insurance contract.
2. If it is non-indemnity, establish whether one of the relationships set down in the statute existed between the purchaser of insurance and the person whose life was insured at the time the contract was made, or whether the latter consented to the insurance being placed on his or her life.
3. If not, the contract is a wager and unenforceable. However, if fraud was not involved, the premiums are refundable because the contract was void from the start.
4. If the contract is indemnity insurance, assess whether, at the time of the loss, the person who bought the insurance stood to benefit from the continued existence of the insured property or to be prejudiced by its destruction.
5. If not, the claim fails because the claimant has not shown that he or she has suffered loss. The contract is not void, the claim merely fails. Premiums are refundable only if it is shown that the contract was entered into on the basis of a mistaken belief about, say, the ownership of the property.
6. An exception applies if one person has intended to insure the interests of others along with his or her own and the contract permits it, provided all relevant facts have been disclosed to the insurer.

---

owned by any person other than the insured, unless the interest of the insured therein is stated in the contract.

Chapter 7

The Role of Agents and
Other Intermediaries

Many insurance transactions are conducted, not between the insurer and the customer directly, but through intermediaries. It is common practice for customers, in buying insurance, to deal with an agent or broker. In settling claims they often deal with adjusters. In this Chapter we examine the role played by such people and the legal consequences in terms of the relations between customer and insurer.

AGENTS

In everyday language the phrases "insurance agent" and "insurance broker" are interchangeable. But, in terms of their role in the making of insurance contracts and in terms of the manner of their regulation by governments, there is a difference between them. For reasons that will become apparent, the explanation of this difference varies depending on whether we are referring to Ontario and Quebec, on the one hand, and all the other provinces on the other. In most provinces, an "agent" is defined as someone who solicits business for an insurer, transmits applications for insurance to insurers on behalf of customers, or who participates in the negotiation or renewal of contracts.[1] The definition of a broker differs only in the exclusion of soliciting.[2] In fact, outside Ontario and Quebec, and for other than health and life insurance, the activities of agents and brokers are almost identical. The main reason for getting a broker's licence is to be able to place insurance with insurers in other provinces and other countries.[3]

In Ontario and Quebec, brokers are self-regulated. Therefore, it is only agents who are licensed by the government. A feature of this separate treatment of agents in Ontario is that, except for life insurance agents in limited circumstances, they are permitted to represent only one insurer.[4] In practice, in both Ontario and Quebec, an agent selling classes of insurance other than life insurance is a virtual employee of an insurer. When a customer deals with an agent in this sense, he or she is not really dealing through an intermediary at all

---

[1] See *e.g.*, New Brunswick *Insurance Act*, R.S.N.B. 1973, c. I-12, s. 1.
[2] *Ibid.*, s. 1.
[3] *Ibid.*, s. 522.
[4] See Ontario *Insurance Act*, R.S.O. 1990, c. I.8, s. 393(12).

but directly with the insurer. In other provinces, agents operate like Ontario brokers in that they place risks among several insurers.

Agents are licensed[5] for specific classes of insurance. In this regard, there is commonly a sharp distinction between life and non-life insurance. Although a separate class, accident and sickness insurance is often combined with life insurance under a single licence. Getting a licence requires passing an exam and paying a fee. Keeping it requires maintaining appropriate standards of honesty and competence.[6]

BROKERS

As we have seen, brokers operate more independently than agents. In provinces other than Ontario and Quebec, they are regulated in the same way as agents in that they are licensed by the provincial Superintendent of Insurance.

In Ontario and Quebec, brokers are self-governing professionals in the same way as lawyers and physicians are. Legislation[7] in each province sets up an incorporated association. The affairs of these associations are managed by boards of directors elected by the members who are the brokers themselves. Each association determines the criteria for admission to membership. In other words, the association rather than the government decides who may be a broker. Each association also controls standards of professional conduct. There are codes of conduct and disciplinary proceedings are instituted when necessary. A broker guilty of misconduct may be struck off the list of those authorized to practise.[8]

ADJUSTERS

Adjusters are people who investigate losses and/or negotiate settlements of claims on behalf, usually, of insurers.[9] Sometimes they are salaried employees of insurers. Sometimes they are self-employed. In some provinces, a self-employed adjuster must have a licence from the Superintendent of Insurance.

---

[5] Licences may be issued to individuals, corporations or partnerships. Individuals employed by a licensed firm may have to be licensed as "salesmen". See *e.g.*, *Saskatchewan Insurance Act*, R.S.S. 1978, c. S-26, s. 422.

[6] See *e.g.*, Ontario *Insurance Act*, R.S.O. 1990, c. I.8, s. 393(8).

[7] Ontario *Registered Insurance Brokers Act*, R.S.O. 1990, c. R.19; Quebec *Act respecting the distribution of financial products and services*, R.S.Q., c. D-9.2.

[8] Decisions like this may be appealed. In Ontario it is to a court. In Quebec it is to the Inspector General.

[9] Here we refer to those for whom this type of work is their profession. Some people, like lawyers, trustees or appraisers, negotiate claims on behalf of others in the course of some other occupation, but they are not required to be licensed as "adjusters".

The requirements for a licence may include passing an examination.[10] In Quebec, adjusters are governed by a code of ethics.[11]

INTERMEDIARIES AND INSURANCE CONTRACTS

Although some insurance is arranged, and some claims are negotiated by direct dealings between the insurer and the customer, frequently an intermediary is involved. Sometimes the process is initiated by an agent soliciting business on an insurer's behalf. Sometimes a person wanting insurance approaches an agent or broker. Faced with a claim an insurer may appoint an adjuster to act on its behalf. In any of these dealings, the intermediary may make statements which appear to be made on behalf of the insurer. It may be asserted, for example, that a contract (either a contract of insurance or an agreement settling a claim) has been concluded between the customer and the insurer. The question here is whether the insurer can be held to such a contract.[12]

The answer to this question depends upon what the insurer has authorized the agent, broker or adjuster to do. If an agent, for example, has been authorized merely to solicit business, and not to enter into binding contracts with customers, then, in the normal course of things, the agent may not commit the insurer to a contract. In the same way, an adjuster who has been authorized only to negotiate but not to conclude a settlement normally may not bind the insurer.

The terms of an intermediary's authority to act on the insurer's behalf are included in an agreement made with the insurer. Some functions are assigned to the intermediary expressly. Any other unstated functions necessary to carry out these expressly authorized functions come within the scope of "implied" authority. An insurer must honour any commitments entered into by an intermediary acting in accordance with express or implied authority.

Not to be confused with implied authority is "apparent" (or "ostensible") authority. Even where an insurer has not delegated express or implied authority, it may have acted in such a way as to cause customers or potential customers reasonably to believe that it has delegated that power. In other words, the agent appears to have the insurer's authority to act on its behalf. It is important to note, however, that this appearance must arise from the conduct of the insurer itself and not merely from the actions of the agent.[13] The following is an example of apparent authority: an insurer gave an agent express authority to commit it to contracts with customers judged by certain criteria to be good risks. Under the agency agreement, applications for insurance from other customers deemed not

---

[10] See *e.g.*, *Insurance Adjusters Licensing Regulations*, N.S. Reg. 245/92, as am. by N.S. Reg. 81/2000.

[11] Quebec Regulation O.C. 1040-99, September 8, 1999, G.O.Q. 1999.II.2938.

[12] Sometimes an intermediary can be the agent of both the insurer and the customer. See *e.g.*, *Walker v. CGU Insurance Co.*, [2003] O.J. No. 4064, 6 C.C.L.I (4th) 150 (Ont. S.C.J.). See also the next section of this chapter.

[13] *Wandlyn Motels Ltd. v. Commerce General Insurance Co.*, [1970] S.C.J. No. 54, [1970] S.C.R. 992 (S.C.C.).

to be such good risks had to be referred to the insurer for acceptance. But the material provided to the agent by the insurer which was intended for showing to customers failed to make the distinction between good and bad risks, and to make the consequences for the agent's authority clear. Accordingly, even bad risk customers might have reasonably assumed that the agent had the authority to conclude contracts with them on the insurer's behalf.[14]

Even where an intermediary acts, intending to commit the insurer, but has no authority, express, implied or apparent, to do so, the insurer may ratify the action after the fact either by positive act or acquiescence, provided it has full knowledge of the transaction.[15]

In some circumstances intermediaries are decreed by statute to be acting on behalf of an insurer whether or not authority has been expressly or apparently granted. When a customer pays a premium to an agent or a broker, it is as good as paying the insurer directly. The agent or broker is deemed by statute to be acting for the insurer for that purpose.[16] An agent or broker who receives insurance money for payment to a customer holds it in trust for the customer.[17]

INTERMEDIARIES AND THE TRANSMISSION OF INFORMATION

Several times during the life of an insurance contract, information passes back and forth between the insurer and the customer. When applying for insurance a customer must disclose relevant information.[18] If, after the contract of insurance comes into effect, changes occur which affect the risk assumed by the insurer, the customer must tell the insurer about them. If either the insurer or the customer wishes to terminate the contract, the other party must be informed.[19] The insurer notifies the customer about renewals or when premiums are due. When making a claim the customer must give the insurer details of loss in a specified manner within a specified time.[20] Whether or not an insurer is entitled to refuse to pay a claim may depend upon its having received or given certain information from or to the customer.[21]

---

[14] *Berryere v. Fireman's Fund Insurance Co.*, [1965] M.J. No. 44, 51 D.L.R. (2d) 603 (Man. C.A.).

[15] *Scott v. Co-operative Hail Insurance Co. of Regina*, [1957] S.J. No. 31, 7 D.L.R. (2d) 648 (Sask. C.A.).

[16] See *e.g.*, Ontario *Insurance Act*, R.S.O. 1990, c. I.8, s. 394. Note also that agents and brokers are accountable to insurers for premiums received. See *e.g.*, Ontario *Marine Insurance Act*, R.S.O. 1990, c. M.2, s. 54. But if a case is not covered by the statute the ordinary rules of agency apply. See *e.g.*, *Moody's Equipment Ltd. v. Royal Sun & Alliance Insurance Co.*, [2004] S.J. No. 113, 9 C.C.L.I. (4th) 60 (Sask. Q.B.).

[17] *Ibid.*, s. 359(2).

[18] See Chapter 5.

[19] See Chapter 4.

[20] See Chapter 10.

[21] For example, an agent with authority limited to receiving and forwarding applications has no authority to excuse a customer from the consequences of breaching a condition of the contract

In all these examples the communication may be made through an intermediary. The question is, when is a communication made to an intermediary, by either party, the equivalent (in terms of legal consequences) of a direct communication to the other party? Here is an illustration of how a problem might arise. An applicant for insurance provides a broker with full and accurate information about everything relevant to the proposed insurance. For whatever reason, fraud or carelessness, the broker fails to transmit the same information to the insurer. The result is that the insurer is misled. From the insurer's perspective, misrepresentation has occurred. In these circumstances, may the insurer deny a subsequent claim on the ground of misrepresentation even though the customer is personally innocent?

The answer to this question turns on the authority the broker has been given by the insurer. If the broker has been authorized, expressly or by necessary implication, to receive this information on the insurer's behalf, then the insurer is considered to have received the information when the broker got it and to have received it in the form it was in when conveyed by the customer to the broker. The result is the insurer cannot invoke misrepresentation as a reason for denying a claim. The same result ensues when the broker has been given authority to finalize contracts on the insurer's behalf. This is because receiving and evaluating information relevant to the insurance is a necessary part of the decision-making involved in accepting or rejecting contracts such that the broker has the implied authority to receive the information.[22] This reasoning also applies in cases where the broker's authority to commit the insurer to contracts is merely apparent.

Similarly, where an adjuster has the authority, express or apparent, to conclude an agreement with the customer settling a claim, this carries with it the implied authority to receive, on the insurer's behalf, information related to the claim.

It is different, however, when the customer has signed a form containing erroneous information. Even if he or she had supplied full and accurate information, the broker having made the mistake in writing it down, the misrepresentation is considered to have emanated from the customer. However, this does not apply in cases where disability, illiteracy or language difficulties make it impossible for the customer to check the accuracy of the written information.[23] Nor does it apply where the insurer's practice is to have the broker or agent complete the forms.[24]

---

[22] unless that authority is separately given. See generally Chapter 11, particularly the discussion about "waiver" and "estoppel".

Blanchette v. C.I.S. Ltd., [1973] S.C.J. No. 71, [1973] S.C.R. 833 (S.C.C.). Note that there are special statutory provisions regarding auto insurance. See *e.g.*, *Ontario Insurance Act*, R.S.O. 1990, c. I.8, s. 133.

[23] *Mahomed v. Anchor Fire and Marine Insurance Co.*, [1913] S.C.J. No. 39, 48 S.C.R. 546 (S.C.C.).

[24] *Blanchette v. C.I.S. Ltd.*, [1973] S.C.J. No. 71, [1973] S.C.R. 833 (S.C.C.).

PERSONAL LIABILITY OF AN INTERMEDIARY

Should a customer be denied a claim because an agent, broker or adjuster, not having the appropriate authority, has failed to transmit information properly to the insurer, he or she may be able to turn instead to the intermediary for redress. On the other hand, an insurer might find itself bound to pay a claim made by a customer it would not have insured in the first place had it known facts that were not passed on by an intermediary acting with the requisite authority. Here, the insurer may seek redress from the intermediary.

These are not the only examples of conduct leading to liability on the part of insurance intermediaries. Some brokers and agents have also had to pay damages to clients for failing to obtain coverage appropriate to their needs or instructions (or advising that the coverage is unavailable)[25], and for failing to arrange renewals.[26] Some have had to pay damages to insurers, for example, for failing to follow instructions to cancel a contract[27] or making undertakings to a customer that prejudice the insurer's rights.[28]

An insurance intermediary might be found liable to pay damages on one or more of several legal bases. The first arises from general agency law. If person A states to person B that A has authority to represent person C in dealings between B and C, and if in fact A has no such authority, A will have to pay damages to B for any loss suffered in reliance on A's assertion. A is said to have given B a warranty that the requisite authority existed.

Another basis for imposing liability upon an intermediary is contract. Apart from any contract that exists between the customer and the insurer, there may be a separate one between the customer and, say, a broker. This second contract obligates the broker to provide certain services for the customer, namely finding appropriate insurance coverage. If the broker fails to live up to this obligation, there is a breach of contract for which the law provides a remedy.[29]

The most common basis for liability is tort, particularly the tort of negligence.[30] Even if a contractual relationship has not been created there may be liability for failing to exercise reasonable care resulting in foreseeable loss to the customer or insurer. If there is a contract between the intermediary and the customer or insurer, the terms of that contract may preclude a tort case, but if

---

[25] But the customer has to show he or she would have acted differently if that information had been provided. *Ken Murphy Enterprises Ltd. v. Commercial Union Assurance Co.*, [2005] N.S.J. No. 114, 231 N.S.R. (2d) 327 (N.S.C.A.).

[26] See Brown, "The Implications of Professional Status: New Directions in the Liability of Agents and Brokers" (1988) 1 Can. Ins. L. Rev. 31.

[27] *Northwestern Mutual Insurance Co. v. J.T. O'Bryan & Co.*, [1974] B.C.J. No. 908, [1974] 5 W.W.R. 322 (B.C.C.A.).

[28] See *e.g.*, *Standard Life Assurance Co. v. Horsburgh*, [2005] B.C.J. No. 385, 209 B.C.A.C. 8 (B.C.C.A.), leave to appeal refused [2005] S.C.C.A. No. 490 (S.C.C.).

[29] See *Fine's Flowers Ltd. v. General Accident Insurance Co. of Canada*, [1977] O.J. No. 2435, 17 O.R. (2d) 529 (Ont. C.A.). The intermediary may also be guilty of a breach of a fiduciary obligation (akin to that owed by bankers to their clients).

[30] *Ibid.*

the contract does not mention it, concurrent actions based on tort and contract are permitted.[31]

Personal liability of an intermediary means that the person either has to provide the coverage to a customer denied it from the insurer, or reimburse an insurer required to pay a claim when, but for the intermediary's mistake, it would not have had to do so.

SUMMARY

Many insurance transactions are conducted through intermediaries such as agents, brokers and adjusters. Whether either party, insurer or customer, is bound or prejudiced by the actions or representations of an intermediary depends on the authority (actual, implied or ostensible) given to that intermediary.

An intermediary may be liable for loss caused to either the customer or insurer by fraudulent or negligent conduct.

---

[31] *Central Trust Co. v. Rafuse*, [1986] S.C.J. No. 52, [1986] 2 S.C.R. 147 (S.C.C.).

Chapter 8

The Form and Content of Insurance Contracts

REQUIREMENTS OF FORM

In everyday language the term "insurance policy" is used interchangeably with "insurance contract". It is common to think of a contract as a piece of paper embodying the terms of an agreement. But a contract and a policy are not the same thing and it is important to distinguish between them. A policy is merely the written evidence that a contract exists.[1] A contract can be proved to exist by other evidence such as the oral testimony of the parties or others; by receipts, application forms or memos; or by a combination of both oral and written evidence. In fact it is usual for property and automobile insurance contracts to come into existence, at least on a temporary basis, before any policy is issued when the customer needs immediate coverage.

One type of insurance, title insurance, must be in writing to have effect. Title insurance protects the customer against financial loss that would occur after he or she purchased land if it turned out the seller of the land did not own it. That these contracts must be in writing is consistent with a requirement pertaining to contracts for the sale and purchase of land generally.[2]

A life insurance contract must also be in writing. Legislation requires that an insurer entering into a contract issue a policy.[3] Moreover the "entire contract" is constituted by that policy, the application, any document attached to the policy when issued, and any amendment agreed upon in writing after the policy is issued.[4] There are also stipulations about what must be in the policy when issued. This will be discussed later in this chapter.

An insurer entering into a contract of accident and sickness insurance with an individual must also issue a policy.[5] Where there is a contract of group insurance, the policy must be issued to the institutional insured (such as an employer

---

[1]   See *e.g.*, Ontario *Insurance Act*, R.S.O. 1990, c. I.8, s. 1. See also *Civil Code of Québec*, S.Q. 1991, c. 64, Art. 2477.

[2]   See *e.g.*, *Statute of Frauds*, R.S.O. 1990, c. S.19, s. 4.

[3]   See *e.g.*, Ontario *Insurance Act*, R.S.O. 1990, c. I.8, s. 174.

[4]   *Ibid.*, s. 174(2). Note that different documents constitute a contract made by a fraternal society (see s. 174(3)).

[5]   See *e.g.*, Ontario *Insurance Act*, R.S.O. 1990, c. I.8, s. 293.

or association) and a certificate issued to each person in the group.[6] However, unlike life insurance, it is not specified that certain documents constitute the "entire contract". The obligation to issue a policy is imposed by statute upon the insurer. The insurer's failure to meet this obligation does not prejudice the customer if the essential elements of a contract — agreement as to the basic terms and an exchange of promises to give something of value — can be demonstrated by whatever evidence is available.[7]

Marine insurance contracts are usually concluded by insurers signing a "slip" setting out the coverage required by the customer. This slip is circulated among several insurers who sign on for a portion of the risk. Each signature on the slip denotes a separate contract between insurer and customer. Normally the policy is issued later, perhaps only when loss has occurred since a lawsuit to enforce a claim may proceed only if there is a policy.[8]

Customers buying auto insurance contracts often get no policy but only a certificate of insurance. This is because standard policies are approved and published by provincial Superintendents of Insurance. However, if the customer wants a policy, he or she is entitled to it on request. Fire insurance (and, more generally, property insurance) contracts are typically evidenced by policies although there is no formal obligation on insurers to issue them. Often, though, fire or general property policies are not issued until some time after the contract has come into effect so that, in the interim, evidence of the contract takes the form of the application, the broker's receipt, or simply the spoken word.

For insurance contracts, except life, accident and sickness, marine, auto and fire insurance, while there is no formal requirement that an insurer issue a policy, consequences follow if it does not. Legislation provides that all the terms of the contract are to be set out in full in the policy and any term not in the policy may not be used by the insurer to its advantage.[9] For example, an insurer may not allege that the customer has breached a condition of the contract if that condition is not included in the policy. But the insurer's failure to include some or all of the terms of the contract in a policy does not mean that there is no contract. The customer may enforce for his or her benefit any term of the contract, assuming it can be established by evidence to exist, even if it is not in the policy or other form of writing.

THE CONTENTS OF POLICIES

When a policy is issued — and for most insurance contracts of any type this happens eventually — there are stipulations in legislation as to what it must, at a

---

[6] *Ibid.*, s. 298. Note that similar considerations apply to group life insurance. See *ibid.*, ss. 176, 177.

[7] This is rarely a practical problem because terms of contracts typically require the delivery of the policy and the payment of the premium before they enter into force.

[8] See *e.g.*, Ontario *Marine Insurance Act*, R.S.O. 1990, c. M.2, s. 23.

[9] See *e.g.*, Ontario *Insurance Act*, R.S.O. 1990, c. I.8. s. 124. But see below regarding temporary contracts.

minimum, contain.[10] For example, a life policy must identify the insured person and the person whose life is insured, the amount of insurance and the conditions under which it becomes payable, the amount of premium and when it must be paid, whether the contract entitles the customer to a share of profits, the conditions upon which the contract may be reinstated if it lapses, and any options for surrendering the contract for cash or obtaining loans or advance payments of insurance money or paid-up or extended insurance.[11]

An accident and sickness policy must identify the person who is to be paid insurance money and the person whose well-being is insured. It must also specify the amount of insurance and the conditions for payment of it, the amount of premium, the conditions for reinstatement if the contract lapses, and the time of commencement and termination of the contract.[12]

The contents of an auto policy are determined in part by direct statutory specification and in part by a process of official approval. The details of so-called no-fault coverage for personal injury sustained in car accidents, for example, are set out in statutes[13] or regulations.[14] These details are not negotiable and form part of every contract. Other parts[15] of the coverage, including

---

[10] See *e.g.*, *Civil Code of Québec*, S.Q. 1991, c. 64, Art. 2399.

[11] See *e.g.*, Ontario *Insurance Act*, R.S.O. 1990, c. I.8, s. 175. See also *Civil Code of Québec, ibid.*, Art. 2415. Note the requirements differ for group policies and certificates.

[12] See *e.g.*, Ontario *Insurance Act*, R.S.O. 1990, c. I.8, s. 294. See also *Civil Code of Québec*, S.Q. 1991, c. 64, Art. 2416. Note that the requirements for group policies and certificates are different, see *e.g.*, Ontario *Insurance Act, ibid.*, ss. 296, 298.

[13] See *e.g.*, British Columbia *Insurance (Motor Vehicle) Act*, R.S.B.C. 1996, c. 231.

[14] See *e.g.*, *Statutory Accident Benefits Schedule*, O. Reg. 776/93.

[15] Auto insurance can be divided into several sub-categories. No-fault coverage pays benefits to the customer or members of his or her household (or, in some cases, passengers in the insured car or pedestrians hit by it) for loss caused by personal injury or death in an auto accident.

Automobile liability insurance pays any legal damages for which the insured person becomes liable when sued by some other person either for personal injury or death or for property damage. Note that, in personal injury cases, this liability is affected by the no-fault benefits available to the person suing. In Quebec an injury victim's sole recovery is from the no-fault scheme. Therefore, for accidents in Quebec, there is no need for liability insurance at all. However, motorists still need liability insurance in case they cause accidents outside Quebec. In Ontario the right to sue is severely restricted but not entirely eliminated, such that liability insurance plays only a residual role in accidents occurring in the province. In some other provinces, while a full right to sue exists, the amount of damages payable is reduced by the amount of no-fault benefits available to the injured person.

Uninsured and under-insured motorist insurance pays money to the customer when the full amount of damages which he or she is entitled to receive from another person judged to be at fault is unavailable owing to the fact that the other person cannot be identified, has no liability insurance, or has some but not enough.

In Quebec and Ontario, the compulsory auto insurance package includes an arrangement whereby the customer's own insurer will make good damage to the insured vehicle where that damage is caused by the fault of someone else. Provided the driver at fault is also insured, there is no lawsuit against him or her. It is thought more efficient simply to have each person go to his or her own insurer and dispense with the business of suing. But in claiming from one's own insurer, one must still demonstrate the other driver's fault. If the customer so elects, no deductible applies but the amount payable will be reduced if the customer was partially to blame.

collision insurance which is optional, are specified by wording which may only be used after it has been approved by the appropriate provincial official, usually the Superintendent of Insurance. But even here, there are elements which are dictated directly by statute. Every policy includes "statutory conditions" dealing with matters like changes in the risk, prohibited uses, termination and the parties' obligations after loss has occurred.[16] In addition, legislation sets out general standards with which all contracts must conform.[17]

Part of a fire insurance policy is mandated in the form of statutory conditions.[18] These are broadly similar to the auto insurance statutory conditions dealing with such matters as misrepresentation, termination and the requirements for dealing with claims. If a policy contains a clause, such as a deductible, limiting the amount of insurance to something less than the amount of the loss, this fact must be spelled out in red ink on the face of the policy.[19] More generally, all contracts must be consistent with the rules pertaining to fire insurance contracts contained in the legislation.[20] In addition, no provision in a contract which is deemed by a court to be unjust or unreasonable is binding on the customer.[21] A provision falls into this category if it imposes a condition having no bearing on the risk insured.[22] Even a provision which is not unjust or unreasonable by this definition will not be given effect if its application in the particular case would be unjust or unreasonable.[23]

THE STRUCTURE OF POLICIES

Apart from those policies whose terms are set out in a statute or regulations and those subject to approval by the Superintendent of Insurance, there is no requirement that policies conform to any particular format. While industry-wide initiatives have produced some standard wordings for some clauses, there is considerable variety when it comes to the way policies are structured.

Components of policies are usually grouped in sections. They may appear under headings such as "insuring agreement", "exclusions", "conditions", "warranties", "endorsements", "declarations", "definitions" and "coverages". Among different insurers there is no consistent usage. Indeed, a term may not

---

Collision or comprehensive coverage are forms of insurance which the customer may choose to buy to provide protection against damage to the vehicle regardless of who is to blame. Comprehensive insurance covers damage by any cause except collision. A customer wanting protection against both collision and other events can buy all-perils coverage. For these types of coverage it is common for customers to opt for deductibles so that the amount of insurance payable will be less than the amount of loss.

[16] See *e.g.*, *Statutory Conditions – Automobile insurance*, O. Reg. 777/93.

[17] See *e.g.*, Ontario *Insurance Act*, R.S.O. 1990, c. I.8, s. 126.

[18] See *ibid.*, s. 148.

[19] *Ibid.*, s. 149.

[20] See *ibid.*, s. 126.

[21] See *e.g.*, *ibid.*, s. 151.

[22] See *e.g.*, *Dunningham v. St. Paul Fire & Marine Insurance Co.*, [1963] B.C.J. No. 181, 45 W.W.R. 463 (B.C.C.A.).

[23] *Marche v. Halifax Insurance Co.*, [2005] S.C.J. No. 7, [2005] 1 S.C.R. 47 (S.C.C.).

necessarily be used by one insurer in the same sense as it is by another. Thus, when it comes to insurance policies, there is no magic associated with the heading under which a particular clause is placed. Headings are intended to make policies easier to read and this can be achieved in a variety of ways. For our purposes we can categorize the clauses in insurance policies under three headings: insuring agreement, exclusions, and conditions and warranties.

The Insuring Agreement

The insuring agreement specifies the subject matter of the insurance such as the house covered by a fire insurance contract or the person whose life is insured by a life insurance contract. The property or person must be identified either specifically or generally (for example, "all the personal property situated at 1 Main St., London").[24] The insuring agreement also sets out the duration of the contract, defined in particular by: the expiry date; the premium, including how and when it is payable; the monetary limits of the coverage and applicable deductibles; and a list of the perils against which insurance is provided.

Terms of policies having to do with the amount of coverage are of several kinds. The most common is a statement of the upper limit of recovery in the event of loss. In indemnity contracts it is also common to find "deductibles". A deductible is an amount of money which the insurer and customer have agreed in advance should be subtracted from the value of the loss when the insurer's contribution is calculated. So, if a policy insuring a car stipulates a deductible of $500, and the car is damaged so that it will take $800 to fix it, the insurer has only to pay $300 to meet its obligation under the policy. The value of the loss is $800 but the insurer is entitled to deduct $500 as agreed.

Another type of clause having to do with the amount of coverage in property insurance is a co-insurance clause. This says that, if the upper limits on the coverage are lower than a given percentage (typically 80 per cent) of the total value of the property, then even for partial damage, the insurer is responsible for only a portion of the loss. Again, an example will illustrate. Assume a stamp collection is worth $50,000. The owner buys theft insurance coverage only for loss up to $30,000, so there is insurance only up to 60 per cent of the value of the property insured. The policy contains an 80 per cent co-insurance clause. If part of the collection, worth $20,000, is stolen, the insurer does not have to pay the full $20,000 even though the limits on the policy are higher than that. The effect of the co-insurance clause is to make the customer a co-insurer of the risk. That is he or she must bear a portion of the risk personally.

If a fire insurance policy includes a deductible or a co-insurance clause, that fact must be stamped in red ink on the face of the policy.[25]

---

[24] Note that there is a distinction between damage to property itself and losses, such as loss of profits, which are consequences of the damage. A contract providing insurance cover for damage to specified property does not automatically cover consequential loss. That has to be covered separately, either in the same contract or in another one (*e.g.*, business interruption insurance).

[25] See *e.g.*, Ontario *Insurance Act*, R.S.O. 1990, c. I.8, s. 149.

Perils are events which lead to loss.[26] They may include fire, flood, theft, vandalism, disease, personal injury, or the incurring of liability. In making a claim, the customer must establish that one of the events stated in the contract has occurred.

Exclusions

Exclusions are events or circumstances which, if they happen in a way that relates to the loss, result in there being no coverage. The insurer must establish that a claim is excluded. Some exclusions deny coverage if the loss is caused or contributed to by a particular peril. For example, a homeowner's insurance contract may provide coverage for damage attributable to flooding unless it is caused by the backup of a sewer. In such a contract sewer backup is an excluded peril. Other exclusions refer to more general situations like a clause in an automobile insurance contract stating that there can be no successful claim if the damage happened while the vehicle was being driven by an unlicensed driver. Another example is a provision in a fire insurance contract denying coverage if the fire happens while the premises are unoccupied.[27]

Most exclusions are stated specifically. However, there are some losses that are presumed to be excluded even if the contract makes no mention of them. These are losses deliberately caused or recklessly allowed to happen by the customer or someone else covered by the contract, or by normal wear and tear.[28]

Conditions and Warranties

Conditions and warranties lay down obligations that the customer must satisfy in order to preserve coverage. These may be affirmative obligations in the sense that the customer is required to do certain things like maintain burglar alarms or hire a minimum number of crew members for a ship. They may be negative obligations, such as refraining from allowing an unlicensed driver to operate a car. They may relate to circumstances before any loss happens, such as the examples just cited, or they may concern matters arising after loss, like giving adequate proof of loss or protecting damaged property against further harm.

The difference between conditions and warranties is that the latter must be strictly observed whereas the former need merely be substantially met. If it is not clear that the provision is a warranty, it will be considered by a court dealing with it to be a condition. In most provinces, legislation dictates that, in fire

---

[26] For more on causation of loss, see Chapter 9.

[27] Sometimes loss is not excluded entirely. Rather, loss occurring in a certain way or in certain circumstances may be covered but subject to lower limits or a higher deductible. See *e.g.*, *British Columbia v. Royal Insurance Co.*, [1991] B.C.J. No. 2959, 4 C.C.L.I. (2d) 206 (B.C.C.A.), leave to appeal refused, [1991] S.C.C.A. No. 506, 10 C.C.L.I. (2d) 309*n* (S.C.C.).

[28] See the remarks about fortuity in Chapter 1 and Chapter 9.

insurance, no condition or warranty is to be given effect if it is unjust or unreasonable.[29]

Except for those contained in fire insurance policies, the distinguishing feature of both conditions and warranties is that failure to satisfy them results in loss of coverage even if the particular instance of default had nothing to do with the loss. This is what makes them different from exclusions. Here is an example. If a policy covering the stock of a jewellery store against theft contains a clause stating that there will be no coverage *while* the property is removed from the store, that is an exclusion. Therefore, if the owner takes some jewellery home, later brings it back to the store and loss caused by an insured peril occurs subsequently, the loss is covered and the insurer must pay. On the other hand, if the policy states that there will be no cover *if* the owner ever removes jewellery from the store, that is a condition. This means that, if jewellery is removed from the store, its return to the store does not revive the coverage and the insurer does not have to pay for any subsequent loss.[30] For provisions in fire insurance policies, however, legislation would protect the insured person on the grounds that application of the condition in the particular case would be unjust and/or unreasonable.[31]

There is another reason it is important to distinguish between conditions and exclusions in those types of insurance contracts for which legislation has provided statutory conditions. Any clause that amounts to a condition is unenforceable against a customer if it amounts to a "variation of or addition to any statutory condition".[32] Thus, a provision in a policy dealing with the same topic (for example, misrepresentation or proof of loss) will be of no use to the insurer if it is a condition.[33]

TEMPORARY CONTRACTS

We saw in the first section of this Chapter that indemnity insurance contracts are not required to be in any particular form. We saw that, although most of them are eventually reduced to writing with the terms set out in full in a policy, temporary arrangements are often based entirely on brief notes or even spoken conversations.

This raises two types of problems. First, given the circumstances in which these temporary arrangements are made, it is unlikely that anything more than the basic terms — subject matter, premium, monetary limits and the time period for coverage — are discussed. The details of most conditions and exclusions are not mentioned. For example, the customer's obligations in the event of loss are rarely, if ever, raised at this stage. But they are invariably spelled out in policies. The

---

[29] See *e.g.*, Ontario *Insurance Act*, R.S.O. 1990, c. I.8, s. 151.

[30] This assumes that there are no other terms in the policy which might save the coverage.

[31] See *Ontario Insurance Act*, R.S.O. 1990, c. I.8, s. 151; *Dunningham v. St. Paul Fire & Marine Insurance Co.*, [1963] B.C.J. No. 181, 45 W.W.R. 463 (B.C.C.A.); and *Marche v. Halifax Insurance Co.*, [2005] S.C.J. No. 7, [2005] 1. S.C.R. 47 (S.C.C.).

[32] See *e.g.*, Ontario *Insurance Act*, R.S.O. 1990, c. I.8, s. 148.

[33] See *e.g.*, *Reynolds v. New Zealand Insurance Co.*, [1961] B.C.J. No. 127, 28 D.L.R. (2d) 374 (B.C.S.C.).

question is, what if a loss happens during the life of such a temporary contract before a detailed policy has been issued? Do the conditions that would be in effect once the policy is issued apply before then as part of the interim arrangement?

There are times when it is clear that policy terms are anticipated so that they do apply before there is a policy. One example is where the brief documentation denoting the interim contract includes a statement that "the insurance effected is subject to the insurer's standard policy form and wording applicable to the class of insurance" or something similar. Even though the customer does not know the precise terms, he or she is presumed to accept that there are some constraints on the rights which the contract confers.[34] On the other hand, where there is no mention, either orally or in writing, that the usual terms apply, it is unclear whether they may be invoked against the customer.[35]

A special case is that involving statutory conditions. Recall that, in most provinces, legislation imposes certain conditions on several types of insurance contracts, notably fire, automobile, and accident and sickness insurance. These conditions are decreed to be "part of every contract".[36] This is not limited to written contracts. Further, the fire and automobile insurance legislation goes on to provide that, while the conditions must be printed in every policy and if they are not, they are not binding on the customer and they need not be included in an "interim binder". So it would seem that the statutory conditions apply to temporary contracts of fire or auto insurance. For accident and sickness insurance, the obligation on the insurer to print the statutory conditions extends to interim binders so that, if they are not printed there they may be invoked by, but not against, the customer.[37]

The second problem that can arise with a temporary contract is a conflict between it and the policy that subsequently appears. In essence, the solution to this problem is that the terms of the contract concluded first in time are to prevail. For fire and automobile insurance, legislation deems policies to be consistent with the terms of any written application for the insurance which the customer has made unless the difference has been pointed out to the customer and he or she has been given the chance to reject the altered contract.[38] More generally, the principle is that the terms agreed at the outset cannot be changed except by further agreement. The unilateral act of the insurer issuing a policy containing terms inconsistent with those originally agreed is not enough.[39]

---

[34] *McQueen v. Phoenix Mutual Insurance Co.*, [1879] O.J. No. 247, 29 U.C.C.P. 511 (U.C. Ct. C.P.)

[35] *Re Coleman's Depositaries Ltd.*, [1907] 2 K.B. 798 (C.A.), an English case, decided that a customer may not be held to terms he or she has not seen or heard about. However, the reasoning in *McQueen, ibid.*, that it is reasonable to expect a customer to know that some conditions must apply, seems to hold even where he or she has not been informed of the existence of "usual" conditions.

[36] See *e.g.*, Ontario *Insurance Act*, R.S.O. 1990, c. I.8, s. 148.

[37] See *North Lethbridge Garage Ltd. v. Continental Casualty Co.*, [1930] A.J. No. 39, [1930] 2 D.L.R. 835 (Alta. C.A.); *Canadian Acceptance Corp. v. Indemnity Marine Assurance Co.*, [1955] B.C.J. No. 123, 15 W.W.R. 322 (B.C.C.A.).

[38] See *e.g.*, Ontario *Insurance Act*, R.S.O. 1990, c. I.8, ss. 146, 232(4).

[39] *Inn. Cor International Ltd. v. American Home Assurance Co.*, [1973] O.J. No. 2229, 2 O.R. (2d) 64 (Ont. C.A.).

SUMMARY

Most types of insurance contracts may be made orally; in fact, that is not uncommon for temporary cover. However, when confirmed, most insurance is reduced to writing in the form of a policy. Policies contain a variety of terms that can be classified as those forming the insuring agreement, those constituting exclusions and those that are conditions or warranties.

Temporary arrangements, whether made orally or by brief written record, usually incorporate the principal terms of the insurer's standard policy for the type of insurance concerned. But where terms agreed to in negotiations differ from those in the policy eventually forthcoming, the agreed terms prevail.

Chapter 9

Interpreting Insurance Policies

In the last Chapter, we examined the structure of the written form of an insurance contract — a policy. Gaining an understanding of structure is the first step to discovering whether or not a particular loss is covered by an insurance contract. The next step is determining the meaning of the words. Once it has been decided that a clause is an exclusion clause, for example, it is necessary to decide further whether it applies in the given case. How we go about this is the subject of this Chapter.

THE "RULES" OF INTERPRETATION

The "rules" of insurance contract interpretation are easy enough to state. A court should give effect to the intention of the parties — the insurer and the customer. If the words used are not clear enough to disclose what this joint intention is, the words are given a meaning that, if reasonable, favours the customer. This is considered fair either because the language was chosen by the insurer or because the meaning adopted (usually by a court asked to resolve a dispute about the meaning) achieves a result that meets the parties' reasonable expectations.

But predicting how a court is going to apply this two-stage approach in a given case can be extraordinarily difficult. Take these facts for example. A builders' risk policy covers all risks of physical damage to a construction project. If the damage is caused by flood, the deductible is 10 times that for other perils. A flood is defined in the policy as "waves, tides, tidal waves, the rising of, the breaking out or the overflow of any body of water whether natural or man-made." This policy is held by the builder on a project involving creek channelling. The work involved reshaping banks and applying concrete. To facilitate the work, the builder diverts the stream through a pipe lying on the original creek bed so that concrete can be placed on either side. While the work is in progress heavy rain falls. It is too much for the pipe. Water spills out and damages the concrete work. But the volume is not so great that it overflows the watercourse. The question is, has the work been damaged by "flood" so that the higher deductible applies? How would you think a court would deal with that?

What, first of all, was the joint intention of the insurer and customer in this regard? Because of the special treatment afforded floods in terms of the deductible (and therefore the premium) it is likely that the matter is something both considered specifically. Indeed, when a case involving these facts got to the

British Columbia Court of Appeal,[1] all three judges thought the parties' intention was clear enough that there was no need to resort to the second level enquiry. From the point of view of understanding the process, the problem was there were two opposing views about what was "clear". Two judges thought it was clear that the intention was not to include facts such as these within the definition of flood. They said the water had to run over the original creek banks. The other judge thought this was the sort of event they would have envisaged as a flood. After all, if this was not a "rising of ... any body of water", what is?

There is a temptation, in the face of decisions like this (majority) one, to conclude that the court's approach is not two-pronged at all. It seems as if the customer-favouring resolution is the only rule in play. But there are enough cases in favour of insurers to undermine this sceptical view. Nonetheless, the process of interpretation remains problematic in its uncertainty. How a particular form of words falls upon a particular set of judicial eyes or ears seems to have as much to do with those eyes and ears as with the form of words.

Against this background, all one can do is provide a framework for organizing thoughts about how a court might construe an insurance contract. What follow are really categories of arguments: arguments about the intention of the parties; about when ambiguity exists; and about how to resolve such ambiguity. But it is only a framework, more to do with asking the right questions than providing the answers.

WHAT THE PARTIES INTENDED

In theory, insurance contracts are like any other contracts in that they are the product of conscious and voluntary actions by the parties who have turned their minds to the terms of their commercial relationship. It would follow that the words they have used capture what was intended by them to be the arrangement.

That the parties' intention is the first point of reference in interpreting insurance contracts is well settled, at least in theory.[2] But practice and theory often diverge. Basic auto insurance, for example, is compulsory for auto owners and most of the terms are mandated by statute or regulation. Fire insurance contracts also contain conditions inserted by statute rather than the parties. To seek the meaning of provisions such as these in terms of the parties' intention is to pursue a fiction. Even where statute has not intruded, it is often inaccurate to speak of a common intention in relation to many of the terms of an insurance contract. Consider the "negotiations" for most contracts involving individuals rather than businesses. The customer has one or two conversations with a broker or agent. Usually only the basic terms — subject matter, limits, premium, deductible and, perhaps, one or two matters of coverage, such as a specific peril to be included or excluded — are discussed. The balance of the policy, which the customer

---

[1]   *British Columbia v. Royal Insurance Co.*, [1991] B.C.J. No. 2959, 4 C.C.L.I. (2d) 206 (B.C.C.A.).
[2]   *Consolidated Bathurst Export Ltd. v. Mutual Boiler and Machinery Insurance Co.*, [1979] S.C.J. No. 133, [1980] 1 S.C.R. 888 (S.C.C.).

typically sees for the first time after the contract has come into force, is the insurer's standard form, the details of which, like claims deadlines, definitions or even conditions of cover, were never considered by the customer during negotiations.

The result is there are cases where the issue turns genuinely on what the parties intended, and there are those where intention cannot realistically be found. In the latter category, a court applies its idea of a fair commercial result. The proper starting point though, is to determine whether the case in point is in the first category; that the dispute involves a term which was specifically negotiated. In making this determination, it is necessary to view the words at issue in the context of the whole policy. For example, words in the body of a printed policy should be read subject to conditions endorsed upon it because the latter are more likely to have been given specific consideration during negotiations. Similarly, the terms of an interim contract, or indeed the application where it has been made part of the contract, prevail over conflicting standard form policy wordings;[3] clearly inoperative parts of a standard general form do not affect the meaning of words in the operative parts,[4] and terms handwritten or typed prevail over those which are printed.[5]

Apart from these relatively obvious examples of evidence of the parties' intention, it is usually possible to say that, on some level, there was a meeting of the minds. It is normally easy to conclude that a customer intended that there be some cover and that words in the contract not have the effect of allowing the insurer to avoid paying any claim. So, if an insurer were to argue for an interpretation of a policy that would render the coverage worthless, it would likely be in vain. By the same token, a customer could not advance an interpretation that would permit recovery for loss that did not occur. The insurer could not reasonably have intended that.

THE PLAIN MEANING OF WORDS

When a court professes to use the "literal" or plain meaning approach to construing words in a policy, it is usually applying the "intention" approach by another name. It is really saying that the words used are so clear that the parties must surely have meant to achieve the meaning they so clearly capture.[6] However, the literal approach is subordinate to the intention of the parties

---

3   See the section of Chapter 8 dealing with temporary contracts.

4   *Home Insurance Co. v. Victoria-Montreal First Insurance Co.*, [1907] A.C. 59 (P.C.).

5   *Poole & Thompson Ltd. v. London & Lancashire Guarantee and Accident Co.*, [1938] S.C.J. No. 52, [1938] 4 D.L.R. 6 (S.C.C.). If there is clear evidence that the words in the policy are completely at odds with what was agreed, a court will give effect to the actual agreement. See *e.g., Inn. Cor International v. American Home Assurance Co.*, [1973] O.J. No. 2229, 2 O.R. (2d) 64 (Ont. C.A.). This is sometimes referred to as "rectification" of the contract.

6   *Progressive Homes Ltd. v. Lombard General Insurance Co. of Canada*, [2010] S.C.J. No. 33, 89 C.C.L.I. (4th) 161 (S.C.C.). See also *e.g., Dimaria v. Pilot Insurance Co.*, [2003] O.J. No. 3958, 5 C.C.L.I. (4th) 191 (Ont. S.C.J.).

approach. Words in policies should not be given their literal meaning if that meaning flies in the face of the parties' intention as gleaned from the document as a whole.[7]

One context in which literal interpretations give way to meanings thought better to reflect the intent, at least of the consumer, is in the approach taken to words and phrases which can be used as terms of art. Here, the general rule is that the ordinary meaning, rather than the technical one is to be preferred.[8]

PRESUMING INTENTION

Where the notion of an intention in respect of particular words used, on the part of the customer at least, is no more than a fiction, courts seek to impose a "sensible" or "commercially realistic" interpretation on the assumption that this is what the parties would have intended if they had turned their minds to it when entering into the contract.[9]

Another way of putting it is that the courts favour an interpretation that gives effect to a viable commercial arrangement over one that nullifies it. While this is true of contracts generally, in insurance it has several specific applications. It means that there is no cover for loss that is not fortuitous, in the sense that it is intentionally caused by the insured or inherent in the nature of the subject matter of the insurance, even where the literal meaning of the policy appears to cover that loss. On the other hand, it means that courts tend to avoid forfeiture of cover if possible. More specifically, coverage provisions are interpreted broadly while exclusions are interpreted narrowly.

AMBIGUITIES

When a court is unable to determine a common intention as to the meaning of a particular word or phrase by applying the rules of construction discussed so far, in other words when the policy is ambiguous, the impasse is resolved by resort to some notion of fairness. It has been stated in the Supreme Court of Canada that this second step is to be taken only after the first step has proved futile.[10]

---

[7] See *Consolidated Bathurst Export Ltd. v. Mutual Boiler and Machinery Insurance Co.*, [1979] S.C.J. No. 133, [1980] 1 S.C.R. 888 (S.C.C.). See also *Jesuit Fathers of Upper Canada v. Guardian Insurance Co. of Canada*, [2006] S.C.J. No. 21, [2006] 1 S.C.R. 744 (S.C.C.); *Co-operators Life Insurance Co. v. Gibbens*, [2009] S.C.J. No. 59, 2009 SCC 59 (S.C.C.).

[8] See *e.g.*, *Model Jewellery Manufacturing Co. v. Western Assurance Co.*, [1963] I.L.R. 560, 42 D.L.R. (2d) 318 (S.C.C.); *Dominion Bridge Co. v. Toronto General Insurance Co.*, [1963] S.C.J. No. 37, [1963] S.C.R. 362 (S.C.C.).

[9] See *e.g.*, *Kingsway General Insurance Co. v. Lougheed Enterprises Ltd.*, [2003] B.C.J. No. 1794, 2 C.C.L.I. (4th) 53 (B.C.S.C.).

[10] *Stevenson v. Reliance Petroleum Ltd.*, [1956] S.C.J. No. 68, [1956] S.C.R. 936 (S.C.C.); *Progressive Homes Ltd. v. Lombard General Insurance Co. of Canada*, [2010] S.C.J. No. 33, 89 C.C.L.I. (4th) 161 (S.C.C.).

But it is worth repeating that we are discussing here a singularly imprecise process. It will be apparent from preceding paragraphs that the inquiry about intention seems itself frequently to dissolve into a search for a fair result, a search not necessarily encumbered by a real belief that a genuine common intent exists.

Be that as it may, it is standard practice for courts to distinguish between words or phrases whose meaning, after due inquiry, can be pronounced to be "clear" and those that are irreducibly ambiguous.

An ambiguity can arise in at least two ways. A form of words might reasonably bear two meanings in the sense that it is fairly arguable both that a given set of facts does and does not fit into it. Another form of ambiguity exists where two or more unambiguous provisions in the same contract are irreconcilable. The terms may be in different parts of the policy or, one may be in the policy and the other in the cover note.

When an ambiguity is identified it is, by and large, resolved in favour of the insured. This is done on one of two theories: *contra proferentem* or reasonable expectation. These two notions need to be examined separately.

CONTRA PROFERENTEM

This is the short form of the Latin maxim *verba chartarum fortius contra proferentem accipuntur*, meaning the words of a contract are to be construed more strongly against the person offering them. For the most part, insurance contracts are evidenced by policies that are drafted almost exclusively by insurers. At least where individual, non-commercial customers are concerned, most of the terms are offered on a take it or leave it basis. The relative sophistication and bargaining power of the parties is markedly unequal. The opportunity for modifying or adding to the text by way of clarification lies almost entirely with insurers. It is therefore considered appropriate that an ambiguity occurring among such terms be resolved against the insurer.[11] The rule applies even where the text has to be submitted to the Superintendent of Insurance for approval.[12] But it does not apply to terms in a contract which are mandated, word for word, by legislation or regulation,[13] unless there is evidence insurers as a lobbying group were influential in the drafting.[14]

---

[11] *McClelland & Stewart Ltd. v. Mutual Life Assurance Co. of Canada*, [1981] S.C.J. No. 60, [1981] I.L.R. 1-1393 (S.C.C.).

[12] *Wigle v. Allstate Insurance Co. of Canada*, [1984] O.J. No. 3422, 10 C.C.L.I. 1 (Ont. C.A.); leave to appeal refused [1985] S.C.C.A. No. 136, 14 D.L.R. (4th) 404*n* (S.C.C.).

[13] *Martin v. Manitoba Public Insurance Corp.*, [1988] M.J. No. 353, [1988] I.L.R. 1-2388 (Man. C.A.); *Squire v. Insurance Corp. of British Columbia*, [1990] B.C.J. No. 633, 44 B.C.L.R. (2d) 65 (B.C.C.A.).

[14] *Guest v. Royal Sun Alliance Insurance Co.*, [2004] N.J. No. 69, 8 C.C.L.I. (4th) 50 (N.L.C.A.); *Donovan v. McCain Foods Ltd.*, [2004] N.J. No. 70, 8 C.C.L.I. (4th) 194 (N.L.C.A.).

REASONABLE EXPECTATION

Disputes about the meaning of terms in insurance contracts are now occasionally resolved by courts determining and applying the "reasonable expectation" of the parties. This development may have created some anxiety among insurers because some courts in the United States, the birthplace of the idea, have looked only at the customer's expectations and have even imposed contractual obligations on insurers in complete disregard even of clear exclusionary language in the policy.[15] But these fears have not so far been borne out. Canadian courts, most notably the Supreme Court of Canada, have been circumspect in their use of the doctrine and have reiterated the following guidelines for the interpretation of insurance policies:[16]

1. The true intent of the parties is to be gleaned from the whole contract.
2. Where two or more meanings are possible, the court is to select that which most reasonably promotes the intent of the parties.
3. Coverage provisions are to be construed broadly and exclusions narrowly.
4. Ambiguities are to be construed against the insurer.
5. The court should avoid an interpretation which will either give a windfall to the insurer or an unanticipated recovery to the insured. In other words the court should give effect to the reasonable expectations of both parties.

CAUSATION

Even if words in a policy are not ambiguous, there may still be questions about whether they cover a particular loss. For there to be coverage, the loss has to have been caused by one of the perils specified and the question of causation can sometimes be problematic. If, for example, a truck is damaged when a branch of a tree, having been split by a bolt of lightning, falls on it, has the truck been damaged "by lightning"? It is clear what the word "lightning" means, but it is not so clear whether the loss has been caused by lightning.

Problems of causation arise when the loss has resulted from several factors, not all of which are insured perils. In our example, if the policy covered loss by lightning but not loss from falling trees, it is easy to see how the insurer and the customer would analyze the matter of causation differently. But whose point of view would prevail?

In general terms the answer turns on what is the "proximate" (or "dominant" or "effective") cause. But, by itself, that test is not very helpful. You could make a case that both the lightning and the falling branch were dominant causes of loss because, without either one, the truck would have been unscathed. For a

---

[15] See the review of American law by Cory J. in his dissenting judgment in *Brissette v. Westbury Life Insurance Co.*, [1992] S.C.J. No. 86, 13 C.C.L.I. (2d) 1 (S.C.C.).

[16] See *Brissette, ibid.*; *Reid Crowther & Partners v. Simcoe & Erie General Insurance Co.*, [1993] S.C.J. No. 10, 13 C.C.L.I. (2d) 161 (S.C.C.).

more meaningful approach, it helps to understand that there are essentially two ways in which there can be multiple causes. One involves a chain of causation where each occurrence causes another to happen in turn, eventually resulting in the loss. If one of those occurrences is mentioned in the policy as a peril against which insurance is provided, and there was a "direct" connection between it and the loss, the test for causation is met. For the connection to be direct, there must be no new, human, intervening cause between the occurrence and the loss[17] except where the intervention is an attempt to prevent or minimize the loss.[18] It does not matter whether the occurrence in question was the originating or an intermediate episode. There may therefore be more than one direct cause of loss.

It is different, however, if one of the occurrences which can be seen as a direct cause of the loss is excluded by a term of the policy. Here the exclusion prevails even if one of the other direct causes is a peril insured against,[19] but it must be remembered that in this, as in other contexts, exclusion clauses are given a narrow interpretation.[20]

The other type of case involving multiple causes is where two independent factors coincide and affect each other to cause loss that would not have happened, or would have been less severe, if only one of the factors had occurred. An example is a case where a man died when he suffered a mild heart attack at the same time he was exposed to toxic fumes. The fumes did not cause the heart attack. Neither the fumes nor the heart attack would have killed him without the presence of the other. But together they were fatal.[21] In this situation, either factor is a proximate cause. This means that there is cover if the policy insures against fatal "accidents" unless death from disease is specifically excluded. Where an accident can be said merely to have "operated on" a pre-existing disease, in that the disease was only a passive factor, the resulting loss is not excluded by a provision confining coverage to loss caused "directly, and independently of all other causes" by accident.[22]

---

[17] *Edwards v. Wawanesa Mutual Insurance Co.*, [1959] B.C.J. No. 101, 27 W.W.R. 413 (B.C.C.A.).

[18] *Drumbolus v. Home Insurance Co.*, [1916] O.J. No. 146, 37 O.L.R. 465 (Ont. H.C.).

[19] *Wadsworth v. Canadian Railway Accident Insurance Co.*, [1914] S.C.J. No. 2, 49 S.C.R. 115 (S.C.C.).

[20] *Derksen v. 539938 Ontario Ltd.*, [2001] S.C.J. No. 27, 33 C.C.L.I. (3d) 1 (S.C.C.).

[21] *Milashenko v. Co-operative Fire & Casualty Co.*, [1970] S.C.J. No, 111, 11 D.L.R. (3d) 128*n* (S.C.C.).

[22] *Marks v. Commercial Travelers Mutual Accident Assn.*, [1956] S.C.J. No. 87, 4 D.L.R. (2d) 113 (S.C.C.). But the mere rarity of the manifestation of disease does not make it an accident without some external factor. See *Co-operators Life Insurance Co. v. Gibbens*, [2009] S.C.J. No. 59, 2009 SCC 59 (S.C.C.); *Wang v. Metropolitan Life Insurance Co.*, [2004] O.J. No. 3525, 16 C.C.L.I. (4th) 69 (Ont. C.A.).

ACCIDENTAL, CERTAIN AND DELIBERATELY CAUSED LOSS

We saw in the previous paragraph that the term "accident" may appear in a policy in opposition to "disease". A similar problem arises in distinguishing accidental occurrences from those certain to happen. Property damage attributable to natural deterioration or normal wear and tear is not "accidental" but the mere fact that the loss happens over time (such as by leaking water) does not mean that it is inevitable and if it is neither intended nor expected is still an accident.[23]

Another problem with the definition of "accident" is defining the line between it and loss deliberately brought about by the person insured. Insurance is about transferring risk of loss, not promising to pay for loss that is virtually certain to happen or which is engineered by the customer's deliberate action. Even if this is not expressly stated in the policy it is deemed to be there since it is implicit in the nature of insurance.

The difficulty in defining an accident in this sense arises when the customer's conduct is so highly reckless as to be beyond mere negligence. At one time courts took the view that, if the conduct was so reckless as to make the occurrence of resulting loss no surprise, the entire matter was beyond the realm of accident. Accordingly, a man's fall from a balcony where he had been performing balancing tricks was held to be no accident.[24] But, more recently, a less strict test has been applied. The traditional definition of an "accident", "an unlooked for mishap or occurrence" has been taken to include even the adverse results of calculated risks.[25] A stunt man who jumped from 188 feet to his death, having failed to land in a barrel of water as intended, was held to have died in an accident because he had not intended to miss.[26] A drug addict who deliberately consumed dangerous amounts of drugs and died as a result was held to have died by "accidental means" because, despite the intentional conduct, death was unexpected.[27] In cases involving liability insurance, this approach has the effect of better protecting third parties harmed by the conduct of an insured person. Under the old approach a third party was out of luck if his or her loss had been caused by the insured person's recklessness.[28] Now, mere recklessness is no

---

[23] *Progressive Homes Ltd. v. Lombard General Insurance Co. of Canada*, [2010] S.C.J. No. 33, 89 C.C.L.I. (4th) 161 (S.C.C.).

[24] *Candler v. London & Lancashire Guarantee & Accident Co. of Canada*, [1963] O.J. No. 763, [1963] 2 O.R. 547 (Ont. H.C.J.).

[25] *Canadian Indemnity Insurance Co. v. Walkem Machinery*, [1975] S.C.J. No. 34, [1976] 1 S.C.R. 309 (S.C.C.); *Stats v. Mutual of Omaha Insurance Co.*, [1976] O.J. No. 2309, 73 D.L.R. (3d) 324 (Ont. C.A.).

[26] *Soucek Estate v. Atlantic Mutual Life Assurance Co.*, [1988] O.J. No. 1482, 35 C.C.L.I. 78 (Ont. Dist. Ct.).

[27] *Martin v. American International Assurance Life Co.*, [2003] S.C.J. No. 14, [2003] 1 S.C.R. 158 (S.C.C.).

[28] *Crisp Estate v. Great American Indemnity Co.*, [1961] O.J. No. 170, [1961] O.W.N. 278 (Ont. C.A.).

longer a bar to recovery provided the insured person did not actually intend the adverse outcome.[29] A related question is whether an insured person may recover under an insurance policy when the loss has resulted from his or her criminal activity. At one time, courts applied a total ban on recovery in these circumstances on the ground that no one should be protected against the consequences of his or her criminal conduct or receive any benefit from it.[30] But, insofar as liability insurance was concerned, this had the unfortunate effect of denying compensation to innocent third parties. Accordingly, legislation in most provinces now stipulates that, unless the contract provides otherwise, the violation of criminal or other law does not, by itself, defeat a claim under an insurance contract.[31] Coverage is barred only if the crime is committed with the intent to bring about the loss. The rule preserving coverage in the face of criminal conduct does not apply to life insurance so that a beneficiary may not receive insurance money if guilty of murder or manslaughter of the person whose life is insured.[32]

SUMMARY

Courts interpret insurance policies so as to give effect, where possible, to the intention of the parties. If that intention is not clear, that there is an ambiguity, a court will apply the meaning most favourable to the customer provided it is what could be reasonably expected.

For there to be coverage, the loss has to have been caused by a peril included in the policy and not specifically excluded. It is also usually required that the loss be accidental and neither deliberately caused nor certain to occur.

---

[29] *Canadian Indemnity Insurance Co. v. Walkem Machinery*, [1975] S.C.J. No. 34, [1976] 1 S.C.R. 309 (S.C.C.).

[30] *Home Insurance Co. of New York v. Lindal*, [1933] S.C.J. No. 63, [1934] S.C.R. 33 (S.C.C.).

[31] See *e.g.*, Ontario *Insurance Act*, R.S.O. 1990, c. I.8, s. 118.

[32] See *Demeter v. British Pacific Life Insurance Co.*, [1983] O.J. No. 3148, 43 O.R. (2d) 33 (Ont. H.C.J.), affd [1984] O.J. No. 3363, 48 O.R. (2d) 266 (Ont. C.A.). But see also *Oldfield v. Transamerica Life Insurance Co. of Canada*, [2002] S.C.J. No. 23, 2002 SCC 22 (S.C.C.), which held that an innocent beneficiary may claim despite the criminal conduct, resulting in death, of the insured person.

Chapter 10

Making Claims

NOTICE OF LOSS

When loss occurs and the customer wants to claim under an insurance contract, the customer's first obligation is to inform the insurer. The details of this obligation are invariably included in the policy. It may be a requirement that the information be given in writing. There will certainly be a time limit. There are at least two reasons insurers want to know about a loss quickly. First, if there are grounds for contesting the claim, then that is more likely to be discovered nearer in time to the event. Second, when a claim for the total loss of property is paid, the insurer is entitled to what is left of the property. The sooner after loss the insurer knows about it, the sooner the insurer is able to take steps to protect this "salvage" interest.

The notice of loss obligations for fire, automobile, and accident and sickness insurance are, in most provinces, set out in statutory conditions. For example, for fire insurance, notice must be given "forthwith" and in writing.[1] For accident and sickness insurance, notice must be written and delivered or sent by registered mail to the insurer or its authorized agent no later than 30 days from the date the claim arises.[2] For automobile insurance, notice of claims must be given "promptly" and in writing and must include all available information about damage and injury.[3]

A time limit expressed in imprecise terms, like "promptly" or "forthwith", can create difficulty because it is not always obvious whether the notice given by a customer meets such a limit. Notice given a month after the event has been held to be too late to be "immediate"[4] and five weeks has been held to be too long to be "prompt".[5] But it depends on all the circumstances including the

---

[1] See *e.g.*, Ontario *Insurance Act*, R.S.O. 1990, c. I.8, s. 148, statutory condition 6(1)(*a*). See also *Civil Code of Québec*, S.Q. 1991, c. 64, Art. 2470.

[2] See *e.g.*, Ontario *Insurance Act*, *ibid.*, s. 300, statutory condition 7(1)(*a*). See also *Civil Code of Québec*, S.Q. 1991, Art. 2435.

[3] See *Statutory Conditions*, O. Reg. 777/93, statutory conditions 5(1)(a), 6(1)(a). Notice of a no-fault personal injury claim must be made within 7 days of the accident "or as soon as practicable": see *e.g.*, *Statutory Accident Benefits Schedule*, O. Reg. 34/10, s. 32(1) (applies to accidents on or after September 1, 2010).

[4] *Shera v. Ocean Accident & Guarantee Corp.*, [1990] O.J. No. 197, 32 O.R. 411 (Ont. H.C.J.).

[5] *Duchene v. General Accident Assurance Co.*, [1926] O.J. No. 161, 31 O.W.N. 59 (Ont. H.C.J.).

difficulties facing the customer and whether the insurer has been prejudiced by the timing of the notice. In one case, notice given four months after an accident was held to be prompt enough, in part because the nature of the injury was unresolved.[6]

Usually, the notice period runs from the date of loss or the date of the accident or other date when a claim arises. When the customer does not become aware of the loss until some time after it has occurred or knows about it but does not at first believe it to be covered by the insurance, the policy wording may permit late notice.[7] Generally, however, the customer is not excused from complying with the time limit if there are reasons to suspect there may be a claim.[8]

An insurer may dispense with the requirement that notice be written if it receives and acts on oral notice. Oral notice effects the same object as the written kind but it is not up to the customer alone to substitute the former for the latter. The insurer must signify to the customer that oral notice is acceptable. Once it has done so, it is unable to go back on its word and later try to deny the claim on the basis that no written notice was provided.[9]

PROOF OF LOSS

In addition to notice, the customer must furnish sufficient evidence to establish the occurrence and extent of the loss.[10] As with notice, policy terms, including statutory conditions where they apply, lay down time limits for this process. The limit may be expressed as a specific period, such as 90 days, or in general terms, such as "promptly" or "as soon as practicable" after the loss.[11] These general terms can present problems similar to those described above pertaining to notice with each case turning on its particular facts.

The customer must supply specific information. For example, a fire insurance claim must include a complete inventory of the destroyed and damaged property, showing in detail quantities, costs, values and the amount claimed as well as a statement of how the loss happened so far as is known.[12] For accident and sickness insurance and automobile insurance, the requirement is for "such proof as is reasonably possible in the circumstances" both of the loss and the customer's right to payment under the policy.[13]

---

[6] *Filiatrault v. Zurich Insurance Co.*, [1981] B.C.J. No. 1937, 126 D.L.R. (3d) 555 (B.C.S.C.).

[7] *Grant v. British Pacific Life Insurance Co.*, [1980] N.S.J. No. 362, 36 N.S.R. (2d) 137 (N.S.T.D.).

[8] *Marcoux v. Halifax Fire Insurance Co.*, [1948] S.C.J. No. 18, [1948] S.C.R. 278 (S.C.C.).

[9] See discussion in Chapter 11 on "Waiver and Estoppel".

[10] See *e.g.*, *Civil Code of Québec*, S.Q. 1991, Art. 2471.

[11] For examples, see *Ontario Insurance Act*, R.S.O. 1990, c. I.8, s. 148, statutory condition 6(1)(a) and s. 300, statutory condition 7(1)(a). See also *Civil Code of Québec*, S.Q. 1991, c. 64, Arts. 2435 and 2470.

[12] See *e.g.*, Ontario *Insurance Act*, R.S.O. 1990, c. I.8, s. 148, statutory condition 6.

[13] See *e.g.*, Ontario *Insurance Act*, *ibid.*, s. 300, statutory condition 7(1)(b); *Automobile Accident Insurance Benefits Regulations*, Alta. Reg. 352/72, s. 3.

Whether a proof of loss is as complete as reasonably possible depends on the circumstances. The object is to enable the insurer to determine if a claim is valid both in nature and amount. If this object is satisfied, proof requirements will generally have been met. Nonetheless, within the limits of the possible, proof must be specific, both as to valuation and loss, and in describing the facts that bring the loss within the terms of the policy. If the first proof submitted is inadequate or inaccurate by mistake, the customer may put in additional or amending information so long as this is done within the prescribed time limit.[14] But if the customer asks if the material submitted is satisfactory and the insurer either states that it is or remains silent, the customer is entitled to assume everything is in order and the insurer may not later try to deny payment on grounds of inadequate proof of loss.[15]

As a safeguard against fraudulent claims, a policy may contain a term requiring that proof be submitted in a particular form, such as a statutory declaration, either in all cases or only in those instances where the insurer demands it.[16] In appropriate cases, medical certificates are also required.[17] However, in dealing with minor claims, most indemnity insurers do not insist on strict compliance with the policy and accept informal proof.[18]

Insurers are obliged to provide customers with claims forms.[19] If no forms are provided, usually within 60 days, or if the insurer fails to assist the customer with the claim in any other way, the insurer may not deny the claim on the basis that the proof was filed too late or otherwise deficient. On the other hand, where forms are provided, the customer is not obliged to use them if the essential information is transmitted to the insurer, unless there is a term in the policy expressly requiring use of the forms.[20]

If absent or otherwise for good reason unable to act personally, the customer may appoint someone else to carry out the requirements relating to notice and proof.[21] If the customer refuses to act or to appoint someone else, any person entitled to some of the insurance money, like the holder of a mortgage on the insured property, may submit the claim.[22]

---

[14] *Kent v. Ocean Accident & Guarantee Corp.*, [1909] O.J. No. 26, 20 O.L.R. 226 (Ont. C.A.).

[15] *Glen Falls Insurance Co. v. Adams*, [1916] S.C.J. No. 54, 54 S.C.R. 88 (S.C.C.).

[16] See *e.g.*, *Statutory Conditions – Automobile Insurance*, O. Reg. 777/93, s. 6(1)(c).

[17] See *e.g.*, Ontario *Insurance Act*, R.S.O. 1990, c. I.8, s. 300, statutory condition 7(1)(c).

[18] See Chapter 11 for more on when customers are excused from meeting the formal requirements laid down in policies.

[19] See *e.g.*, Ontario *Insurance Act*, R.S.O. 1990, c. I.8, s. 135.

[20] *Marks v. Commercial Travelers Mutual Accident Assn.*, [1956] S.C.J. No. 87, 4 D.L.R. (2d) 113 (S.C.C.).

[21] See *e.g.*, Ontario *Insurance Act*, R.S.O. 1990, c. I.8, s. 148, statutory condition 8.

[22] *Stevens v. Queen Insurance Co.* (1894), 32 N.B.R. 387 (N.B.C.A.).

FRAUDULENT CLAIMS

Unless the policy deals with it some other way, fraud by the customer when making a claim entitles the insurer to deny that claim, and any other claim made under the contract, without having to refund premiums.[23] The policy may give the insurer rights which are narrower than this. For example, a statutory condition required to be in fire insurance policies in most provinces states that "any fraud or wilfully false statement" in the proof of loss "vitiates the claim of the person" making it. Note that the power to vitiate relates only to the particular claim, not any claim, and only to the claim of the individual guilty of the fraud.[24] The consequences of fraud in a claim may be dictated by statute in other ways. In some provinces, automobile insurance legislation states that, if a claimant wilfully makes a false statement in respect of the claim, it is invalid and the right to indemnity is forfeited.[25]

It makes no difference if the fraud is in the form of positive assertion or omission as long as it is deliberate and it is material to the claim.[26] Inadvertent errors do not count.[27]

The insurer has to prove that there has been fraud. Although to assert that the customer is guilty of fraud is to allege that a crime has been committed, it is not necessary that the insurer establish its case according to the criminal law standard of proof, that is, beyond a reasonable doubt. However, while the standard applied in civil cases pertains so that it is theoretically sufficient if the insurer demonstrates that it is more likely than not that the customer committed fraud, courts in fact vary this standard in accordance with the seriousness of the offence alleged.[28] The evidence must amount to more than suspicion or conjecture and the allegation proven to a "high degree" of probability.[29] This test is met if the customer, having claimed on account of fire damage, later pleads guilty to or is convicted of the crime of arson in relation to the same fire.[30] The fraud here is the attempt to conceal the fact that the fire was set deliberately, deliberate loss being excluded from coverage.

---

[23]   *Royal Insurance Co. v. Dimario*, [1987] O.J. No. 1144, 29 C.C.L.I. 67 (Ont. Div. Ct.).

[24]   If the policy is silent on the matter, fraud by a customer relating to a claim in which another person has an interest will not prejudice that other person's rights unless the subject matter of the insurance is not divisible. *Truglia v. Travelers Indemnity Co.*, [1965] O.J. No. 1095, [1966] 1 O.R. 364 (Ont. H.C.J.); *Siountres v. United States Fire Insurance*, [1981] O.J. No. 723, 128 D.L.R. (3d) 493 (Ont. H.C.J.). But see Chapter 15 for the special rights of mortgage holders and other third parties.

[25]   Ontario *Insurance Act*, R.S.O. 1990, c. I.8, s. 233.

[26]   *Mortgage Corp. of Nova Scotia v. Law Union & Rock Insurance Co.*, [1936] S.C.J. No. 48, [1937] S.C.R. 74 (S.C.C.).

[27]   *Lindsay v. General Accident Assurance Co.*, [1981] N.B.J. No. 71, 34 N.B.R. (2d) 78 (N.B.Q.B.); *I.C.B.C. v. Phung*, [2003] B.C.J. No. 1986, 3 C.C.L.I. (4th) 83 (B.C.S.C.).

[28]   *Continental Insurance Co. v. Dalton Cartage Ltd.*, [1982] S.C.J. No. 116, 131 D.L.R. (3d) 559 (S.C.C.); *Hanes v. Wawanesa Mutual Insurance Co.*, [1963] S.C.J. No. 8, [1963] S.C.R. 154 (S.C.C.).

[29]   *Smetana v. Manitoba Public Insurance Corp.*, [1986] M.J. No. 240, 21 C.C.L.I. 95 (Man. Q.B.).

[30]   *Wawanesa Insurance Co. v. Levesque* (1939), 6 I.L.R. 139 (Ont. H.C.J.).

SUMMARY

To succeed in making a claim, a customer must give timely and otherwise proper notice and proof of the loss to the insurer. Fraud in connection with the claim, the onus of proof for which is on the insurer, disqualifies the claim.

Chapter 11

Excusing Defects in Claims and Other Defaults

As we have seen in previous Chapters, customers face forfeiture of coverage if they fail to meet their obligations under insurance contracts. A customer breaching a condition, such as a requirement to maintain a burglar alarm or file proof of loss on time, gives the insurer a valid reason for denying payment of a claim. So does misrepresenting or withholding information relevant to the insurance. But in some cases it is possible for a claim to succeed despite the customer's default. This can occur if the circumstances come within the terms of legislation allowing "relief from forfeiture". It may also happen if the insurer has "waived", or is "estopped" from raising its right to withhold payment. In this Chapter, we shall examine these concepts.

RELIEF FROM FORFEITURE

In all provinces, except Quebec, insurance legislation contains a section giving a judge the discretion to rule that a claim should not be forfeited where the customer has been guilty of "imperfect compliance" with one of the obligations arising after loss, such as the timely submission of notice or proof.[1] To exercise this discretion, a judge must be convinced that it would be unfair, in the circumstances, to deny payment to the customer. This means that the customer's mistake was innocent and not wilful, such as deliberately misrepresenting the claim.[2] It also means that the insurer has not been prejudiced by the customer's default.[3] Lateness in giving notice of loss, for example, may make it impossible for the insurer properly to investigate the loss.[4]

Use of the section is restricted in two other ways. First, it may be invoked only where there has been imperfect compliance with an obligation, not where

---

[1] See *e.g.*, Ontario *Insurance Act*, R.S.O. 1990, c. I.8, s. 129. See also s. 328 applying to accident and sickness insurance. Note that these sections apply to neither life insurance nor marine insurance.

[2] *Canadian Indemnity Insurance Co. v. Erickson*, [1959] S.C.J. No. 48, [1959] S.C.R. 672 (S.C.C.).

[3] *Hua v. Optimum West Insurance Co.*, [2005] B.C.J. No. 412, 2005 BCCA 123 (B.C.C.A.); *Donovan v. McCain Foods Ltd.*, [2004] N.J. No. 70, 8 C.C.L.I. (4th) 194 (N.L.C.A.).

[4] *Rayko v. Insurance Corp. of British Columbia*, [1986] B.C.J. No. 1302, 21 C.C.L.I. 196 (B.C.S.C.).

there has been complete non-compliance, such as the failure to provide any proof of loss at all. But the requirements for proving a loss are, for these purposes, considered as a package, and non-compliance with only part of the package is mere imperfect compliance with the whole so that relief may be granted where that happens.[5] Second, the section only applies where the customer's default relates to one of the obligations arising after loss has occurred.[6] Thus, there may be relief against forfeiture for inadequate or late proof of loss, but not for a customer's failure to disclose relevant information at the time the insurance is taken out.

On the matter of deadlines, it is important to distinguish between the one that limits the time within which various aspects of a claim must be submitted to the insurer and that which limits the time within which a lawsuit must be launched against the insurer in the event of disagreement about the customer's entitlement to payment. Missing the former amounts to imperfect compliance with an obligation and is something a court may excuse. But failure to meet the latter (the "limitation" date) may not be excused in this way because it relates to legal procedure as opposed to the substantive rights and obligations under the contract.[7]

More general authority for a court to grant relief may be found in legislation constituting a province's superior courts. In Ontario, the relevant provision is section 98 of the *Courts of Justice Act.*[8] This section is not constrained by the same limiting factors as the section in the *Insurance Act,*[9] but it still does not allow a court to create contractual obligations where they do not exist, for example, where a customer has breached a condition, such as the requirement to pay premiums, which is the basis of the contract.[10]

WAIVER AND ESTOPPEL

There are five categories in which an insurer is considered to have given up (or "waived") its right to refuse payment even though the customer has defaulted on one of the obligations in the contract. Once one of these situations has arisen, the insurer may not change its mind and try to invoke the right it has relinquished.

---

[5] *Schwartz v. Providence Washington Insurance Co.,* [1963] M.J. No. 82, 45 W.W.R. 617 (Man. C.A.).

[6] *Williams v. York Fire & Casualty Insurance Co.,* [2007] O.J. No. 2517, 86 O.R. (3d) 241 (Ont. C.A.).

[7] *Presco Industries Ltd. v. Saskatchewan Government Insurance Office,* [1967] S.J. No. 225, 65 D.L.R. (2d) 120 (Sask. C.A.); *National Juice Co. v. Dominion Insurance Co.,* [1977] O.J. No. 2462, 18 O.R. (2d) 10 (Ont. C.A.); *Chiasson v. Century Insurance Co. of Canada,* [1978] N.B.J. No. 65, 21 N.B.R. 192 (N.B.C.A.). This is so even though the limitation period may be set by the contract (see Chapter 12).

[8] R.S.O. 1990, c. C.43, s. 98.

[9] R.S.O. 1990, c. I.8, s. 129.

[10] *Pluzak v. Gerling Global Life Insurance Co.,* [1999] O.J. No. 1401, 44 O.R. (3d) 49 (Ont. S.C.J.), revd [2001] O.J. No. 34, 195 D.L.R. (4th) 293 (Ont. C.A.), leave to appeal refused [2001] S.C.C.A. No. 110 (S.C.C.).

The five categories are "estoppel by representation", "promissory estoppel", "election of remedy", "variation of contract" and "repudiation".

Estoppel By Representation

If an insurer has told a customer that he or she has satisfactorily complied with a particular obligation, and the customer, relying on that assurance, does nothing further in connection with the obligation, the insurer may not later allege that the customer did not meet the obligation. The insurer is said to be "estopped" from raising the matter even if the customer did in fact fail to fulfil the obligation.

Here is an example. A term of a policy requires the customer to provide written notice of loss within three weeks if a claim is to succeed. Loss occurs and the customer telephones the insurer and gives the relevant information orally. The insurer's claims officer tells the customer that the phone call is sufficient and that there is no need to put the notice in writing. The customer assumes nothing further need be done and takes no further action even though the deadline for submitting written notice is several days away. The deadline passes. Later the insurer tries to deny payment on the ground that the customer failed to provide written notice of loss within three weeks. Here the insurer is estopped from using that failure as a reason for denying payment. In other words, if the customer sues for payment, he or she will succeed despite not having complied with the letter of the contract.

In situations like this, the estoppel arises from the insurer's representation to the customer. This representation can be expressed or implied by the insurer's conduct. For example, cashing a premium cheque which is sent in late amounts to a representation that late payment is, at least on the particular occasion, acceptable. Accordingly, if the customer relies on that implied assurance by, say, doing nothing about getting alternative insurance, the insurer may not later take the position that the late payment on that occasion entitles it to refuse payment in the event of loss.[11] In some cases, the "representation" may be construed from complete silence. If the insurer has an obligation to communicate certain information to the customer, like the form in which it wants proof of loss submitted, and does not do so, it cannot later say, with any legal effect, that the customer did not comply with its requirements as to form of proof.[12]

Promissory Estoppel

Estoppel by representation arises where an insurer has, in effect, excused a prior default by the customer. Where the insurer excuses the default in advance, it is called promissory estoppel because the insurer is prevented from going back on its promise not to insist on future compliance with a particular obligation.[13]

---

[11] *Tattersall v. People's Life Insurance Co.*, [1905] O.J. No. 159, 9 O.L.R. 611 (Ont. Div. Ct.). See also *Whitehorn v. Canadian Guardian Life Insurance Co.*, [1909] O.J. No. 154, 19 O.L.R. 535 (Ont. Div. Ct.).

[12] *Caldwell v. Stadacona Fire & Life Insurance Co.*, [1882] S.C.J. No. 37, 11 S.C.R. 212 (S.C.C.).

[13] *Maracle v. Travelers Indemnity Co.*, [1991] S.C.J. No. 43, 3 C.C.L.I. (2d) 186 (S.C.C.). Some cases may involve both estoppel by representation and promissory estoppel. In the above example of the insurer's employee telling the customer that written notice was not necessary, there was estoppel by representation in that there was a statement that the notice already given,

An example of promissory estoppel is an insurer telling a customer, after it has received notice of a loss but before proof of loss, that a clause in the policy requiring proof of loss to be in the form of a statutory declaration may be ignored and that informal proof will be sufficient. When the customer acts or rather fails to act on the strength of this assurance, the insurer may not go back on it.

As with estoppel by representation, the "promise" creating promissory estoppel may be express or implied. Consider again the example of late premiums. Just as the insurer may excuse a previous late payment, it may also excuse future late payment. One way this might happen is by the insurer consistently accepting late payments over a period of time. For a while, each acceptance merely creates an estoppel by representation with respect to that payment. But, eventually the cumulative effect will be to establish a customary practice wherein the customer comes reasonably to assume that late payment is always acceptable to the insurer. A late payment submitted after this point is reached, even if it is rejected by the insurer, will not prejudice the customer's rights under the contract of insurance.[14]

Election of Remedy

One of the central features of estoppel, of either variety, is the response by the customer to the statement made by the insurer. There must be some reliance placed on the assurance given by the insurer. The customer must have acted or refrained from acting in a way which would have been to his or her benefit, like going ahead and complying with the strict requirements of the policy or buying alternative insurance to be safe in the face of any change of heart on the insurer's part. If there has been no reliance, estoppel does not apply.

But there are circumstances in which an insurer will be bound by its statement or conduct forgiving a customer's default even where no reliance is placed on it by the customer. In other words, it is possible for an insurer to choose to ignore the default and to treat the contract of insurance as continuing in effect.

Occasionally a contract expressly deals with the consequences of its breach. That is, if one party breaks the contract by failing to live up to his or her obligations under it, the contract might give the other party specific remedies. If the contract is silent about that, breach of the contract gives the party not in breach a choice. In the context of insurance cases where the customer has broken the contract by, for example, not paying premiums on time, this choice falls to the insurer. The choice is between: (1) bringing the contract to an end; and (2) treating it as continuing in effect and calling for future performance by the customer of his or her obligations. This decision will be taken because the

---

although defective because it was not in writing, was acceptable. There was also promissory estoppel in that the insurer promised that it would not be necessary to comply with the writing requirement in the future, that is, the time between when the statement was made and the deadline.

[14] *Whitehorn v. Canadian Guardian Life Insurance Co.*, [1909] O.J. No. 154, 19 O.L.R. 535 (Ont. Div. Ct.).

insurer expects to benefit from the continuation of the contractual relationship in that premiums will keep coming in.

This choice also arises in respect of defaults that occur in connection with claims. If a customer is delinquent in filing proof of loss, the insurer's remedy is to deny the claim. But, in some situations, the insurer may choose to ignore the delinquency and treat the claim as one in good standing. This may be because the insurer is unsure of its ground and prefers, on balance, to keep the claim alive and benefit from the continued cooperation of the customer in the investigation of the claim. This is especially likely in the context of liability insurance because the claim involves injury done allegedly by the customer to a third party. The third party may have a claim directly against the insurer and, if it involves an auto accident, this claim may survive any default on the customer's part.[15]

When making its choice, the insurer is electing which remedy it prefers. Once that choice is made unequivocally, it is irrevocable. The customer's default is excused. It does not matter what response, if any, is made to it by the customer.

Although the choice may be made by implication, such as by cashing a late premium cheque, it must be clear. This means that the insurer knew that it was indeed in a position to choose. In other words, it must have been aware that the customer had breached an obligation and that there was therefore an opportunity to treat the contract as at an end or the claim as invalid. Once this is known to the insurer, the insurer must make its election and, if the choice is to carry on despite the breach, it must be signalled unequivocally. Courts require clear evidence that a party to a contract is voluntarily and irrevocably giving up rights.[16]

The insurer may elect to ignore, not only those delinquencies which arise directly from the contract, such as missed claims deadlines, but also statutory limitations on the time for filing lawsuits to resolve coverage disputes.[17]

Variation of the Contract

One way a customer may overcome an insurer's contention that the contract has been breached is by showing that the clause, of which he or she has supposedly fallen foul, no longer applies, the contract having been amended. To prove that this has occurred, the customer must show that he or she and the insurer entered

---

[15] See Chapter 15.

[16] *Reierson v. Northern Life Assurance Co. of Canada*, [1976] S.C.J. No. 28, [1977] 1 S.C.R. 390 (S.C.C.). In most provinces, legislation underscores this by requiring a "waiver", if it is to be binding on an insurer, to be in writing. See *e.g.*, Ontario *Insurance Act*, R.S.O. 1990, c. I.8, ss. 131, 300, statutory condition 1. This does not apply to life insurance or marine insurance. Section 131 (and the equivalent in other provinces) also provides that neither party shall be deemed to have waived any term of the contract by any act relating to the appraisal of loss, the delivery of proofs or the investigation of a loss, thus greatly reducing the scope for election by implication.

[17] *Miller v. Toronto General Insurance Co.*, [1966] P.E.I.J. No. 5, 59 D.L.R. (2d) 507 (P.E.I.S.C.). Note that this election of remedies differs from relief from forfeiture in this respect.

into a new contract changing the old one. Like any contract, this new arrangement must be characterized by agreement, in the sense that both parties desired the same thing. It must also be shown that each party promised to give the other something of value.[18]

A contract to vary the old contract might arise as follows. A contract of insurance contains a term stating that, in the event of a dispute about the customer's entitlement to payment, the customer must commence legal proceedings against the insurer within one year from the date of loss. The parties find themselves in dispute and the customer contemplates legal action. It is a complicated claim and the insurer feels it needs more than one year to deal with it. As the one-year deadline approaches, the insurer asks the customer to defer starting legal proceedings, saying it needs more time. The customer agrees, only too pleased to save the legal costs. Both parties have received a benefit from the mutually agreed arrangement. They have made a new contract extending the one-year limitation period. The insurer may not later assert successfully that a lawsuit, commenced by the customer after one year has elapsed since the loss, is too late.[19]

Repudiation

An insurer may refuse to pay a claim saying the contract is no longer in effect because the customer breached one of its conditions prior to the loss. For example, if it is a condition of a contract of insurance on a building that a security system be maintained, failure to do so allows the insurer to avoid its obligations under the contract. When the insurer announces it intends to do this, it is repudiating the contract.

If an insurer refuses to pay because it believes the particular loss is not covered by the policy or the customer has failed to live up to obligations arising after loss, such as timely submission of proof of loss, it is said to be repudiating the claim, although the insurance usually remains in effect for other instances of loss if proper claims procedures are followed for them.

When an insurer repudiates the entire contract, it may not also insist that the customer continue to abide by the terms of the contract. When it repudiates a claim, it may not insist on continued compliance with claims requirements. In other words, an insurer may not have it both ways. It may not both refuse to recognize the continued existence of a contract or claim under the contract, as the case may be, and invoke the terms of that very contract. Accordingly, actions by a customer inconsistent with his or her obligations under a contract, taken after the insurer has renounced, do not prejudice the customer.

Here are two examples. A customer makes a claim in relation to damage to a house. The insurer rejects it on the ground that a condition requiring continuous occupation of the house has not been met. The customer proceeds with the claim

---

[18] See Chapter 4, generally, concerning the formation of contracts.
[19] See *Miller v. Toronto General Insurance Co.*, [1966] P.E.I.J. No. 5, 59 D.L.R. (2d) 507 (P.E.I.S.C.).

anyway, but in a form inconsistent with that laid down in the policy. Subsequently, the insurer discovers that its suspicion regarding the occupation issue is without foundation so it changes its objection. Now the insurer says it does not have to pay because the claim did not conform to the requirements in the policy. This ploy will not succeed because the insurer repudiated the contract thereby relinquishing its right to insist on further compliance with it. The same result ensues if an insurer rejects a claim on the basis of its belief that the particular loss is excluded by the terms of the policy. If it turns out that the loss is not excluded and the customer, subsequent to the insurer's rejection of the claim, fails to cooperate in preserving the damaged property or in settling the amount of the claim, contrary to contractual obligations, that failure may not be held against him or her.[20]

Insurers' Tactics for Preserving Their Rights

There are steps insurers can take to avoid relinquishing contractual rights. The need to do so arises most often in relation to liability insurance claims. An insurer may be inclined to reject a claim but may be unsure whether it has the grounds to do so. As we saw, rejecting a claim entails giving up rights. For liability insurance claims, this includes losing the right to influence the outcome of the lawsuit brought by the third party against the customer. If it eventuates that the insurer has no grounds for rejecting the claim, giving up this right would have been a substantial sacrifice because the outcome of that lawsuit determines how much the insurer has to pay.

A solution to this dilemma is to conclude a "non-waiver agreement" with the customer wherein the customer allows the insurer to deal with the third party but acknowledges that, in doing so, the insurer relinquishes no rights. Thus, the insurer is not prevented, simply by its involvement in the case, from later raising its objection to the claim. However, the insurer enjoys this form of immunity only in respect of actions permitted by the agreement. If the insurer goes beyond that, it risks losing rights through estoppel or one of the other ways previously discussed in this Chapter.[21]

If the customer refuses to sign a non-waiver agreement, the insurer can nonetheless preserve most of its rights by sending the customer an appropriately-worded[22] "reservation of rights" letter. This letter informs the customer that the

---

[20] This is particularly important in liability insurance. The insurer requires the customer to keep out of settlement negotiations with the third party claimant. Normally, if the customer interferes, the insurer is excused from paying and the customer is left to his or her own devices. But, if the insurer takes the position that it is not liable for anything, and the customer negotiates a settlement, the insurer may not later seek to avoid responsibility on the different ground that the customer interfered.

[21] *Federal Insurance Co. v. Matthews*, [1956] B.C.J. No. 129, 18 W.W.R. 193 (B.C.S.C.); *Northwest Casualty Co. v. Fritz*, [1941] O.J. No. 363, [1941] O.R. 287 (Ont. C.A.).

[22] If not carefully worded, the letter will not have its intended effect. See *Beattie v. United States Fidelity & Guarantee Co.*, (*sub nom. Home Insurance Co. of New York v. Lindal*), [1933] A.J.

insurer maintains the position that it may or may not be required to pay the loss and that its participation in the settlement or litigation process should not be viewed as detracting from that. In other words, the insurer reserves its right to reject the claim despite its actions in dealing with that claim. This makes it more difficult (though not impossible) for the customer to establish that he or she has relied on any undertaking by the insurer not to deny the claim. Therefore, there is less likely to be an estoppel. It is clear that there is no unequivocal forgiveness of past delinquencies which the customer might have committed, so there is no election. The contract of insurance is specifically invoked. No variation is contemplated. Finally, because the insurer is proceeding, in the meantime, to honour its obligations in dealing with the third party's lawsuit against the customer, it is more difficult for the customer to show that the contract or the claim has, as yet, been repudiated.

SUMMARY

When a customer defaults on an obligation under an insurance contract, it usually means cover is forfeited. However, in some cases, the default may be excused. If the breach is minor and does not prejudice the insurer, a court may grant relief from forfeiture. Alternatively, if the insurer caused the customer to assume the breach was excused, either in prospect or in retrospect, the insurer may be estopped from relying on the breach as a reason for denying a claim. The insurer may have irrevocably elected to excuse the breach. By repudiating the contract, the insurer may have given up its right to invoke a term of the contract. The term of the contract invoked by the insurer may have been amended by agreement.

To avoid being denied the right to deny coverage, an insurer may act under a reservation of rights arrangement. If so, it is less likely that estoppel, election, revocation or amendment will apply.

No. 31, [1933] 1 W.W.R. 334 (Alta. C.A.), revd on other grounds [1933] S.C.J. No. 63, [1933] S.C.R. 33 (S.C.C.).

Chapter 12

Settling Claims and Resolving Disputes

Once a customer making a claim has provided the insurer with evidence that loss covered by the insurance contract occurred and evidence of the monetary extent of that loss, it is then up to the insurer to respond. If the insurer accepts the evidence, and agrees that the contract applies, it will meet the claim. But, if the insurer considers the evidence of loss or value to be unconvincing, or that the loss claimed does not come within the coverage of the contract, or that the customer has failed to fulfil his or her obligations under the contract, it will dispute the claim and refuse to pay some or all of it. This Chapter is about the process which leads to either payment or resolution of the dispute when payment is refused.

INVESTIGATION

When a claim is lodged, it is investigated by a representative of the insurer to determine whether it is valid and, if so, the appropriate amount for payment. The insurer may have employees who do this work. They are typically called adjusters or claims examiners. It is also common for insurers to retain "independent" adjusters on a contractual basis for specific claims. These people are not independent in the sense that they are impartial as between the insurer and the customer. They represent the insurer's interest in dealing with a claim. Such a person is described as independent merely to distinguish him or her from an adjuster who works for only one insurer as a member of its staff.

An adjuster may consult experts such as health care professionals and valuers. In any event, the adjuster determines whether or to what extent a claim should be paid. This determination may be referred to the insurer or a supervisor as a recommendation or the adjuster may have authority to commit the insurer to payment personally.[1]

PAYMENT

If the decision is taken to accept the claim and the amount payable is agreed, the insurer usually has a time limit for payment. This is specified in the policy. For

---

[1] The general principles concerning the role of intermediaries, discussed in Chapter 7, apply here.

fire insurance, it is included in statutory conditions which state that payment must be made within 60 days after completion of loss unless the contract provides a shorter period.[2] Where the policy provides for periodic payments, like benefits for income replacement, the waiting period is usually shorter. For example, income replacement benefits available under Ontario's no-fault automobile insurance regime must be paid within 10 days of the insurer's receipt of the application[3] and "loss of time benefits" payable under accident and sickness insurance must be paid within 30 days of completion of the proof of loss.[4]

THE AMOUNT PAYABLE

The amount the insurer has to pay is determined, at least in part, by the terms of the policy. The most obvious example is a life insurance policy which provides for the payment of a specified amount on the happening of a particular event, usually a death. When a person whose life is insured dies, the insurer pays the specified amount. With indemnity insurance the calculation of the amount payable is less straightforward and the policy often provides only guidelines rather than a precise formula. These guidelines include an upper limit. It is also common for there to be a lower limit. By the use of a "deductible", the customer agrees to bear the first level of loss personally. For example, if there is a deductible of $500, the insurer is not required to pay for any loss smaller than $500 and, for losses greater than that, it is allowed to deduct $500 from the value of the loss when calculating what it has to pay.

Another term bearing upon the extent of the insurer's liability is a "replacement cost" clause. This is a clause which requires the insurer to pay an amount sufficient to restore lost or damaged property to its pre-loss condition without making any deduction to account for the fact that the restoration increased its value. Without such a clause, an insurer is obligated to pay only the "actual cash value" of the loss meaning it is entitled to deduct from the cost of restoration the increased value, or "betterment" that has resulted from the fact that new products or materials were used. A replacement cost clause may allow the insurer to withhold the difference between actual cash value and replacement cost until it has received satisfactory proof that replacement has actually occurred.[5]

---

[2] See *e.g.*, Ontario *Insurance Act*, R.S.O. 1990, c. I.8, s. 148, statutory condition 12.

[3] *Statutory Accident Benefits Schedule*, O. Reg. 34/10, s. 36(4).

[4] See *e.g.*, Ontario *Insurance Act*, R.S.O. 1990, c. I.8, s. 300, statutory condition 11.

[5] See *e.g.*, Ontario *Insurance Act*, *ibid.*, s. 148, statutory condition 13. It is common for property insurance policies to allow insurers to arrange for replacement or repair of lost or damaged property directly without paying anything to the customer personally: see *e.g.*, Ontario *Insurance Act*, s. 148, statutory condition 13.

The amount to be paid for a given loss may be predetermined and included as a term of the policy as a "scheduled loss endorsement". A policy with this type of clause is sometimes called a "valued policy". These clauses are used when the parties foresee difficulties in establishing the value of loss, should it occur, because of the nature of the property. Take, for example, an art object or a collection of jewellery. If either is stolen, it might be difficult to value after the fact and there is considerable prospect for dispute. To minimize this, the customer and the insurer would find it useful to have the item valued when the insurance is taken out. If it is valued at $5,000, that amount is put into the policy and that is what is paid if the item is stolen or destroyed.

But these clauses can present problems when there is only partial loss. In one case,[6] where some paintings had been damaged but not destroyed, the amount payable under the valued policy that covered them was calculated by determining the percentage by which the actual value had diminished and then applying that percentage to the agreed value. This yielded something less than the full loss suffered by the customer; something less than would have been paid had the specified sum been a limit rather than an agreed valuation.

Where the policy limit is lower than the actual value of the insured property, there may be a shortfall in recovery in cases of partial loss as well as total loss even where the extent of partial loss is within the limit specified. This will happen if there is a "co-insurance" clause. This provides that if the limit is below a stated percentage (*e.g.*, 80 per cent) of the actual value of the insured property, the insurer's liability is limited to the proportion of the loss that the limit bears to the actual value.

Unless something in the policy directs otherwise, the standard measure of indemnity is actual cash value. As we saw, this can be the cost of replacement less an amount for betterment (or "depreciation" as it is sometimes called). But sometimes other measures may be more appropriate. When a tavern burned down in an era of prohibition, it made no sense to think in terms of rebuilding it. The loss, if there was one, was the difference between the value of the tavern before the fire and its value as a pile of ashes. This may have been very little, certainly less than the cost of replacing it.[7] The appropriate measure of loss was the diminution in value. This might also be so in cases involving damage to but not destruction of unique items like art or family heirlooms.[8]

The term "market value" is sometimes applied to the valuation of property. This may simply be another way of saying replacement value in that the measure of loss is what it takes to go into the marketplace and buy a substitute. In the case of a building, it may mean the value of comparable property, or the amount a prudent person would have paid for it prior to the loss taking into

---

[6] *Re Art Gallery of Ontario and Eaton*, [1961] O.J. No. 539, [1961] O.R. 329 (Ont. H.C.J.).

[7] See *Canadian National Fire Insurance Co. v. Colonsay Hotel Co.*, [1923] S.C.J. No. 31, [1923] S.C.R. 688 (S.C.C.).

[8] *Re Art Gallery of Ontario and Eaton*, [1961] O.J. No. 539, [1961] O.R. 329 (Ont. H.C.J.).

account its capacity for earning rent.[9] It depends upon what best reflects the loss in money terms in all the circumstances.

SETTLEMENTS

An agreement between the insurer and the customer about how much is to be paid and other details of the settlement of the claim is a binding contract. The insurer promises to meet the claim and the customer promises to release the insurer from further liability for that claim. This exchange of promises creates mutual obligations which may not be broken without consequences. Nor, in the usual course, may they be altered without further agreement.

But what if new information comes to light? May either the insurer or the customer reopen the matter? Consider the case in which the insurer agreed to replace jewellery which had been lost. After the new items of jewellery had been provided, the old ones were found. An English court[10] said the settlement, being binding, had to stand so the customer kept the new jewellery and the insurer got the old stuff under its right of salvage.[11] Only in rare circumstances will a settlement be set aside. If both the insurer and the customer were mistaken about something fundamental to the settlement, like the common belief that loss which did not actually happen did, the settlement may be dismantled.[12] The English jewellery case did not fall into this category because, at the time of the settlement, a loss had in fact occurred. Another ground for setting aside an agreement is unconscionable conduct by the insurer in extracting the settlement from a vulnerable customer.[13]

THE DUTY OF GOOD FAITH

In Chapter 5 we saw that insurance contracts are contracts of utmost good faith. There, the focus was on how the principle of utmost good faith gives rise to obligations on the part of a customer to disclose information relevant to the risk to be covered by the insurance. The rationale is that, without some legal protection, an insurer would be at a disadvantage in contract negotiations because most of this information is known only to the customer. In other words, the good faith principle applies to redress an imbalance in the bargaining process.

Now, when it comes to negotiating the settlement of a claim, the shoe is often on the other foot. It is the customer who is vulnerable. In the wake of property loss or personal injury, he or she may be physically, emotionally or financially

---

9   See *e.g.*, *Leger v. Royal Insurance Co.*, [1968] N.B.J. No. 32, 70 D.L.R. (2d) 344 (N.B.C.A.).
10 *Holmes v. Payne*, [1930] 2 K.B. 301.
11 See Chapter 13 for more on salvage.
12 *Magee v. Pennine Insurance Co.*, [1969] 2 K.B. 301.
13 *Pridmore v. Calvert*, [1975] B.C.J. No. 752, 54 D.L.R. (3d) 133 (B.C.S.C.).

weakened. An unscrupulous insurer might be tempted to play on this vulnerability to extract a settlement agreement for less than the claim is worth. By unreasonably delaying or quibbling about a claim, an insurer may hope to force a needy customer to accept its terms. The principle of good faith exists to prevent this by imposing penalties on insurers if they fail to deal with a claim fairly and with reasonable dispatch.

This is not to say that an insurer cannot refuse to pay a claim if there are reasonable grounds for denial or take reasonable steps to make sure the claim is valid. If there are genuine reasons for disputing evidence, policy interpretation or the law an insurer is entitled to maintain its position without penalty until the matter is resolved. But if there are no such reasons, the insurer may be found guilty of committing an unfair or deceptive act[14] which may result in loss or suspension of licence or a fine, or, more commonly, it may be required to pay punitive damages[15] or aggravated damages when its conduct has caused its customer additional loss[16] such as the unreasonable denial of the peace of mind an insurance contract is supposed to provide.[17]

Customers also have a duty of good faith in making and negotiating claims. If a customer acts in bad faith, for example by lying, not only will the claim fail, the customer may have to pay the insurer punitive damages.[18]

RESOLVING DISPUTES

If the insurer rejects a claim or makes an offer of settlement which is rejected by the customer, and negotiations have reached the point of impasse, the next step is to invoke a dispute resolution procedure. Technically, there is no dispute until the deadline for payment has passed without payment being made. Once that happens the customer may start proceedings to enforce his or her entitlement under the contract of insurance.

For many insurance contracts, this will mean suing in the court with appropriate jurisdiction. Depending on the amount in dispute this could be in small claims court, county court, provincial court or a superior court.[19] Adverse decisions there might be appealed, perhaps all the way to the Supreme Court of Canada.

The policy may contain terms requiring that disputes be referred to other forms of dispute resolution. Statutory conditions for fire insurance require that

---

[14] See *e.g.*, Ontario *Insurance Act*, R.S.O. 1990, c. I.8, s. 438.

[15] *Whiten v. Pilot Insurance Co.*, [2002] S.C.J. No. 19, 2002 SCC 18 (S.C.C.).

[16] *Clarfield v. Crown Life Insurance Co.*, [2000] O.J. No. 4014, 23 C.C.L.I. (3d) 266 (Ont. S.C.J.).

[17] *Fidler v. Sun Life Assurance Co.*, [2004] B.C.J. No. 982, 2004 BCCA 273 (B.C.C.A.), vard [2006] S.C.J. No. 30, 2006 SCC 30 (S.C.C.).

[18] *Andrusiw v. Aetna Life Insurance Co.*, [2001] A.J. No. 789, 289 A.R. 1 (Alta. Q.B.).

[19] These have different names in different provinces: *e.g.*, Supreme Court, Queen's Bench, and Court of Justice (General Division).

disputes about valuation of loss be resolved by appraisal.[20] This involves a three-person panel deciding the questions in issue. Each party appoints one appraiser and those two people appoint an umpire to deal with the situation where the appraisers cannot agree.[21] Although the language of the condition mandates reference to appraisal, in practice parties sometimes agree to have the dispute dealt with another way, even by a court.

It is also possible for the parties to agree to refer disputes about things other than valuation to a form of alternate dispute resolution (ADR). This may be mediation or arbitration. This agreement might be part of the contract of insurance or it might be arrived at only after a dispute has arisen. Factors influencing a choice of alternate dispute resolution may include the availability of evidence, the amount of money at stake, cost and speed of proceedings (ADR may be cheaper and faster than litigation), the parties' desire for privacy or publicity (including the desire to obtain or avoid a judicial precedent), a desire to have decisions made by an expert (such as an engineer) and the state of certainty of the legal issues involved.[22]

Mediation is a process wherein a third party, mutually acceptable to the disputants, seeks to facilitate a settlement by, for example, helping to clarify and narrow the issues and otherwise overcome barriers such as poor communication, different views of the facts and emotional considerations. A mediator may be brought in simply to clarify issues and provide an independent assessment of the merits of the case, or he or she may be asked to play a wider role by promoting dialogue and suggesting solutions. Generally, a mediator has no authority to impose a binding solution. In an arbitration, on the other hand, the third party is given authority, after hearing the evidence and argument presented by both sides, to reach a decision for the disposal of the dispute that is binding on both sides.

Unless some other intention is indicated in the contract of insurance, the proceedings are governed by the relevant provincial *Arbitration Act*.[23] There can be a single arbitrator or a panel. It may be empowered to decide one issue or all matters in dispute. Decisions are binding but usually appealable to a court on points of law or mixed questions of law and fact.

In Ontario, people disputing entitlements under the no-fault automobile insurance scheme are obliged, before any litigation is commenced, to submit their disputes to a mediation process provided by the Financial Services Commission.[24] If mediation fails, the customer must then choose between suing the insurer in court and launching an arbitration. If the choice is arbitration, the proceedings are either in accordance with the Ontario *Insurance Act* or the

---

[20] See *e.g.*, Ontario *Insurance Act*, R.S.O. 1990, c. I.8, s. 148, statutory condition 11.

[21] See *e.g.*, Ontario *Insurance Act*, *ibid.*, s. 128.

[22] For an excellent treatment of ADR in relation to insurance disputes, see A. Grant, *Dispute Resolution in the Insurance Industry* (Aurora: Canada Law Book, 2000).

[23] See *e.g.*, Ontario *Arbitration Act, 1991*, S.O. 1991, c. 17.

[24] One caveat, however, is that a court action will be allowed to proceed if the Financial Services Commission has not provided a mediation within 60 days.

Arbitration Act.[25] If the former, the parties do not select the arbitrator. He or she is supplied by the Commission. Each side presents evidence and cross examines the other side's witnesses. The arbitrator's decision may be appealed to the Director of Arbitrations.

Where an unsatisfied customer resorts to litigation in the courts, the lawsuit must be started before the end of the relevant "limitation" period. Like all civil litigation, insurance cases are subject to deadlines for their commencement. The idea is to prevent disputes from persisting indefinitely. The deadlines vary with different types of cases and are usually imposed by statute. The provincial insurance statutes provide periods which usually range from one to two years after the accident or loss. By way of example, here are the deadlines that apply in Ontario. A suit to enforce a claim under a fire insurance policy must be started within one year from the date of the loss.[26] In most provinces, for accident and sickness insurance, the period is two years from the date the claim is payable.[27] An action to enforce rights under the liability part of an auto policy has to start within two years of the accident but the deadline for claims under the collision part of the policy is only one year.[27] Disputes about no-fault entitlements may not be litigated or arbitrated after two years from the date the insurer refused to pay the benefit in dispute.[28]

LIABILITY INSURANCE CLAIMS

The disposal of liability insurance claims is complicated by the fact that it is a two tier process. Recall that liability insurance protects customers against the financial consequences of lawsuits brought against them. The insurer's ultimate liability requires not only a determination of its rights and obligations in respect of the customer (as with other types of insurance) but also a resolution of the lawsuit against the customer.

For this reason, a liability policy invariably reserves for the insurer the exclusive right to deal with the person bringing the lawsuit against its customer in negotiating a settlement or otherwise managing the litigation. The insurer chooses the lawyer who will defend the action and gets to decide questions such as whether to settle the case, what witnesses to call and whether to appeal.

This right to control the litigation from the defence point of view carries with it certain obligations. In particular, the insurer must conduct itself in accordance with a duty of good faith and fair dealing in relation to its customer. In addition to the general obligation to treat its customer fairly, discussed earlier in this Chapter, good faith imposes an additional requirement on a liability insurer. If the person bringing the lawsuit makes an offer of settlement within the policy limits, the insurer may not reject it without taking account of its customer's

---

[25] See *e.g.* Ontario *Insurance Act*, R.S.O. 1990, c. I.8, ss. 279-88.
[26] See *ibid.*, s. 148, statutory condition 14.
[27] *Ibid.*, s. 259.1.
[28] *Ibid.*, s. 281.1.

interest. Remember, if, in the normal course, a case is allowed to go to judgment, and the court awards the person bringing the action damages in excess of the policy limits, the customer has to pay the extra amount personally. It is therefore in the customer's interest that a settlement offer within the policy limits be accepted. But the insurer may consider it to be in its own interest to let the matter go to court, calculating that the case is winnable by the defence. An insurer must resolve this dilemma with care. If it has guessed wrong and loses the case and the damages exceed the policy limits, it may have to pay the full amount despite the limits.[29] The test is, did the insurer give at least equal consideration to the customer's interest as it did its own interest?[30] In practice, insurers seek to meet this standard by obtaining independent legal advice on whether a case is winnable or what damages are likely to be awarded.

The other duty that goes with the insurer's right to control the defence of an action brought against its customer, is the duty to pay the costs of that defence. The package of promises made by the insurer in the contract of insurance requires not only that the insurer pay damages on behalf of its customer in appropriate cases, but also that it must provide a defence. This is no small obligation as legal costs are often significant, sometimes greater than any damages paid.

The scope of the duty to defend depends on the terms of the policy, but generally it extends to even groundless actions brought against the customer, provided the allegations made in the statement of claim would, if true, require the insurer to pay the damages.[31] For example, if a policy provided for indemnity where the customer was liable to pay damages resulting from the customer's professional negligence, and a suit was brought against the customer alleging professional negligence, the insurer would have to pay the defence costs even if, on investigation, there turned out to be no facts to support the allegation. On the other hand, if the suit alleged negligence by the customer in a personal capacity, the insurer would have to pay neither the damages, if there were any, nor the defence costs.[32] However, if it is unclear whether or not the policy provides coverage, a court will usually give the customer the benefit of the doubt and order that defence costs be paid.

An insurer is excused from paying defence costs, just as it is excused from its other obligations under the policy, if the customer has breached one of his or her obligations under or in connection with the policy, such as material misrepresentation, failure to pay premiums, or deliberate causing of loss. But the insurer may raise an issue like this only if it has undisputed evidence. Disputed evidence about, for example, the customer's conduct may seriously prejudice the customer in the main lawsuit. Accordingly, the insurer is precluded from introducing it at the preliminary stage when the duty to defend is being

---

29 *Dillon v. Guardian Insurance Co.* (1983), 2 C.C.L.I. 227 (Ont. H.C.J.).

30 *Shea v. Manitoba Public Insurance Corp.*, [1991] B.C.J. No. 711, 1 C.C.L.I. (2d) 61 (B.C.S.C.).

31 *Bacon v. Mcbride*, [1984] B.C.J. No. 2813, 6 D.L.R. (4th) 96 (B.C.S.C.).

32 *Nichols v. American Home Assurance Co.*, [1989] O.J. No. 238, 72 O.R. (2d) 799 (Ont. C.A.), revd [1990] S.C.J. No. 33, [1990] 1 S.C.R. 801 (S.C.C.). See also *Sansalone v. Wawanesa Mutual Insurance Co.*, [2000] S.C.J. 26, [2000] 1 S.C.R. 551 (S.C.C.).

decided.[33] The result is the insurer must proceed with the defence and hope to recover its costs from the customer later.

When an insurer refuses to provide a defence the customer may ask the court to declare that it has an obligation to do so. Alternatively, the customer may seek damages from the insurer for breach of contract after the main litigation has been resolved.[34]

SUMMARY

When an insurer accepts a claim, or when its counter-offer for terms of settlement of the claim is accepted by the customer, there is a contract of settlement which binds both parties. However, like any contract, a settlement may be set aside if based on a common mistake about something fundamental, or if achieved by unconscionable conduct by the insurer taking unfair advantage of a customer's vulnerability.

If negotiations fail and there is no settlement because the insurer denies that the loss is covered, the parties cannot agree how much the claim is worth, or both, the issues in dispute must be resolved either by litigation or some form of alternate dispute resolution, subject to the normal rules applicable to those procedures.

Throughout the claims process, an insurer owes a duty to its customer to act in good faith by not unreasonably denying liability or delaying its response. Bad faith may result in an insurer having to pay punitive or aggravated damages, in addition to the amount of the claim. Insurers' good faith has an additional aspect in liability insurance where an insurer manages its customer's response to legal action brought against him or her by a third party. In performing this role, an insurer must be careful not to put its own interests above those of the customer.

---

[33] *Slough Estates Canada Ltd. v. Federal Pioneer Ltd.*, [1994] O.J. No. 2147, 20 O.R. (3d) 429 (Ont. Gen. Div.); *Cooper v. Farmers' Mutual Insurance Co.*, [2002] O.J. No. 1949, 59 O.R. (3d) 165 (Ont. C.A.).

[34] *Great West Steel Industries Ltd. v. Simcoe & Erie General Insurance Co.*, [1979] O.J. No. 4503, 106 D.L.R. (3d) 347 (Ont. C.A.).

Chapter 13

Insurers' Rights on Paying Claims

Recall our discussion of the indemnity principle. That principle requires that a person insured by an indemnity insurance contract who incurs loss should recover the value of that loss, but no more. In furtherance of this principle, in certain circumstances, when an insurer has paid a claim made under an indemnity insurance contract, it inherits some of the rights formerly enjoyed by the customer. Among these are "salvage rights" and "subrogation rights". These are what this Chapter is about.

INSURERS' SALVAGE RIGHTS

When insured property is severely damaged, the insurer may treat is as if it is totally destroyed and pay for the total loss. This does not necessarily mean that the property is actually destroyed. It means merely that it would cost more to repair it than to replace it so it is "written off". The damaged goods may still have some value, say, for spare parts. In cases where the insurer has paid out for the loss or theft of an item which is later recovered, the insured property still has considerable value.

However, it would offend the indemnity principle to allow the insured customer to keep both the insurance money received for a total loss and what is left or recovered of the insured property. Then he or she would be overcompensated and that would represent an inappropriate incentive. Unscrupulous customers might be tempted to bring about loss in the hope of profiting from it.

To prevent this, insurance law grants an insurer ownership of property which has been treated as totally lost or destroyed and for which a full indemnity has been paid. This is the salvage right. But, unless the policy or a statute provides differently, the insurer must have paid for the full value of the loss.[1] Thus, if a policy limit or deductible applies, so that the customer does not get full value for the loss, the salvage right does not arise. If the insurer wants the advantage of salvage, it must pay the customer a full indemnity. However, this rule, insofar as it relates to deductibles, does not apply to automobile insurance. Legislation allows an insurer to take salvage even where there is a deductible.[2]

---

[1]   See *Dane v. Mortgage Insurance Corp.*, [1894] 1 Q.B. 54 (C.A.).

[2]   See *McNaughton Automotive Ltd. v. Co-operators General Insurance Co.*, [2005] O.J. No. 2436, 23 C.C.L.I. (4th) 191 (Ont. C.A.), leave to appeal refused [2005] S.C.C.A. No. 388 (S.C.C.).

To protect the insurer's interest in the property, the terms of the policy usually require the customer to take reasonable steps, after loss has happened, to
protect property from further damage.[3]

Except for marine insurance, the decision about whether a loss is total or
partial is for the insurer to determine.[4] Marine insurance legislation allows the
insured person, if circumstances reasonably require it, to abandon insured
property to the insurer to be treated as a total loss.[5]

SUBROGATION

Where a customer with a claim under an indemnity[6] insurance contract has an
alternative source of compensation for the same loss, other than another
insurance contract,[7] over-recovery is prevented by application of the doctrine of
subrogation.

Subrogation operates where there is a legally enforceable right to tap the
alternative source of compensation. Examples are a right to damages from a
negligent causer of loss,[8] a landlord's right (contained in the lease) to claim
from a tenant for damage to rented property,[9] or a right of an unpaid vendor of
a building to the purchase price.[10] The insurer is "subrogated" to the right so
that its customer may not receive both insurance money and the proceeds of
the claim against the other person. In general terms, it works in one of three
ways:

1. If the insurer has paid out under the insurance contract, it is permitted to
   sue the other person although this is done in the name of its customer.
   The amount recovered in this suit goes first to reimburse the insurer.
   Anything left over goes to the customer.[11]

2. If the customer has already obtained the money from the other person, and
   has thereby been fully compensated, the insurer need not pay anything.[12]

---

3   See *e.g.*, Ontario *Insurance Act*, R.S.O. 1990, c. I.8, s. 148, statutory condition 9 (fire insurance).
4   *Ibid.*, statutory condition 10.
5   See *e.g.*, Ontario *Marine Insurance Act*, R.S.O. 1990, c. M.2, s. 61.
6   While subrogation generally applies only to indemnity insurance (*i.e.* not life insurance and some
    forms of accident insurance), this is not so where the right of subrogation is created by statute.
    Gurniak v. Nordquist, [2003] S.C.J. No. 60, 4 C.C.L.I. (4th) 1 (S.C.C.).
7   To see how this is resolved, see Chapter 14.
8   *Gough v. Toronto & York Radial Railway*, [1918] O.J. No. 205, 42 O.L.R. 415 (Ont. C.A.).
9   *United Motor Service Inc. v. Hutson*, [1937] S.C.J. No. 19, [1937] S.C.R. 294 (S.C.C.).
10 *Castellain v. Preston* (1883), 11 Q.B.D. 380 (C.A.).
11 *Ledingham v. Ontario (Hospital Services Commission)*, [1974] S.C.J. No. 53, 46 D.L.R. (3d) 699
    (S.C.C.). The obligation to account to the customer for excess recovery distinguishes subrogation
    from an assignment by the customer of the right of action. Under an assignment, an insurer may
    keep everything recovered. See *Compania Colombiana de Seguras v. Pacific Steam Navigation
    Co.*, [1965] 1 Q.B. 101 (Q.B.D.).
12 *Glynn v. Scottish Union & National Insurance Co.*, [1963] O.J. No. 781, [1963] 2 O.R. 705
    (Ont. C.A.).

3. If the customer has been paid by both the insurer and the other person, the customer must pay the insurer back.[13]

Subrogation exists independently of statute or the express terms of policies. However, for some classes of insurance, the general rules have been modified by statute. For other types, these rules may be modified by the parties to particular contracts of insurance. More on that follows, but first, let's explore the general rules.

An insurer's right of subrogation is derivative. As against the third party, the insurer can be in no better position than the customer.[14] If the customer has no enforceable right against the third party, neither does the insurer. Any impediments to a successful lawsuit brought by the customer, such as a lapsed limitation period[15] or a contractual undertaking not to sue,[16] can impede the insurer as well. The right to the alternative source of compensation must be enforceable and not a gift or other gratuitous form of payment.[17]

The right of subrogation does not arise until the customer has been fully indemnified for the loss, even if the insurer has paid to the full extent of its liability.[18] Applied to the three ways in which subrogation can arise, this results in the following:

1. An insurer seeking to enforce the customer's right against a third party must first have completely indemnified the customer. Until a full indemnity is paid, the insurer can neither recover from the third party nor control the litigation or settlement process.[19]
2. If the customer has already received some, but not full, compensation from the third party, the insurer must pay (up to its limits) the balance of the loss plus the expenses incurred by the customer in achieving the recovery it did.[20]
3. If the insurer has made a payment and the customer has received something from the third party, the insurer may seek reimbursement from the customer only if the total amount paid to the customer by both sources exceeds the amount of loss (including the amount spent by the customer to pursue the third party) and then only that amount in excess of the loss.[21]

However, an insurer has some rights even when it has not paid the customer a full indemnity. The customer has a duty to pursue any rights against a third party in good faith and sue, not only for the uninsured portion of the loss, but also the

---

[13] *Castellain v. Preston* (1883), 11 Q.B.D. 380 (C.A.).

[14] *Royal Insurance Co. v. Aguiar*, [1984] O.J. No. 3399, 8 C.C.L.I. 300 (Ont. C.A.).

[15] *Ibid.*

[16] See *e.g.*, *Ross Southwood Tire v. Pyrotech Products*, [1975] S.C.J. No. 62, [1976] 2 S.C.R. 35 (S.C.C.); *Smith v. T. Eaton Co.*, [1977] S.C.J. No. 125, [1978] 2 S.C.R. 749 (S.C.C.).

[17] *Burnard v. Radocanachi, Sons Co.* (1882), 7 App. Cas. 333 (H.L.).

[18] *National Fire Insurance Co. v. McLaren*, [1886] O.J. No. 98, 12 O.R. 682 (Ch. D.).

[19] *Globe & Rutgers Fire Insurance Co. v. Truedell*, [1927] O.J. No. 24, [1927] 2 D.L.R. 659 (Ont. C.A.).

[20] *Ibid.*

[21] *Ledingham v. Ontario (Hospital Services Commission)*, [1974] S.C.J. No. 53, 46 D.L.R. (3d) 699 (S.C.C.).

full extent of the claim. Remember, before a full indemnity is paid, the customer retains control of the lawsuit. It is a breach of this duty if the customer chooses to settle with the third party for a fraction of what he or she could get in court, presumably counting on the insurer to pay the rest. The consequence of breaching this duty is that the customer has to pay the insurer damages equal to the amount the insurer would have received by way of reimbursement if the third party had been pursued diligently.[22]

For fire insurance these rules have been modified by statute. The main change gives insurers subrogation rights where they have made or assumed liability for *any* payment.[23] Thus an insurer may bring an action in the name of the customer to enforce all rights the customer may have against a third party in respect of the loss, even where the insurer has paid for only part of the loss (perhaps because of low policy limits or a deductible). If the sum recovered from the third party is not sufficient both to top up the customer's compensation and reimburse the insurer, that sum is shared by the insurer and the customer in the proportions in which they bore the loss. For example, if the insurer paid for two thirds of the loss, it gets to keep two thirds of the amount recovered from the third party, even if the remaining one third is not enough to provide the customer with a complete indemnity.

If the insurer chooses not to exercise this expanded right of subrogation, perhaps because it has an agreement with the third party's liability insurer not to do so, the customer may sue the third party for any shortfall in compensation.[24]

In most provinces, legislation similar to that pertaining to fire insurance applies to insurance against damage to automobiles.[25] The exceptions to this are Ontario and Quebec. These provinces have enacted schemes that require automobile property damage claims to be handled exclusively on a "first party" basis. This means that a person whose vehicle is damaged must seek compensation from his or her own insurer regardless of who is to blame for the damage[26] (although it may still be necessary to show that someone else was to blame). The insurer is precluded from seeking reimbursement from the person at fault or that person's liability insurer except in rare circumstances.[27]

All provinces and territories have some form of no fault auto insurance. This provides compensation for personal injury and death suffered in motor vehicle accidents. Payment is made by an insurer to its own customer, or sometimes to a

---

[22] *Globe & Rutgers Fire Insurance Co. v. Truedell*, [1927] O.J. No. 24, [1927] 2 D.L.R. 659 (Ont. C.A.); *Davis v. MacRitchie*, [1938] N.S.J. No. 5, [1938] 4 D.L.R. (2d) 187 (N.S.T.D.).

[23] See *e.g.*, Ontario *Insurance Act*, R.S.O. 1990, c. I.8, s. 152.

[24] *Burnett v. New Brunswick Electric Power Commission* (1965), 51 M.P.R. 350 (N.B.C.A.); *Morley v. Moore*, [1936] 2 K.B. 359 (C.A.).

[25] See *e.g.*, Alberta *Insurance Act*, R.S.A. 2000, c. I-3, s. 546(1).

[26] See *e.g.*, Ontario *Insurance Act*, R.S.O. 1990, c. I.8, s. 263.

[27] See *e.g.*, *Automobile Insurance*, R.R.O. 1990, Reg. 664, ss. 6-8. The insurer of a vehicle that is towed may seek reimbursement from the owner or the insurer of the vehicle towing it if the tower is in that business or if the towing vehicle is heavier than 4,500 kilograms. The insurer of a vehicle the contents of which suffer damage in excess of $20,000 may seek reimbursement from the insurer of another vehicle involved in the accident. In both cases, it is necessary to establish fault on the part of the driver of the other vehicle.

person injured while a passenger in a customer's vehicle or who is struck by that vehicle. For the most part, entitlement to payment is not contingent on fault. If damages are recoverable from someone who was at fault, those damages are reduced by the amount of no fault payments available.[28] The accident victim does not get doubly compensated. Therefore, in the normal run of things, there is no subrogation.[29]

In Quebec, there is no access to damages outside the no fault system so there can be no subrogation there either.[30] In Ontario, lawsuits outside the no fault scheme are severely restricted.[31] Again, the no fault system is intended to be primary and the proceeds of lawsuits, such as are allowed, do not duplicate no fault benefits. Because any rights an injury victim has to damages do not relate to the losses compensated by no fault benefits, there is nothing to which the no-fault insurer can be subrogated. However, in limited circumstances a no fault insurer is permitted to seek reimbursement from another insurer. Where the injury victim was an occupant of a motorcycle hit by a car or truck, or an occupant of a car hit by a heavy truck, the victim's insurer is entitled to be reimbursed by the insurer of the other vehicle if the driver of that vehicle was at fault.[32]

Marine insurance legislation allows insurers rights of subrogation even in the event of partial payment, but only to the extent to which they have made insurance payments.[33]

The general principles of subrogation may be modified for a contract of insurance even if it is not affected by legislation dealing with the topic. The contract itself may contain a clause giving the insurer wider, or indeed narrower, rights of subrogation. It is not uncommon for wider rights to be cast in terms similar to that provided by statute for fire insurance. A narrowing effect is achieved when the insurer agrees not to pursue certain classes of people even if their fault causes the insured customer loss. A standard term of auto collision coverage, for example, is a clause waiving subrogation against anyone driving the insured vehicle with the permission of the insured customer.

The insurer's subrogation rights may also be narrowed by implication. If a policy covers the interests of more than one person in the same property, the insurer may not subrogate to any rights enjoyed by one of those people against the other in respect of damage to the property. Here is an example. In *Commonwealth Construction Co. v. Imperial Oil Ltd.*,[34] an oil company engaged a contractor to build a fertilizer plant, and the project was insured by a policy

---

[28] See *e.g.*, *Stokes v. Desjardins Groupe D'assurances Générales*, [2009] O.J. No. 3608, 97 O.R. (3d) 634 (Ont. S.C.J.).

[29] In the government auto insurance schemes in British Columbia, Manitoba and Saskatchewan, the insurer is subrogated to claims against out-of-province drivers and drunk or unlicensed drivers. See *e.g.*, Manitoba *Public Insurance Corporation Act*, R.S.M. 1987, c. P215, s. 26(2).

[30] Quebec *Automobile Insurance Act*, R.S.Q. 1977, c. A-25, s. 120.

[31] Ontario *Insurance Act*, R.S.O. 1990, c. I.8, ss. 266, 267.

[32] Ontario *Insurance Act*, *ibid.*, s. 275; *Automobile Insurance*, R.R.O. 1990, Reg. 664, s. 9.

[33] See *e.g.*, *Marine Insurance Act*, S.C. 1993, c. 22, s. 81.

[34] *Imperial Oil Ltd. v. Commonwealth Construction Co.*, [1976] S.C.J. No. 115, [1978] 1 S.C.R. 317 (S.C.C.), revg [1974] A.J. No. 261, [1975] 2 W.W.R. 72 (Alta. C.A.).

covering the oil company, the contractor and subcontractors. One subcontractor caused a fire that destroyed some of the property used in the project. The insurer sought, through subrogation, to obtain reimbursement from the subcontractor by enforcing a right thought to be enjoyed by the principal contractor. The Supreme Court of Canada held that there was no case for subrogation because the interests of the contractor and the subcontractor in the property were too closely interconnected. But, if the two people do not share an interest in the damaged property, subrogation applies, even if they are named in the same policy. For example, when parents' property is destroyed by their son, and it is property in which the son himself has no insurable interest, their insurer may pursue a subrogated action against the son despite the fact that the son's own property is insured by the same policy.[35]

SUMMARY

When it has paid a claim for indemnity, an insurer may recoup some of its outlay. This is so in property insurance if payment is for a full indemnity and any of the lost or damaged property is recovered. The insurer gets the salvage value. It will also happen if there is a claim against a third party arising out of the loss. The insurer is subrogated to the rights the insured customer has against, for example, the negligent causer of the loss. Subrogation also requires full indemnity unless that requirement is modified by statute or the insurance contract.

---

[35] *Morawietz v. Morawietz*, [1986] O.J. No. 582, 18 C.C.L.I. 108 (Ont. C.A.).

Chapter 14

Claims Against More Than One Insurer

Occasionally more than one insurance contract covers the same loss. It is not unusual, for example, for someone to have several insurance policies on his or her own life. Property or liability insurance can be duplicated too. A firm might have insurance on its factory including the contents. Inadvertently, or through an abundance of caution, it might also have taken out insurance on, say, its computer system. If computers are damaged, claims could seemingly be made under both policies. This Chapter is about the rights and obligations of the various parties when a situation like this arises.

LIFE AND OTHER NON-INDEMNITY INSURANCE

If there are multiple life insurance policies in effect on the same life, each insurer must pay the full value of its policy when the person whose life is insured dies. No account is taken of the fact that other insurance is payable to the same beneficiaries. This is because life insurance is not indemnity insurance. It is payable whether or not the beneficiaries were financially dependent on the deceased before he or she died.

The same is true for other non-indemnity insurance like some forms of accident insurance. For example, the kind of insurance that pays accident victims according to a schedule — so much if the use of an arm is lost, and so forth — is usually not conditional upon proof of financial loss. The claimant must merely show that there was an injury which deprived him or her of the use of an arm. The fact that there is more than one policy providing similar benefits does not reduce the liability of any of the insurers.

INDEMNITY INSURANCE

It is entirely different when it comes to indemnity insurance. Remember that the indemnity principle holds that people should not receive from insurance any more than has actually been lost. The possibility of being in a better financial position after a loss, thanks to insurance, than before it, is thought to be too big a temptation to fraud or carelessness. As we have seen, this explains the requirements of insurable interest and strict proof of loss, and justifies the insurer's right of subrogation. It also leads to the conclusion that a person should not be allowed to recover his or her loss more than once even if he or she has two or more insurance contracts whose total limits exceed the amount of loss.

When Multiple Insurance Exists

The first thing to determine is whether there is, in fact, multiple insurance at all. It will be the case only if more than one insurance contract covers the same interest in the same subject matter and the same risk. It is usually not difficult to see whether the same subject matter and same risk are covered.[1] But whether or not the same interest is covered by each policy can be a more subtle question. This is illustrated by a case involving a man who obtained insurance on the house he owned jointly with his wife. The insurance covered both spouses' interests. Subsequently the couple separated and the wife took out insurance on her interest in the house. There was multiple, or overlapping coverage only on the wife's half interest even though both policies covered the same house.[2] Other examples of separate interests in the same house are those of the owner and the mortgage holder,[3] landlord and tenant[4] and vendor and purchaser.[5] In these situations over-compensation is prevented by subrogation.[6]

Preventing Multiple Recovery

Once it is clear that there is indeed overlapping coverage, the next step is to decide how over-compensation is to be prevented. There are essentially two possibilities. An order of priority can be established with one insurer paying first up to the limit on its policy and, if that is not sufficient to cover the loss, the next one on the list paying, and so forth until the loss is covered or the limits are exhausted. The alternative is for every insurer to contribute a proportion of indemnity regardless of whether any one of them could have covered the loss within its limits.

In the absence of anything on point, either in any of the policies or in a statute, this second rule applies. The customer may choose to claim from any of the insurers with whom he or she has a contract. But the customer may only lodge claims which, in total, match the amount of loss. Once it has met the claim, the selected insurer may then turn to the other insurers, each of whom must reimburse it for a proportion of the loss. The method of calculating the amount of each insurer's contribution varies depending on the nature of the policies involved. There are two options, the "maximum liability" method and the "independent liability" method.

The maximum liability method applies when the policies are "concurrent". This means that both or all policies cover the same subject matter and neither

---

[1] See *Pacific Forest Products Ltd. v. AXA Pacific Insurance Co.*, [2003] B.C.J. No. 937, 46 C.C.L.I. (3d) 1 (B.C.C.A.).

[2] *Re Wawanesa Mutual Insurance Co.*, [1951] 3 D.L.R. 703 (B.C.S.C.).

[3] *Clarke v. Fidelity-Phoenix Insurance Co.*, [1925] O.J. No. 144, [1926] 1 D.L.R. 303 (Ont. C.A.).

[4] *United Motors Service Inc. v. Hutson*, [1937] S.C.J. No. 19, [1937] S.C.R. 294 (S.C.C.).

[5] *Econ. Mut. Ins. Co. v. Federation Ins. Co.* (1961), 27 D.L.R. (2d) 539 (B.C.S.C.).

[6] See Chapter 13.

one covers anything else. The formula for calculating an insurer's contribution in a case like that is:

amount of insurer's limit   x   amount of loss (to the limit
total of all insurers' limits   under the policy)

The term maximum liability refers to the fact that the proportion is based on the total of all insurers' maximum limits. This is appropriate given the concurrence of the coverage.

But where the coverage is not concurrent, that is, where one of the policies covers more subject matter than the other(s), this formula works to the disadvantage of the insurer providing the wider coverage because the wider coverage usually means the policy has higher limits. Take, for example, a case involving a bank which insured itself against the dishonesty of a specified employee.[7] It also had another policy, with a different insurer, covering loss arising from the dishonesty of any employee or the destruction of documents by fire or burglary. The limits on the wider policy were, because they related to a considerably greater risk, several times higher than the limits on the narrow one. When the named employee caused the bank loss, both insurers had to contribute. However, had the maximum liability formula been used, the insurer providing the wider coverage would have had to pay the lion's share of the loss. Given that loss had occurred which was precisely that for which the narrow policy had been purchased, the court considered that the insurer which had issued that policy should pay more than a small fraction. It therefore applied the independent liability formula. This formula works like this:

insurer's liability if no other policy   x   amount of loss (subject
total of amounts of liability of each   to the policy limit)
insurer if each the only insurer.

This approach also applies to liability insurance.[8] Whereas the limits in property insurance policies are related specifically to the value of the property insured and therefore the value of loss should it occur, with liability insurance, the limits are somewhat arbitrary and the highest likelihood is that any loss will be much lower than the limits.

These contribution rules may be altered by the terms of one or more of the policies involved.[9] There are various types of "other insurance" clauses but they fall into three general categories. First, the insurer's liability to the customer may be limited to a pro-rated amount so that the customer, and not the insurer, is obliged to seek contribution from the other insurers. Second, coverage under the policy may be limited to the amount of loss in excess of that covered by other

---

[7] *American Surety Co. v. Wrightson* (1910), 103 L.T. 663 (K.B.).

[8] *Commercial Union Assurance Co. v. Hayden*, [1977] Q.B. 804 (C.A.); *Dominion of Canada General Insurance Co. v. Wawanesa Mutual Insurance Co.*, [1985] B.C.J. No. 1394, 16 C.C.L.I. 69 (B.C.S.C.).

[9] See *Family Insurance Corp. v. Lombard Canada Ltd.*, [2002] S.C.J. No. 49, 2002 SCC 48 (S.C.C.).

policies. Third, the insurer may be excused entirely from paying a claim if there is other insurance about which it has not been informed and, perhaps, for which it has not given its consent.

There can of course be some difficulty in sorting out the respective obligations of the insurers if each of the policies contains an "other insurance" clause. Essentially it is a matter of interpretation based, usually, on common sense. Where a person is insured by two policies, each of which contains a clause stating that the insurer is not liable to pay anything if there is other insurance covering the risk, it is considered unreasonable to read the policies as cancelling each other out. The policies are interpreted to apply only with respect to other insurance which is not itself cancelled by the existence of co-existing insurance.[10] Therefore each insurer has to contribute to the loss.

Another example is a case where one policy contained a clause stating that coverage would not be provided if there was other insurance. Subsequently, another policy was taken out which contained a clause stating that the coverage was void if there was any insurance already in place. The court said the second policy never took effect because of its clause. Therefore the clause in the first policy was not infringed. So the first insurer had to pay.[11]

Questions involving multiple insurance may be resolved by statute, even where one or more of the policies contain apparently relevant clauses. Legislation in each province, except Quebec, governing fire insurance has a section dealing with overlapping coverage. The effect of this legislation is to limit each insurer's liability to its pro-rated share.[12] An insurer will know whether it can take advantage of this because a statutory condition obliges the customer to include information about other insurance in the proof of loss.[13] Any "excess only" clause in a fire policy is of no effect except that insurance on identified property is "first-loss" insurance as against any other insurance which covers the property without mentioning it specifically. Limits of coverage on specified property (for example, jewellery or computers) and deductible and co-insurance clauses remain valid and the pro-rating formula must take them into account. Indeed, the legislation provides guidance on how to deal with deductibles.

Automobile liability insurance is treated as follows:

1. If the loss is covered by auto insurance and also nuclear energy hazard liability insurance, the auto policy is excess only, meaning the insurer has to pay only if the loss exceeds the limits of the nuclear policy.[14]

2. Where there are two auto policies, one insuring the owner of the vehicle is first loss insurance as against one insuring the driver if the driver is not the owner.[15]

---

[10] *Family Insurance Corp. v. Lombard Canada Ltd.*, [2002] S.C.J. No. 49, 2002 SCC 48 (S.C.C.).

[11] *Home Insurance Co. v. Gavel*, [1927] S.C.J. No. 40, [1927] S.C.R. 481 (S.C.C.).

[12] See *e.g.*, Ontario *Insurance Act*, R.S.O. 1990, c. I.8, s. 150.

[13] *Ibid.*, s. 148, statutory condition 6(1)(b)(iv).

[14] *Ibid.*, s. 255.

[15] *Ibid.*, s. 277. An exception is where the driver is insured by a "garage policy" and the accident occurs while the vehicle is operated by garage personnel in the course of servicing.

3. If the same named insured customer has two policies, the insurers each pay a rateable proportion based on a version of the independent liability formula.[16]

4. Where more than one insurer is liable and they cannot agree about who is to defend the customer against the third party's lawsuit, they must apply to a court for directions as to who should do it. However all have to contribute to the cost of the defence.[17]

The various provincial auto no fault insurance schemes provide medical, rehabilitation and income replacement benefits to the victims of auto accidents. Sometimes similar benefits are available to those victims from other sources. Legislation, regulations and policies providing for no fault benefits invariably include terms designed to prevent duplication. Usually the no fault benefits are secondary to other sources of compensation,[18] including public health insurance, wage and salary continuation plans, employment insurance and Canada Pension. Where the accident is covered by a workers' compensation plan, the no fault insurer is usually excused entirely.[19] Where the alternative source is another auto no fault policy (because, for example, the injured person was riding in a car insured by one policy and owned another car insured by a second policy), most schemes provide that the insurer of the owner of the vehicle involved in the accident pays the benefits.[20] But in Ontario the opposite rule applies with each injury victim required to go first to his or her own insurer.[21] If recovery is unavailable from that source, only then does the claim lie against the insurer of the vehicle in which the claimant was riding at the time of the accident.[22]

Marine insurance legislation deals with multiple insurance by allowing the customer to claim the total loss from any of the insurers.[23] The insurer selected must pay, up to the limit of its policy, the actual loss, but it then may claim contribution from the other insurers.[24] If double insurance arises inadvertently, the customer is entitled to a refund of a portion of the premiums paid to the second insurer.[25]

Many of the insurers who write property insurance in Canada subscribe to an agreement of "guiding principles with respect to overlapping coverages relating to property insurance" under the auspices of their trade association, the Insurance Bureau of Canada. This agreement contains some 23 rules for dealing with

---

[16] *Ibid.*, s. 277(2), (3).

[17] *Ibid.*, s. 257. See *ING Insurance Co. v. Federated Insurance Co.*, [2005] O.J. No. 1718, 75 O.R. (3d) 457 (Ont. C.A.).

[18] See *e.g.*, Ontario *Insurance Act*, R.S.O. 1990, c. I.8, s. 268(6). (But tort damages are excess).

[19] See *e.g.*, *Statutory Accident Benefits Schedule*, O. Reg. 34/10, ss. 47, 61.

[20] See *e.g.*, Alberta *Insurance Act*, R.S.A. 2000, c. I-3, s. 591(1).

[21] Ontario *Insurance Act*, R.S.O. 1990, c. I.8, s. 268(2).

[22] The next step, if the claimant is still unable to recover, is to collect from the insurer of any other vehicle involved in the accident.

[23] See *e.g.*, *Marine Insurance Act*, S.C. 1993, c. 22, s. 86.

[24] *Ibid.*, s. 87.

[25] *Ibid.*, s. 85.

specific examples of double insurance. The rules are grouped under the following headings:

- A. Rules Dealing with Primary Insurances.
- B. Rules Dealing with Insurance by Bailees in Relation to Bailors.
- C. Rules Dealing with Reduced Amount of Contribution in Certain Cases.
- D. Rules Dealing with Boiler and Machinery Insurance and Other Insurances.
- E. Rules Dealing with Building and Contents Insurance Including Condominiums.
- F. Rules Applicable when Loss Deductible Clause(s) are in Question.
- G. Rules Applicable to Non-concurrent Apportionments.
- H. Rules for Concurrent Insurance Subject to Limitation Clauses.
- I. General Rules.

For property insurance this agreement is the most important practical source of rules for resolving disputes about multiple insurance because most insurers in the field are party to it. Of particular practical significance are the rules about non-concurrent coverage because the most common way for overlapping coverage to arise is for a specific policy to be taken out when a more general one already exists. The agreement favours the independent liability approach in this situation.

SUMMARY

If there is more than one indemnity insurance contract applicable to the same interest, subject matter and risk, a customer may claim the value of the loss only once. Unless there is legislation or contract terms dictating otherwise, each insurer must contribute its *pro rata* share of indemnity. A clause in a policy may modify this. A common modification has the insurer, if there is other insurance, having only to pay if the loss exceeds the limits of that other insurance. The allocation of responsibility may also be affected by prior agreement between the insurers.

Chapter 15

Rights of People not Party to the Insurance Contract

A contract of insurance may give rights to people who are not party to it or who were not party to it when it was made. The rights enjoyed by the customer who originally bought the insurance may be transferred to someone else. This is called "assignment". Alternatively, certain people may be entitled to claim under a contract of insurance, even though not a party to it, because the contract or a statute says they can. In this Chapter we look at the situations when these rights arise and how they are enforced.

ASSIGNMENT

In relation to insurance, the term "assignment" is used in several different ways. When insured property is sold or otherwise transferred by the person who took out the insurance to another person, it is sometimes said that the subject matter of the insurance has been assigned to that other person. If the transfer of the property is complete, the insurance ceases to have any effect. The seller no longer has an insurable interest.[1] Unless the insurer is involved in the deal, the buyer has no rights in the insurance either. This is because an insurance contract is personal in the sense that the risk transferred has to do, not only with the nature of the property insured, but also with personal characteristics, including the moral character, of the customer. Normally, the insurer does not have the opportunity to assess the buyer in this respect. Therefore, the insurance does not pass automatically with title to the property.[2]

However, with the consent of the insurer, the buyer may be substituted as the insured in the policy.[3] This is referred to as an assignment of the policy, but the expression is misleading. With the appearance of a new customer there is really an entirely new contract in place. The rights and obligations apply to a new relationship. The new customer may sue on the contract. Of particular

---

[1] *Caledonian Insurance Co. v. Edmonton Terminal Grain Co.*, [1932] S.C.J. No. 37, [1932] S.C.R. 581 (S.C.C.).
[2] *Rayner v. Preston* (1881), 18 Ch. D. 1 (C.A.).
[3] See *e.g.*, *Civil Code of Québec*, S.Q. 1991, c. 64, Art. 2475.

importance, any defaults on the part of the old customer may not be held against the new one who starts with a clean slate.[4]

Assignment of life insurance contracts is permitted by statute if the terms of the policy do not forbid it and the insurer has been given notice.[5] The arrangement may be permanent and transfer all the customer's rights under the contract including the right to surrender the policy or to make further assignments of it. Or it may be temporary, done to provide security for a loan, in which case the only right transferred is the right to receive the proceeds of the contract when the person whose life is insured dies (if that happens before the loan is repaid). A complication arises if there are beneficiaries designated. If they are irrevocable beneficiaries, their interests may not be changed without their consent. In any case, the rights obtained by the assignee are no better than those held by the assignor prior to the assignment. Any grounds for refusing payment, such as failure to disclose relevant facts when the contract was originally made, remain available to the insurer after the assignment.[6] An assignment of a policy differs from the designation of a beneficiary in that, on the death of the assignee, the benefit of the policy passes to the assignee's estate and does not revert to the assignor.

The device of assigning the benefit of an insurance contract, while keeping the essentials of the contract itself in place, is used for non-life insurance too. This may be useful, for example, to protect the security interest of someone lending money and taking a mortgage on the insured property. While the lender could take out separate insurance, it is usually more convenient for that person to require the borrower to insure the property and agree that, should the property be destroyed or damaged, the insurance money will be used either to pay off the loan or to restore the property, so the lender's interest is protected that way. We shall see later that further measures are usually available to bolster the protection of mortgagees. For now, however, we should note an important point. Without these additional measures, the insurer's obligations are owed entirely to the borrower who purchased the insurance. If that person made a material misrepresentation, violated a warranty, or the like, any claim is defeated and the assignee has no recourse against the insurer. Claims, and lawsuits to enforce them, must be brought by the insured customer. If the insurer wishes to cancel the policy, notice to the customer is sufficient.

Another example of assignment of the proceeds of insurance is an arrangement often made in connection with an agreement for the sale and purchase of a building. Unless there is some protection for the purchaser in place, he or she must go ahead with the deal any time after it is signed, even if the building is damaged or destroyed before the formal transfer of title. The purchaser could buy separate insurance to cover this period but, since the seller normally has insurance already in place, the convenient course is for the seller to agree to

---

[4] *Springfield Fire and Marine Insurance Co. v. Maxim*, [1946] S.C.J. No. 30, [1946] 4 D.L.R. 369 (S.C.C.).

[5] See *e.g.*, Ontario *Insurance Act*, R.S.O. 1990, c. I.8, s. 200.

[6] *Venner v. Sun Life Insurance Co.*, [1890] S.C.J. No. 15, 17 S.C.R. 394 (S.C.C.).

assign the proceeds of that insurance to the purchaser, should damage occur before completion of the sale.[7] But the effectiveness of this arrangement depends on the seller having insurance with high enough limits and the absence of any problems such as the seller having breached a condition of the coverage. Further, the purchaser cannot bring suit against the insurer independently. The seller must be involved.[8]

ASSIGNMENTS BY MORTGAGORS

We saw above that mortgage holders can protect their security interests by insisting that borrowers agree to assign to them proceeds that may become payable under the insurance on the mortgaged property. In fact this is done routinely. Mortgage agreements contain clauses requiring the borrower to have adequate insurance and, in the event of destruction of the mortgaged property, to use the insurance money to pay off the loan.

But we saw too that this protection is not watertight. If the borrower has defaulted on premium payments or otherwise breached a condition of the policy, the lender will receive nothing. The lender cannot sue the insurer without the involvement of the borrower. The insurer may cancel the insurance without telling the lender.

Some of these adverse possibilities are eliminated if the lender's right to the insurance money is included as a term of the policy. The lender is then in the same position as a party to the contract and is able to sue the insurer for payment. If the claim is good, the insurer must pay the lender directly without going through the borrower, even though it is the borrower who took out the insurance. If the amount of the lender's claim equals or exceeds the policy limits, the insurer satisfies its entire obligation under the policy by paying the lender.[9] In addition, cancellation of the policy by the insurer is not effective against any "loss payee" named in the policy unless that person is notified of the cancellation.[10]

The protection is further enhanced by the inclusion in policies of "mortgage clauses", which state that the lender's interest is not invalidated by any act or neglect by the borrower. This means that even if the borrower defaults on an obligation under the policy or ceases to have an insurable interest in the

---

[7] In cases of substantial damage, the purchaser usually has the option of cancelling the deal entirely. In Manitoba, legislation provides that, even without an agreement, the purchaser can apply for a court order that the seller's insurance be used to restore the damaged property: see Manitoba *Law of Property Act*, C.C.S.M. c. L90, s. 36(1).

[8] See Brown, "Protecting the Purchaser's Interest Pending the Completion of the Sale of a Building" (1984) 62 C.B.R. 498.

[9] *Mitchell v. City of London Fire Assurance Co.*, [1888] O.J. No. 21, 15 O.A.R. 262 (Ont. C.A.).

[10] See *e.g.*, Ontario *Insurance Act*, R.S.O. 1990, c. I.8, s. 147; *Bonser Estate v. London & Midland General Insurance Co.*, [1972] S.C.J. No. 70, [1973] S.C.R. 10 (S.C.C.).

property, the lender may still claim under the policy.[11] If an insurer pays out in these circumstances, it is subrogated to the rights of the lender and may seek reimbursement from the borrower.

In most provinces, the lender may insist that the borrower use insurance money either to restore a building over which the lender has a mortgage or to pay down the loan, even if that is not mentioned in the policy.[12]

ASSIGNMENT ON DEATH

Contracts of insurance, other than life insurance, may cease to have effect on the death of the insured customer. The terms may specify this or it may be implicit in the nature of the coverage, such as the provision of benefits for accident and sickness. But, in some cases, the death of the customer does not immediately cause the insurance contract to die as well.

Automobile insurance remains in effect after the death of the person named in the policy as the owner of the vehicle covered by it. This is the clear implication of a statutory condition stating that, while in general the insurer must be notified of changes affecting the insurance, there is no such requirement where the change is a change of ownership of the vehicle resulting from death.[13] The insurance remains in effect while title to the vehicle is held by the executor or estate administrator pending its transfer.[14] When it comes to automobile liability insurance, the rule does not have to be inferred; it is spelled out. The definition of "insured" includes the spouse of a deceased insured, any person having proper, temporary custody of the vehicle pending confirmation of the executor or appointment of an administrator of the estate, and the estate executor or administrator.[15]

Fire insurance continues after ownership of the insured property has changed "by succession ... or by death".[16] This means that the executor or administrator and probably an heir[17] inherits the insurance on the property along with the property itself.

In cases where neither a statute nor the policy address the question of the death of the insured customer, the insurance does not survive that death without the insurer's consent. However, if the loss happened before death, the executor or administrator may enforce the claim like any other debt owed to the estate.[18]

---

[11] *Royal Bank of Canada v. State Farm Fire & Casualty Co.*, [2005] S.C.J. No. 34, [2005] 1 S.C.R. 779 (S.C.C.).

[12] See *e.g.*, Ontario *Mortgages Act*, R.S.O. 1990, c. M.40, s. 6. See also the *Fires Prevention (Metropolis) Act 1744* (U.K.), s. 83, a British imperial statute, which still applies in Alberta, British Columbia and Saskatchewan.

[13] See *e.g.*, *Statutory Conditions – Automobile Insurance*, O. Reg. 777/93, statutory condition 1.

[14] *Global General Insurance Co. v. Finlay*, [1961] S.C.J. No. 32, [1961] S.C.R. 539 (S.C.C.).

[15] See *e.g.*, Ontario *Insurance Act*, R.S.O. 1990, c. I.8, s. 239.

[16] See *e.g.*, *ibid.*, s. 148, statutory condition 3.

[17] This is made clear in Quebec: see *Civil Code of Québec*, S.Q. 1991, c. 64, Art. 2476, which applies to all "damage insurance".

[18] *Durrant v. Friend* (1852), 64 E.R. 1145.

In some provinces, this right to claim even passes to a beneficiary to whom the insured property was specifically bequeathed.[19]

A claim brought by an executor or an administrator under a policy will fail if the insurer can point to any default by the deceased while still alive. In other words, the claim by the representative is no better than a claim by the customer if he or she had survived.

ASSIGNMENT ON BANKRUPTCY

Apart from the legislation dealing with automobile liability insurance, the rules about the survival of insurance after the death of the insured customer are virtually identical to those that apply if he or she goes into bankruptcy. The only difference, in the latter case, is that it is the trustee in bankruptcy, rather than the executor or administrator, who inherits the right to enforce the policy should loss occur.[20]

ASSIGNMENT OF MARINE INSURANCE

A marine insurance contract is assignable, even without notice to the insurer, unless the policy contains a term stating the contrary. The practice is that the original insured endorses the policy on the back and delivers it to the assignee. Any claim by the assignee under the policy may be defeated by any defences which would have been available to the insurer against the original insured.[21] An insured person may not assign a policy insuring property in which he or she no longer has an interest.[22] On the other hand, the transfer of title to property in which the transferor has an interest does not necessarily entail the assignment of insurance on that property.[23]

BENEFICIARIES UNDER LIFE OR ACCIDENT AND SICKNESS INSURANCE

It is common for a life insurance policyholder who has insured his or her own life to designate a specific person who is to receive the proceeds of the insurance when the insured event happens. This designation, which may be made irrevocably, enables the beneficiary so designated to claim, and if necessary sue for, the proceeds directly from the insurer. But the claim will fail if the insured

---

[19] See *e.g.*, Ontario *Succession Law Reform Act*, R.S.O. 1990, c. S.26, s. 20.

[20] See *e.g.*, Ontario *Insurance Act*, R.S.O. 1990, c. I.8, s. 148, statutory condition 3; *Statutory Conditions – Automobile Insurance*, O. Reg. 777/93, statutory condition 1. See also Canada *Bankruptcy and Insolvency Act*, R.S.C. 1985, c. B-3, s. 24(2).

[21] See *e.g.*, Ontario *Marine Insurance Act*, R.S.O. 1990, c. M.2, s. 51.

[22] *Ibid.*, s. 52.

[23] *Ibid.*, s. 16.

customer breached a condition of the coverage or was otherwise in default under the policy.[24] If a beneficiary predeceases the person whose life is insured, the entitlement passes to other beneficiaries. If there are no others, it reverts to the estate.[25] If the beneficiary and the person whose life is insured die in a common disaster, the beneficiary is presumed to have died first.[26] Designations of beneficiaries may be changed by the policyholder unless they are declared to be irrevocable. In Quebec, any designation of a spouse lapses on divorce.[27]

JUDGMENT CREDITORS

The insurer's responsibility under a liability insurance contract is to defend and, if necessary, pay a claim brought by a third party against the insured customer. As with other types of insurance, the insurer's obligation, being contractual, is owed to its customer. But the obligation does not end there. Legislation extends it so that, if certain conditions are met, it is owed directly to the third party who may sue to enforce it.

Quebec's rule is the simplest. It states that "an injured third person may bring an action directly against the insured or directly against the insurer, or against both".[28] In other provinces, there are two pieces of legislation on point. One deals with automobile insurance, the other with other types of insurance.

Let us look first at the section dealing with all liability insurance except auto.[29] To take advantage of it, a person must first have obtained a judgment against the insured customer. Since the judgment establishes that the customer owes the third party a certain amount of money, the third party is a "judgment creditor". Armed with the judgment, the third party may then commence a new lawsuit against the insurer. In this second action, the third party need only establish the fact of insurance and the fact of the judgment.[30] The insurer may be able to reopen the merits of the original claim, but only if it produces appropriate evidence.[31]

There is a difference of judicial opinion about whether the section is available when the loss suffered by the third party is purely economic, unrelated to any property damage or personal injury. The wording of the section includes the

---

[24] See *e.g.*, Ontario *Insurance Act*, R.S.O. 1990, c. I.8, s. 195, *Civil Code of Québec*, S.Q. 1991, c. 64, Art. 2550. For a similar treatment of accident and sickness insurance, see Ontario *Insurance Act*, s. 314.

[25] See *e.g.*, Ontario *Insurance Act*, *ibid.*, s. 194. For accident and sickness insurance, see s. 314.

[26] See *e.g.*, Ontario *Insurance Act*, *ibid.*, s. 215; *Civil Code of Québec*, S.Q. 1991, c. 64, Art. 2448. For accident and sickness insurance, see *e.g.*, Ontario *Insurance Act*, s. 319.

[27] *Civil Code of Québec*, S.Q. 1991, c. 64, Art. 2459.

[28] *Ibid.*, Art. 2501. This does not apply to auto accidents which are dealt with entirely on a first-party basis.

[29] See *e.g.*, Ontario *Insurance Act*, R.S.O. 1990, c. I.8, s. 132.

[30] *Global General Insurance Co. v. Finlay*, [1961] S.C.J. No. 32, [1961] S.C.R. 539 (S.C.C.).

[31] *Carwald Concrete & Gravel Co. v. General Security Insurance Co. of Canada*, [1985] A.J. No. 1086, 42 Alta. L.R. (2d) 224 (Alta. C.A.).

phrase, "injury or damage to the person or property of another". The Ontario Court of Appeal has held that this excludes pure economic loss, such as that suffered by the client of a lawyer who was negligent in investigating a land title, so that the client has no claim against the insurer when the lawyer cannot or will not pay the judgment.[32] On the other hand, a Saskatchewan court has held that the term "property" is wide enough to encompass monetary loss and that "if the legislature had intended such an exclusion, it would have said so in clear terms".[33]

Another limit on the utility of the section is that a claim by a third party against the insurer is subject to "the same equities as the insurer would have if the judgment had been satisfied". This means that any grounds entitling the insurer to refuse payment had the customer paid the judgment and then turned to the insurer for reimbursement, remain good against the third party. For example, if the customer had been guilty of misrepresentation or breached a condition of the policy, the insurer would not be liable to the third party just as it would not have been to the customer.[34]

In contrast, the section dealing with auto liability insurance preserves the third party's direct claim against the insurer even in the face of defaults by the customer.[35] If the customer violated an obligation owed the insurer before or after the loss, the third party may nonetheless succeed in pressing the claim up to an amount equivalent to the minimum compulsory limits of coverage.[36] However, the insurer will not have to pay if the policy has lapsed at the time of the accident, if the accident did not fall within the basic coverage (for example, if it is covered by extended garage risk coverage), or if the judgment was obtained outside Canada. It should also be noted that where an insurer has to pay a claim under the section, and there would have been grounds for denying it if it had been brought by the customer instead of the third party, the insurer may seek reimbursement from the customer.

UNNAMED INSUREDS

The coverage provided in an insurance contract may extend to a class of people not individually named in it. For example, homeowner's insurance often includes the property, not only of the person named in the policy, but also that of family members living in the household. This is permissible and enforceable,

---

[32] *Perry v. General Security Insurance Co. of Canada*, [1984] O.J. No. 3300, 7 C.C.L.I. 231 (Ont. C.A.).

[33] *Kallos v. Saskatchewan Government Insurance*, [1983] S.J. No. 897, 3 C.C.L.I. 65 at 72 (Sask. Q.B.).

[34] *Rocovitis v. Dominion of Canada General Insurance Co.*, [2004] O.J. No. 4326, 16 C.C.L.I. (4th) 207 (Ont. C.A.). But a post-loss agreement between the insured and insurer excusing the insurer does not prejudice a third party. See *Azevedo v. Markel Insurance Co.*, [1999] A.J. No. 1201, 14 C.C.L.I. (3d) 137 (Alta. C.A.).

[35] See *e.g.*, Ontario *Insurance Act*, R.S.O. 1990, c. I.8, s. 258.

[36] Usually $200,000. See *e.g.*, Ontario *Insurance Act*, *ibid.*, s. 251. See *Joachin v. Abel*, [2003] O.J. No. 1484, 47 C.C.L.I. (3d) 1 (Ont. C.A.). Where more than one insurer is involved, each is liable up to the limit. See *Canadian General Insurance Co. v. MacKinnon*, [1975] S.C.J. No. 92, [1976] 2 S.C.R. 606 (S.C.C.).

even without disclosing the details of the other people to the insurer, provided the named insured has more than a nominal interest in some of the property insured.[37] If loss occurs, the named insured can sue on behalf of the others and holds any proceeds which relate to their property in trust for them.[38]

Defaults by the named insured prejudice the rights of unnamed insureds. The opposite can also be true. Where an unnamed insured commits an act in breach of the coverage, even claims of innocent named insureds may be forfeited. Where a son, who was unnamed in the policy but whose property was covered by it because he lived in the household, deliberately set fire to his parents' house, even the parents' claim in respect of their own property was denied.[39] The policy contained a clause excluding claims resulting from "wilful acts of an insured or any person whose property is insured hereunder". However, the decision would have been the same without this clause because the delinquent son shared an interest in the property he destroyed.

The various forms of automobile insurance also extend coverage to unnamed insureds. For automobile liability insurance, anyone driving the insured vehicle with the consent of the named insured is covered as if he or she was a party to the contract.[40] Under the standard auto policy, insurance against damage to the vehicle or property carried in it also applies when someone other than the named insured is driving, as long as it is with the consent of the named insured. For both these types of insurance, the key issue is consent. Problems tend to arise when the consent is not express but alleged to have been impliedly given. Whether consent can be inferred is a question of evidence in the individual case.[41] This is also true in defining the scope of the consent which has been given. Permission to drive a car "to the garage" does not include permission to drive around town for a few hours.[42] Similarly, permission given to one driver does not necessarily imply that that person may, in turn, allow someone else to drive the car.[43]

First-party personal injury benefits may be payable to persons other than the named insured. Uninsured motorist coverage extends to "any person who sustains bodily injury or death while driving, being carried in or upon or entering or getting on to or alighting from the described automobile" as well as the named insured, that person's spouse[44] and any dependent relatives living in

---

[37] *Marks v. Commonwealth Insurance Co.*, [1973] O.J. No. 2255, 2 O.R. (2d) 237 (Ont. C.A.).

[38] *Maldover v. Norwich Union Fire Insurance Co.*, [1917] O.J. No. 123, 40 O.L.R. 532 (Ont. H.C.). See also *Keefer v. Phoenix Insurance Co. of Hartford*, [1901] S.C.J. No. 6, 31 S.C.R. 144 (S.C.C.).

[39] *Scott v. Wawanesa Mutual Insurance Co.*, [1989] S.C.J. No. 55, [1989] 1 S.C.R. 1445 (S.C.C.).

[40] See *e.g.*, Ontario *Insurance Act*, R.S.O. 1990, c. I.8, ss. 239, 243.

[41] See *e.g.*, *Judgment Recovery (Nova Scotia) Ltd. v. London and Edinburgh Insurance Co.*, [1975] N.S.J. No. 353, 11 N.S.R. (2d) 602 (N.S.C.A.); *Usher v. Goncalves*, [1969] B.C.J. No. 451, 9 D.L.R. (3d) 15 (B.C.S.C.).

[42] *Lloyd v. Dominion Fire Insurance Co.*, [1940] 2 D.L.R. 707 (Sask. C.A.).

[43] *Ontario (Minister of Transport) v. Canadian General Insurance Co.*, [1971] S.C.J. No. 104, [1972] S.C.R. 234 (S.C.C.).

[44] In Ontario, a same-sex partner would also qualify: O. Reg. 113/00.

the same household.[45] No fault schemes generally provide for the same class with the addition of people struck by the insured vehicle.[46]

Although there are significant differences among provincial no fault schemes, there are some issues which are common to most of them. One such issue is who qualifies as a member of the household, especially in cases involving separated spouses.[47] Occasionally, unusual circumstances make it difficult to decide if a person has been "struck by" the insured vehicle. For example, where a wheel fell off a tractor being towed by the insured vehicle and hit a pedestrian, there was held to be no coverage because the tractor did not fit the meaning of "trailer" in the policy.[48] In contrast, where a car hit another one and propelled it into the owner standing nearby, he was held to have been struck by the first car.[49]

SUMMARY

In some circumstances, the benefit of an insurance contract operates in favour of a person not originally party to that contract. A third party may have been assigned the benefit of the contract by the named insured. A common example is the assignment by a borrower to a lender of the right to proceeds of insurance on property mortgaged to secure the loan. In the case of the death or bankruptcy of the named insured, the statute assigns the benefit of certain insurance to a personal representative or trustee in bankruptcy. Purchasers of life insurance commonly designate beneficiaries. Legislation affords rights in liability insurance contracts to judgment creditors. Some insurance is extended by its terms to cover classes of persons not specifically named and not party to the contract.

Unless otherwise provided by statute or by agreement with the insurer, a third party cannot enforce his or her rights directly and the claims may be defeated by defences available to the insurer against the named insured.

---

[45] See *e.g.*, Alberta *Insurance Act*, R.S.A. 2000, c. I-3, s. 586.

[46] *Ibid.*, ss. 587-588. See Chapter 14 for how the matter is resolved when a person qualifies for benefits under more than one policy, being, for example, the named insured in one policy and entitled to claim under another which insures the car which struck him or her.

[47] See *e.g.*, *Goodland v. Gore Mutual Insurance Co.*, [1978] O.J. No. 3341, 19 O.R. (2d) 521 (Ont. C.A.).

[48] *Thompson v. Sharpe*, [1977] O.J. No. 2245, 16 O.R. (2d) 24 (Ont. C.A.).

[49] *Re MacGillivray*, [1975] I.L.R. 1-695 (Ont. H.C.). See also *Ezard v. Warwick*, [1979] O.J. No. 4328, 25 O.R. (2d) 577 (Ont. C.A.), leave to appeal refused (1979), 31 N.R. 89n (S.C.C.).

Chapter 16

Regulation of the Insurance Industry

INTRODUCTION

The other Chapters in this book are concerned primarily with the relationship between an insurer and its customer or other persons having rights under insurance contracts. The focus of this Chapter is the relationship between insurers and government. To promote the solvency of insurers so that they can meet their financial obligations to policyholders, governments at both the federal and provincial level have schemes for the regulation of insurers and their activities. These schemes concern corporate structure, financing and investment, and impose licensing, auditing and deposit requirements.

DEFINING INSURANCE

For regulatory purposes, insurance is defined as:

> ... the undertaking by one person to indemnify another person against loss or liability for loss in respect of certain risk or peril to which the object of insurance may be exposed, or to pay a sum of money or other thing of value, upon the happening of a certain event, and includes life insurance.[1]

While this is broad enough to include many transactions not normally thought of as insurance, the courts tend to construe the definition narrowly. For example, it has been held not to apply to annuities.[2] On the other hand, services offered by automobile clubs — towing, emergency repairs, legal assistance in connection with motoring accidents — have been held to fit the definition in that they involve indemnity against risk[3] and correspond to one of the classes of insurance dealt with by provincial insurance legislation, namely, auto insurance. A key distinguishing feature of arrangements caught by the definition is that they involve the right of the "insured" to demand payment or the provision of a service on the happening of some uncertain misfortune. If the "premium" is

---

[1] See *e.g.*, Ontario *Insurance Act*, R.S.O. 1990, c. I.8, s. 1.

[2] *Kerslake v. Gray*, [1957] S.C.J. No. 62, [1958] S.C.R. 3 (S.C.C.). Note, however, that legislation in most provinces now expressly includes annuities within the definition of life insurance. See, for example, the definition of "life insurance" in Alberta *Insurance Act*, R.S.A. 2000, c. I-3, s. 639.

[3] *R. v. Anderson*, [1940] 3 W.W.R. 505 (Alta. C.A.).

merely an advance payment for services that may be accessed at any time, it is not insurance. But a manufacturer's extended warranty, by which a promise is made to provide goods or services in the event that the product malfunctions, is not insurance even though the event giving rise to the warrantor's obligation is not certain to happen. This is because the warranty is merely an expression of confidence in the quality of the product.[4]

There is a distinction between insurance and non-insurance contracts of indemnity such as performance bonds, guarantees and sureties.[5] Those issuing bonds or acting as guarantors or sureties are generally not caught by the regulatory scheme of the Insurance Acts.[6] Potential for confusion lies in the fact that insurers often issue performance bonds. It also arises from the fact that certain types of insurance, like credit insurance and guarantee insurance,[7] resemble their non-insurance cousins. The crucial point of distinction is that insurance protects the customer against the financial risks of non-performance of a contract or non-payment of a debt, whereas a guarantor or surety undertakes to assume the obligation to the third party directly.

THE FORM AND ORGANIZATION OF INSURANCE COMPANIES

Insurers may be organized as joint-stock companies, mutual insurance corporations (including cash-mutual insurance corporations), fraternal societies, mutual benefit societies, reciprocal or inter-insurance exchanges, or underwriters or syndicates of underwriters operating through Lloyd's.[8]

Joint stock companies' capital consists of shares either held privately or purchased by the public (depending on the terms of incorporation). Incorporation may be according to either federal[9] or provincial[10] legislation which governs such matters as capital structure, ownership, corporate governance and payment of dividends. An insurer may also be incorporated outside Canada but, in that case, it must obtain authorization to carry on business in Canada. This is a process that requires an insurer to, among other things, demonstrate its ability to

---

[4]　*Bedard v. Gervais* (1933), 55 Que. K.B. 195.

[5]　*Whalen v. Union Indemnity Co.*, [1932] O.J. No. 114, 41 O.W.N. 208 (Ont. H.C.J.).

[6]　There is an exception in Saskatchewan where guarantee companies must be licensed under the *Saskatchewan Insurance Act*, R.S.S. 1978, c. S-26. See *Guarantee Companies Securities Act*, R.S.S. 1978, c. G-9 (as am. R.S.S. 1978 (Supp.), c. 26).

[7]　See *e.g.*, New Brunswick *Insurance Act*, R.S.N.B. 1973, c. I-12, s. 1.

[8]　See *e.g.*, Ontario *Insurance Act*, R.S.O. 1990, c. I.8, s. 42.

[9]　*Insurance Companies Act*, S.C. 1991, c. 47, Part III, ss. 22-48.

[10]　See *e.g.*, Ontario *Corporations Act*, R.S.O. 1990, c. C.38, Part V. For discussion of the Constitutional authority of each level of government to legislate with respect to the incorporation of companies, see P. Hogg, *Constitutional Law in Canada*, 2d ed. (Carswell, Scarborough, 1992), Chapters 23, 24.

meet the obligations imposed on insurers by Canadian (both federal and provincial) law.[11]

Mutual insurance corporations are pooling arrangements whereby members contribute to a fund to cover future claims from individual members. Members may be liable to make additional contributions (or "assessments") should the pool prove insufficient. Excess amounts are returned as dividends. A mutual company is called a "cash mutual" if it has sufficient reserves to make liability for assessments unnecessary, and if issued the appropriate letters patent.[12] Mutual companies may be licensed to write the same coverages as joint-stock companies,[13] however, it is common for mutual companies to be limited both in terms of scope and geographical area. A typical example of a mutual company is one covering only agricultural property in a particular district. As few as 10 owners of agricultural property may organize initial meetings and only 50 need subscribe.

Fraternal societies are organizations licensed to enter into non-profit contracts of life, accident and sickness, disability or funeral insurance with their members or members' families. There must be at least 75 members.[14]

Mutual benefit societies are non-profit organizations such as trade unions licensed to provide limited sickness and funeral benefits for their members only. They may not provide other classes of insurance.[15]

Reciprocal exchanges are similar to mutual insurance corporations except they usually involve fewer participants, and subscribers assume liability individually and not collectively through an incorporated body.[16]

Some Canadian insurance business, particularly in the field of marine insurance, is placed with Lloyd's insurance market in London, England. That market is made up of numerous syndicates of individuals willing to underwrite risks. A syndicate may be licensed to do business in Canada or business may be brought to underwriters in England by a Canadian broker authorized by Lloyd's to do so. It is common for brokers to spread risks among several underwriters (or syndicates of them). Contracts are with the underwriters directly and not with Lloyd's.

ACCESS TO BUSINESS

An insurer must obtain authorization from the government of a province or territory of Canada before conducting business in that jurisdiction.[17] Authorization

---

[11] *Insurance Companies Act*, S.C. 1991, c. 47, s. 574. See also Ontario *Insurance Act*, R.S.O. 1990, c. I.8, s. 48(10).

[12] See *e.g.*, Ontario *Corporations Act*, R.S.O. 1990, c. C.38, s. 153.

[13] See *e.g.*, Ontario *Insurance Act*, R.S.O. 1990, c. I.8, ss. 42-43, and Ontario *Corporations Act*, *ibid.*, s. 149(13).

[14] *Insurance Companies Act*, S.C. 1991, c. 47, ss. 540-542. See Ontario *Insurance Act*, *ibid.*, Part X for detailed rules concerning the regulation and operation of Societies.

[15] See *e.g.*, Ontario *Insurance Act*, R.S.O. 1990, c. I.8, s. 40(5), providing that mutual benefit societies are not insurers and are thus not entitled to being licensed as such.

[16] See *e.g.*, Ontario *Insurance Act*, *ibid.*, Part XIII.

[17] *Ibid.*, s. 40.

by one provincial government is usually accepted by other provincial governments as sufficient evidence of financial viability, and it is not generally necessary, for example, for an insurer to duplicate the payment of the required deposit. Cancellation or suspension of authority to carry on business in one province may result in cancellation or suspension in other jurisdictions.

The federal government also operates a scheme of authorization of insurance companies.[18] A company authorized under the federal statute must obtain separate authorization from the government of each province where it intends to do business, but this second step is usually little more than a formality. An insurer wishing to do business throughout Canada therefore has a choice. It may obtain an initial licence from one province (usually the one where its head office or chief Canadian agency is located) by satisfying the various requirements and then seek authorization elsewhere without having to duplicate the deposit and other requirements. Alternatively, the insurer may obtain federal authorization which, in turn, provides relatively easy access to provincial licences.

The Federal System

The federal system is administered by the Minister of Finance and the Superintendent of Financial Institutions. If satisfied that the company is viable as an insurer, the Minister of Finance issues letters patent to it.[19] Where the applicant is a foreign company seeking to incorporate a subsidiary in Canada, the Minister must be satisfied that the company would be capable of making a contribution to the financial system of Canada and that similar access is available to a Canadian company in the relevant foreign jurisdiction.

Before starting operations, within one year after obtaining letters patent, an insurer must apply to the Superintendent for an order to commence and carry on business.[20] Obtaining such an order is conditional upon, among other things, paid up capital of at least $10 million.

Foreign companies must also apply for an order permitting them to operate in Canada.[21] Before granting such approval, the Superintendent must also be satisfied that the company is capable of making a contribution to the financial system of Canada and, further, that similar access to the relevant foreign market is available to Canadian companies, the company has appointed an actuary and an auditor for its insurance business in Canada, it has established the location of its chief agency, and that all other requirements have been satisfied.

An insurer is restricted to writing the classes of insurance specified in the Superintendent's order allowing it to commence and carry on business.[22] A life insurer may not insure other classes of risk except those falling within accident

---

[18]　*Insurance Companies Act*, S.C. 1991, c. 47.
[19]　*Ibid.*, Part III.
[20]　*Ibid.*, s. 52.
[21]　*Ibid.*, s. 573.
[22]　*Ibid.*, s. 443.

and sickness insurance.[23] Nor may it engage in specified activities such as: acting as executor, administrator, trustee or, in certain circumstances, guarantor; lending on the security of a mortgage against residential property where the amount of the loan exceeds 75 per cent of the value of the property; entering into excessive (relative to assets) debt obligations; leasing of personal property, and becoming a general partner in a limited partnership without the approval of the Superintendent.[24]

Provincial Systems

Since 1989, British Columbia has operated a system of authorization of involvement broadly similar to that in place federally. A single statute[25] governs both incorporation and authority to enter into the business of insurance. The "business authorization" issued by the Financial Institutions Commission differs from the old licensing system in that it need not be renewed annually.

All other provinces and territories adhere to a system of licensing under their Insurance Acts. This is separate from the incorporation process which is governed by general company law.[26] Licences permit dealing in a specified class or classes of insurance.[27]

In most provinces an insurance company must pay a deposit before receiving a licence, although this does not usually apply to mutual companies, fraternal societies or Lloyd's syndicates.[28] In Ontario, deposits are payable when, and in the amount and form, considered necessary by the Superintendent.[29]

It is also usually a condition of obtaining a licence that the insurer have a minimum amount of paid-up capital. For example, in Ontario, a company applying for a licence to transact life insurance must have a paid-up capital and surplus of at least $2 million. At least $1 million must be paid up capital and at least $500,000 must be unimpaired surplus. For other than life insurance, the amount is $3 million for joint-stock companies.[30] In the case of mutual insurance corporations or Lloyd's underwriters, there must be a net surplus of assets over liabilities of $2 million for life insurers and $1 million for others.

---

[23] *Ibid.*, s. 445.

[24] *Ibid.*, ss. 466-478.

[25] *Financial Institutions Act*, R.S.B.C. 1996, c. 141.

[26] In Ontario, the *Corporations Act*, R.S.O. 1990, c. C.38, contains a part (Part V) devoted entirely to the incorporation of insurance corporations, but this is separate from the legislation dealing with licensing (authorization) which is contained in the *Insurance Act*.

[27] See *e.g.*, Ontario *Insurance Act*, R.S.O. 1990, c. I.8, s. 43.

[28] *Ibid.*, s. 66.

[29] *Ibid.*, s. 66.

[30] *Ibid.*, s. 48.

SUPERVISION

The Federal System

The federal system of control is contained in the *Insurance Companies Act*.[31] Administration of the Act is the responsibility of the Minister of Finance. The Superintendent of Financial Institutions is the civil servant who reports to the Minister and who has considerable power of supervision over the activities of insurers.

Insurers are required to make annual reports to the Superintendent setting out details of their financial situation.[32] In addition, the Superintendent has the power to examine or inquire into the affairs of a company as he or she deems necessary to ensure the Act is being complied with and that the company is in sound financial condition.[33] If the Superintendent considers that a company is involved in unsound business practices, he or she may direct the company to rectify the situation. In serious cases, the Superintendent may take immediate control of the assets for at least seven days during which time the company is given an opportunity to explain, or to put things right.

Some of the obligations imposed on individuals or corporate bodies with the aim of ensuring solvency carry criminal sanctions. For contravening a provision of the Act, a natural person may be fined up to $100,000 and/or imprisoned up to 12 months. Any other entity may be fined up to $500,000. Additional fines may be levied to eliminate any monetary benefit gained by the convicted person.[34]

Provincial Systems

The British Columbia legislation[35] is administered and enforced by the Superintendent of Financial Institutions under the aegis of the Financial Institutions Commission. Insurers must file detailed annual financial reports and such additional reports as may be required by the Superintendent. If a problem is evident, the Superintendent may order the insurer to remedy the situation. The Superintendent also has power to freeze property and obtain court orders to enforce his or her directives. Failure to comply with directives exposes an insurer to revocation of its business authorization.

Setting aside slight differences, the other provinces have broadly similar regulatory systems. In Alberta, for example, insurers must file annual reports with the provincial Superintendent of Insurance showing the condition of their financial affairs.[36] If a company's assets are found to be insufficient to justify continuance of the insurer or to provide proper security to persons effecting

---

[31] *Insurance Companies Act*, S.C. 1991, c. 47.
[32] *Ibid.*, s. 665.
[33] *Ibid.*, s. 674.
[34] *Ibid.*, ss. 705, 706.
[35] *Financial Institutions Act*, R.S.B.C. 1996, c. 141.
[36] Alberta *Insurance Act*, R.S.A. 2000, c. I-3, s. 43.

insurance in Alberta, conditions may be attached to the insurer's licence or remedial measures ordered. If the insurer fails to comply, the insurer's licence may be suspended or cancelled. Some provinces such as Alberta and Ontario which, unlike British Columbia, retain the system of annual licences, require that insurers maintain deposits. In New Brunswick, if the Superintendent of Insurance considers it necessary for the protection of policyholders, a deposit may be used to reimburse all or some of the insurer's contracts of insurance.[37] Alternatively, deposits may be applied directly for the benefit of insureds in payment of claims or refunds or unearned premiums.[38]

Industry Compensation Plan

Since 1988, there has been in place in Canada a compensation plan designed to come into operation on the insolvency of a property and casualty insurer.[39] This plan, which is operated by a federal non-profit corporation (the Property and Casualty Insurance Compensation Corporation) funded by members of the industry, has effect in all Canadian jurisdictions. It does not apply to life, accident and sickness, aircraft, credit, crop, directors' and officers', employer's liability, fidelity, financial guarantee, marine, mortgage, surety and title insurance. Neither does it apply to provincial government automobile insurers where they exist. Otherwise an insurer is required to participate as a condition of its licence. The plan only comes into play on the formal winding up of an insurer. It pays outstanding claims to a maximum of $250,000 per insured and repays 70% of unearned premiums to a maximum of $700 per policy.

SUPERVISION OF CONTRACT TERMS

Supervision of contract terms is one of the ways governments exercise control over insurers. For some classes of insurance, legislation sets out rules for various aspects of the contractual relationship. Any term inconsistent with these rules cannot be enforced by the insurer although the contract remains valid for the benefit of the insured. Fire, automobile, and accident and sickness insurance contracts are automatically deemed to include certain terms, called statutory conditions. They are required to be printed in every policy to which they apply but still have effect, at least for the benefit of the insured, when they are not printed. Statutory conditions deal with such matters as disclosure and misrepresentation, material change in the risk, termination of contracts, requirements after loss, salvage, appraisal and limitation periods.

Additional control is exercised by the insurance authorities in all provinces over automobile insurance policies. No form of policy (and, in most provinces, application, endorsement or renewal) may be used without the approval of the

---

[37] New Brunswick *Insurance Act*, R.S.N.B. 1973, c. I-12, s. 44.

[38] *Ibid.*, s. 45.

[39] Kennedy, "Compensation Plan for Property and Casualty Insurers" (1989) 1 Can. Ins. L. Rev. 203.

Superintendent of Insurance.[40] It is the common practice that standard forms are approved for all insurers leaving relatively few matters (such as amount of premium and deductible) to be agreed in individual cases. For certain sub-categories of automobile insurance, notably no fault benefits for personal injury and death, all the terms are provided by regulation.[41] In British Columbia, Manitoba, Quebec and Saskatchewan, compulsory automobile insurance coverages are provided directly by government through specially created insuring organizations. Accordingly, government control over the terms of contracts is direct.

RESERVES AND INVESTMENTS

Reserves

Insurers authorized to transact business under both the federal and provincial systems of insurance regulation must maintain minimum levels of capital and liquidity. The federal regime requires life companies and fraternal benefit societies to maintain "adequate capital and adequate and appropriate forms of liquidity", as determined by the superintendent of Financial Institutions.[42] Foreign companies authorized under the federal system must maintain an adequate margin of assets in Canada over liabilities in Canada and a prescribed value of assets in Canada in respect of each class of insurance transacted.[43] Provincial legislation also obliges insurers doing business in the respective jurisdictions to have adequate reserves in relation to liabilities.[44]

Investment Restrictions

1. Federal Regulation

Insurers incorporated and/or authorized under the federal system of regulation are subject to constraints on investment. In general, directors of companies and fraternal benefit societies[45] must adopt lending policies and procedures that "a reasonably prudent person would apply in respect of a portfolio of investments and loans to avoid undue risk of loss and obtain a reasonable return".[46] Specifically, insurers are restricted in respect of commercial loans they may make,[47] real estate they may hold,[48] shares they may own,[49] and dealings they may have

---

40 See *e.g.*, Ontario *Insurance Act*, R.S.O. 1990, c. I.8, s. 227.
41 See *e.g.*, *Automobile Insurance*, R.R.O. 1990, Reg. 664.
42 *Insurance Companies Act*, S.C. 1991, c. 47, s. 515.
43 *Ibid.*, ss. 608-609.
44 See *e.g.*, British Columbia *Financial Institutions Act*, R.S.B.C. 1996, c. 141, s. 77.
45 *Insurance Companies Act*, S.C. 1991, c. 47, s. 551.
46 *Ibid.*, s. 492.
47 *Ibid.*, ss. 503-504, 562.
48 *Ibid.*, ss. 506, 563.
49 *Ibid.*, ss. 508, 565.

with their own directors, officers (or families of either) or significant shareholders of companies in which any officer or director has a substantial investment.[50]

Foreign insurers authorized under the federal regime to conduct business in
Canada are also subject to restrictions on investments in Canada. Investment in
loans is limited to a prescribed percentage of the value of assets in Canada.[51]

2. Provincial Systems

In British Columbia, insurers must submit their investment and lending policies
to the Superintendent of Financial Institutions for approval.[52] Such a policy must
conform to "prudent standards" avoiding undue risk and creating a reasonable
expectation of a fair return. Dealings with officers, directors, family members
and companies in which they have substantial investments are subject to
restrictions broadly similar to those contained in the federal legislation.[53]

In other provinces, permitted investments are set out specifically. Typical of
permitted investments are government securities of Canada and other specified
countries, municipal bonds, securities issued by the International Bank for
Reconstruction and Development, and, subject to various restrictions, other
bonds, debentures, mortgages, shares and real estate.[54] Insurers are expressly
empowered to own real property obtained by way of foreclosure and an office
building larger than necessary for their own business purposes (intending to earn
rents for the extra space).[55]

Some general restrictions are superimposed on otherwise permissible investments.[56] For example, it is usual for insurers to be precluded from holding more
than a certain percentage of the shares of a corporation from having more than a
stated percentage of its assets invested in a single security or corporation (except
government securities), or from having more than a stated percentage of assets
in the form of real estate, or shares. Moreover, no insurer is allowed to invest in
or loan funds on the security of its own shares or those of any other insurance
company. As with other systems discussed above, transactions with parties
related to the insurer are also prohibited.

ACCOUNTING REQUIREMENTS

All Canadian insurance regulatory regimes have two basic accounting requirements. One requirement is that any insurer transacting life insurance must
maintain separate funds (and therefore accounts) for that class of business.

---

[50] *Ibid.*, s. 518.

[51] *Ibid.*, ss. 616, 617.

[52] *Financial Institutions Act*, R.S.B.C. 1996, c. 141, ss. 135-137.

[53] *Ibid.*, ss. 142-154.

[54] See *e.g.*, Ontario *Insurance Act*, R.S.O. 1990, c. I.8, s. 433.

[55] *Ibid.*, s. 107.

[56] *Ibid.*, s. 435.

The other is that all insurers must prepare and submit to the relevant authorities annual returns.

Under the federal system, life insurers are required to maintain segregated funds in respect of their life policies.[57] Moreover, they must maintain accounts for participating policies separate from those relating to other policies. The allocation of investment income, losses and expenses to participating policy accounts must be "fair and equitable" to participating policyholders, and an actuary's report to that effect is required. Payments may be made to shareholders from the participating account, but only in accordance with a complex formula set out in the legislation.

In British Columbia, an insurer must keep separate funds for each class of insurance it sells and account separately for all premiums and claims in relation to each such separate fund. However, investments relating to one fund need not be kept separate from those relating to others.[58] In the other provinces, the segregated fund requirement usually relates only to life insurance. For example, in Ontario, insurers must maintain at least one separate fund in respect of their life policies with separate assets for each fund.[59] Transfers between segregated funds are subject to limitations.

REGULATION OF PREMIUMS

In New Brunswick, Nova Scotia, Newfoundland, Alberta and Ontario, premium rates for automobile insurance are regulated by public authorities. Nova Scotia's system is a "file and use" one whereby insurers file with the regulator their premium rates together with supporting financial information. Upon filing its rates, an insurer may use them immediately although changes may subsequently be required by the regulatory body. Alberta, New Brunswick, Newfoundland and Ontario have prior approval systems. Insurers submit their proposed rates. The rates must be approved before use. The approval process may involve a hearing.

REINSURANCE

If an insurer's reserves are insufficient to cover a particular risk or group of risks, it may protect itself by contracting with another insurer who assumes part or all of the risk. Although the risk is thus shared between the two (or more) insurers, either on a proportional or excess basis, the original insurer retains the liability to its customers. The second insurer in an arrangement of this type is a "reinsurer".[60] Provincial legislation addresses itself to reinsurance in several

---

[57] *Insurance Companies Act*, S.C. 1991, c. 47, ss. 451, 452, 593.

[58] *Financial Institutions Act*, R.S.B.C. 1996, c. 141, s. 80.

[59] See *e.g.*, Ontario *Insurance Act*, R.S.O. 1990, c. I.8, s. 109.

[60] Reinsurance may be concluded *ad hoc* or under a general agreement known as a "treaty". A treaty may provide for automatic reinsurance for specified classes of policies as soon as they are

contexts. It permits contracts of reinsurance made with reinsurers not licensed in the province.[61] In some situations, it restricts the percentage of risk that may be reinsured.[62] In New Brunswick, where any insurer's reserves are considered to have fallen to an inadequate level, the provincial Superintendent of Insurance may use that insurer's deposit to effect reinsurance.[63]

SUMMARY

To reduce the chance of insolvency, insurance companies are regulated by the federal and provincial governments. If an insurer satisfies the federal regulatory requirements, or those in one of the provinces, with minimum additional formality, then that will usually be accepted by the authorities in other jurisdictions.

Before commencing business, an insurer must satisfy certain requirements relating to incorporation and also obtain the requisite approval, or licence, for trading in insurance. These requirements involve, among other things, a minimum level of capitalization. Once in business, an insurer must submit annual reports on its financial well-being. In the event of problems arising, an insurer may be ordered to take remedial measures or, in serious cases, may be subject to direct supervision of its affairs.

Insurers must maintain reserves sufficient to underwrite their liabilities. They must also maintain separate accounts for life insurance and are subject to restrictions on the investments they may hold. For auto insurance, some provinces regulate the level of premiums that may be charged.

---

entered into between an insurer and its customer or be "facultative" in that specific acceptance is required in individual cases.
[61] See *e.g.*, Ontario *Insurance Act*, R.S.O. 1990, c. I.8, s. 41.
[62] See *e.g.*, *Reinsurance*, O. Reg. 129/08.
[63] New Brunswick *Insurance Act*, R.S.N.B. 1973, c. I-2, s. 44.

Chapter 17

Different Classes of Insurance

In Chapter 3 we saw that some rules of insurance law are different depending on the class of insurance to which they apply. In this chapter we identify the principal types of insurance and describe some of the distinctive features of each, particularly those features that the law treats in a particular way.

ACCIDENT AND SICKNESS INSURANCE

Accident and Sickness insurance provides cover for loss arising from accidents causing personal injury or illness that occurs, usually without pre-existing symptoms. To the extent the insurance responds to financial loss such as lost income or medical or other expenses incurred, it is indemnity insurance. When the insurance provides for a lump sum payment upon the occurrence of a specified event, like an accident causing total disability, without the claimant having to verify any associated financial loss, it is non-indemnity insurance. It is important to determine whether a claim relates to indemnity or non-indemnity insurance, because an insurer's subrogation rights[1] and its right to claim contribution from any other insurer covering the loss[2] apply only to claims under indemnity insurance.

If insurance covers loss from accidents and not illness, it may be necessary in a particular case to determine whether the claim arises from one and not the other. The mere fact that illness is an unexpected and even rare consequence of a physical event external to the claimant's body does not make it an accident in the sense that personal injury would. In *Co-operators Life Insurance Co. v. Gibbens*,[3] the Supreme Court of Canada dealt with the case of a man who had contracted genital herpes from unprotected sex which led to a rare condition that left him paralyzed. The Court held that this was not covered by an accident policy since diseases frequently arise from external factors such as bacteria or mosquito bites, and to treat all of these as accidents would be contrary to the reasonable expectations of the parties to insurance contracts.

Unlike some other forms of insurance, accident and sickness insurance policies are, for the most part, not uniform. The exception to this general observation is the segment of every policy appearing under the heading "Statutory Conditions". Statutory conditions are imposed by provincial Insurance Acts

---

[1] See Chapter 13.
[2] See Chapter 14.
[3] [2009] S.C.J. No. 59, 2009 SCC 59 (S.C.C.).

(except in Quebec) and deal with such matters as changes in the insured's occupation, termination of the contract, notice and proof of claims, waiver and payment of benefits.[4] Otherwise, while precise wording is not prescribed, contracts must be consistent with statutory or common law rules relating to such matters as the duty of disclosure,[5] insurable interest,[6] beneficiaries,[7] relief against forfeiture,[8] as well as interpretation of the contract, causation and fortuity.[9]

An issue that raises interpretation, causation and fortuity relates to a common exclusion in accident policies by which cover is limited to injury caused "solely by accident and independent of all other causes". This limitation has been held to apply only where a contributing factor such as a pre-existing illness or physical defect is an active cause. Thus where the pre-existing factor has merely been activated by the accident, and would otherwise not have manifested itself, the accident is nonetheless the sole cause of the injury.[10]

MARINE INSURANCE

Marine insurance covers losses arising from "(a) losses that are incidental to a marine adventure, including losses arising from a land or air peril incidental to such an adventure, if they are provided for in the contract or by usage of the trade; or (b) losses that are incidental to the building, repair or launch of a ship."[11] The subject matter of marine insurance may be a ship, cargo, crews' wages, freight, commissions on profits, mortgage or loan monies (including a form of security called "bottomry", or liability to third parties).[12]

There is a federal *Marine Insurance Act*,[13] and British Columbia, Manitoba, New Brunswick, Nova Scotia, Ontario and Quebec each have almost identical legislation because of uncertainty about constitutional authority. These statutes are all modelled on the British *Marine Insurance Act* of 1906,[14] and consequently much British case law is relevant in Canada.

Any person interested in a marine adventure, in the sense that he/she stands to lose if an insured event occurs, has an insurable interest in that adventure.[15]

Marine insurance may be in the form of a voyage policy insuring cargo at and from one specified place to another,[16] or a time policy the usual time limit being a set time following delivery at the end of the voyage. In such a case, coverage

---

4   See *e.g.*, Ontario *Insurance Act*, R.S.O. 1990, c. I.8, s. 300.
5   See *e.g.*, *ibid*, s. 308*ff* and Chapter 5.
6   See *e.g.*, *ibid*, ss. 305, 306 and Chapter 6.
7   See *e.g.*, *ibid*, s. 313*ff*.
8   See *e.g.*, *ibid*, s. 328.
9   See Chapter 9.
10 *Voison v. Royal Insurance Co. of Canada*, [1988] O.J. No. 3115, 66 O.R. (2d) 45 (Ont. C.A.).
11 See *Marine Insurance Act*, S.C. 1993, c. 22, s. 6; and Ontario *Marine Insurance Act*, R.S.O. 1990, c. M.2, ss. 2, 3.
12 See generally, *e.g.*, *ibid.*, Ontario *Marine Insurance Act*, R.S.O. 1990, c. M.2, s. 4.
13 S.C. 1993, c. 22.
14 (U.K.), 6 Ed. 7.
15 See *e.g.*, Ontario *Marine Insurance Act*, R.S.O. 1990, c. M.2, s. 6.
16 *Ibid.*, s. 26.

may apply with respect to modes of transport in addition to ships. Floating policies specify the cargo insured without reference to the ship(s) on which it is to be carried. Unless the policy provides otherwise, coverage attaches when the insurer is notified of the identity of the ships(s).[17] Under an open policy, the insured is permitted to issue certificates relating to several cargo consignments for specified classes of risks and amounts. This avoids the need for separate policies although separate premium quotations are usually required. The terms of coverage are governed by the underlying policy rather than the certificate.

The subject matter of marine insurance is invariably insured against losses proximately caused by the "perils of the sea". This means fortuitous accidents or casualties of the seas and not the ordinary action of wind and waves.[18] The risks covered may be extended or limited by statute or the terms of the policy. Legislation provides that, unless otherwise indicated in the policy, coverage extends to losses caused by the misconduct of master or crew, but does not extend to consequences of delay, ordinary wear and tear, leakage and breakage, inherent vice or nature of the subject matter, or loss caused by rats or vermin.[19] Other risks may be excluded or included by endorsement. The standard cargo clauses exclude war risks unless expressly incorporated. The "free from particular average" cargo clause restricts coverage to losses arising from stranding, sinking or burning. It is also common for restrictions to be placed on recovery for partial loss. The broadest coverage available is under an all risks endorsement but, even here, it is necessary that the loss be accidental or fortuitous.

It is usual for marine insurance policies to contain warranties and conditions of various kinds. A warranty may be a true warranty in that it must be strictly complied with whether or not it is material to the risk.[20] Examples are clauses warranting that a vessel be towed during a specified part of a voyage,[21] or that it be "laid up and out of commission" from a specified date.[22] A warranty found by a court to be merely a delimitation of the risk (as opposed to a true warranty) need not be strictly complied with. Failure by the insured to comply merely suspends coverage until there is compliance. For example, breach of a requirement that a small craft be used only for private pleasure has been held to mean only that the vessel is not insured at the time it is used for commercial purposes.[23] It is similar for clauses restricting navigation to specified waters.[24]

In addition to express warranties, several are implied by statute. These include a warranty that the nationality of the vessel shall not be changed during

---

[17] *Ibid.*, s. 30.

[18] See the rules for construction of policies contained in Ontario *Marine Insurance Act, ibid.*, Sch. See also *C.C.R. Fishing Ltd. v. British Reserve Insurance Co.*, [1990] S.C.J. No. 34, [1990] I.L.R. 1-2592 (S.C.C.).

[19] Ontario *Marine Insurance Act, ibid.*, s. 56.

[20] *Ibid.*, ss. 34-36.

[21] *Provincial Ins. Co. of Canada v. Connolly*, [1879] S.C.J. No. 33, 5 S.C.R. 258 (S.C.C.).

[22] *Dolbel v. U.S. Fire Ins. Co.*, [1963] B.R. 153 (C.A.).

[23] *Staples v. Great American Insurance Co.*, [1941] S.C.J. No. 4, [1941] S.C.R. 213 (S.C.C.).

[24] *Britsky Building Movers Ltd. v. Dominion Ins. Corp.*, [1981] I.L.R. 1-1420 (Man. Co. Ct.).

the life of the policy,[25] one, applicable to voyage policies, that the ship is
seaworthy at the commencement of the voyage,[26] and one that the adventure
insured is a legal one.[27]

Payment for total loss may be claimed in the event of actual total loss[28] or
constructive total loss.[29] Constructive total loss arises at the instigation of the
insured who, when actual total loss seems unavoidable or avoidable only at
prohibitive cost, may give the insurer notice of abandonment. This distinguishes
marine insurance from other classes of insurance where determination of total
loss is the prerogative of the insurer.

Partial loss may also be recoverable along with expenses incurred to protect
the subject matter from loss or further damage.[30] Where property is intentionally
jettisoned or otherwise destroyed to preserve the ship or cargo, those who
benefit are each liable to make a "general average contribution" to indemnify the
owners of the property destroyed. This liability is usually insured.[31]

AUTOMOBILE INSURANCE

In Canada, the provinces and territories differ in their approach to automobile[32]
insurance. In some cases there is a single public insurer, while in other cases
multiple private insurers are permitted to compete in the marketplace. Moreover,
some jurisdictions emphasize no-fault benefits, while others focus on tort
liability. In all of the jurisdictions, however, there are four types of automobile
coverage: third party liability coverage; first party coverage for no-fault benefits;
coverage for victims of uninsured or unidentified motorists; and first party
coverage for damage to the vehicle and contents.

In British Columbia, Manitoba, Quebec and Saskatchewan, automobile insurance is delivered by way of a public corporation which maintains a monopoly
over the area. In these provinces, the terms of compulsory coverage are dictated
by legislation.[33] In the other provinces, where private insurers compete, a

---

[25] See *e.g.*, *Ontario Marine Insurance Act*, R.S.O. 1990, c. M.2, s. 38.

[26] *Ibid.*, s. 40.

[27] *Ibid.*, s. 42.

[28] *Ibid.*, s. 58.

[29] *Ibid.*, s. 61.

[30] *Ibid.*, ss. 65, 66, 79.

[31] *Ibid.*, s. 67.

[32] The term "automobile" is defined in the various provincial statutes to include a trolley-bus and
self-propelled vehicle and the trailer, accessories and equipment of automobiles, but does not
include railway rolling stock that runs on rails, watercraft or aircraft. See *e.g.*, Manitoba, S.M.
2007, c. 10, s. 2. With the exception of Ontario, the definition of automobile is broad enough to
include snowmobiles and all-terrain vehicles.

[33] See *Insurance (Vehicle) Act*, R.S.B.C. 1996, c. 231; *Manitoba Public Insurance Corporation
Act*, 1987, C.C.S.M. c. P215; *Automobile Insurance Act*, R.S.Q., c. A-25; and *Automobile
Accident Insurance Act*, R.S.S. 1978, c. A-35.

government regulator has established a standard form policy.[34] Whether through a standard form policy or legislation, it is mandated across Canada that all vehicles on public highways be covered by a liability policy.[35] This obligation falls on both the owner and operator of a vehicle.[36] The jurisdictions differ, though, in terms of whether other types of coverage are mandatory. In Manitoba and Saskatchewan, for example, first-party coverage for damage to vehicles is compulsory, whereas it is optional in other provinces like British Columbia.[37]

One of the principal issues that arises with liability coverage is whether or not a named insured granted permission to a person who was driving the automobile at the time of an accident. In the absence of consent, there will be no coverage under the owner's policy.[38] The determination is one that is made based on the facts of each individual case. In one case, the owner of a vehicle hired someone to drive him across the country. After several days at a stop, the owner left the keys in the truck and disappeared for the evening. The driver took the truck and ended up in an accident. Prior to that, the driver had not driven without the owner being present. The court determined that there was insufficient evidence to support a finding of implied consent.[39] Even in cases where it is clear that the owner has provided his or her consent, issues can arise if the individual who receives the consent chooses to allow others to drive the vehicle. A majority of the Supreme Court of Canada found that the consent given to an owner's son did not extend to others, even though such permission "might have" been granted had the father turned his mind to the issue.[40]

In addition to liability coverage, all Canadian jurisdictions offer some type of no-fault benefits, such as income replacement benefits, medical and rehabilitation benefits, or permanent impairment benefits.[41] However, the provinces and territories vary in terms of the extent to which the no-fault system is relied upon to compensate accident victims. In general, the more robust that a jurisdiction's no-fault benefits system is, the higher the restrictions are on tort recovery. In Newfoundland, for instance, which might be referred to as a tort jurisdiction, the no-fault benefits system is optional, leaving many victims with no option but to pursue recovery through the tort system. At the other end of the spectrum is Manitoba, a province which has a pure no-fault system. In Manitoba, all tort rights with respect to bodily injury or death resulting from an automobile accident have been removed for accidents occurring on or after March 1, 1994.[42] Ontario lies somewhere between the two extremes and has a minimum

---

[34] See *e.g.*, for Ontario OAP (Ontario Automobile Policy) #1.

[35] See *e.g.*, *Traffic Safety Act*, R.S.A. 2000, c. T-6, s. 54(1).

[36] *Ibid.*, s. 54(1)(c).

[37] These requirements are not in the provincial Insurance Acts, but rather in other statutes, such as the Saskatchewan *Automobile Accident Insurance Act*, R.S.S. 1978, c. A-35, s. 38.

[38] See *e.g.*, Ontario *Insurance Act*, R.S.O. 1990, c. I.8, s. 239(1).

[39] *Judgment Recovery (N.S.) Ltd. v. London & Edinburgh Insurance Co.*, [1975] N.S.J. No. 353, [1976] I.L.R. 1-724 (N.S.C.A.).

[40] *Ontario (Minister of Transport) v. Canadian General Insurance Co.*, [1971] S.C.J. No. 104, [1972] S.C.R. 234 (S.C.C.).

[41] See *e.g.*, *Statutory Accident Benefits Schedule*, O. Reg. 34/10.

[42] *Manitoba Public Insurance Corporation Act*, C.C.S.M. c. P215, s. 72.

threshold[43] and pre-set deductibles[44] for general damages, limits on the recovery of income losses in tort and a comprehensive no-fault regime.

One thorny issue with no-fault benefits is whether or not an insured's injuries arise out of the operation, use or operation of a vehicle. The Supreme Court of Canada was faced with this issue in *Amos v. Insurance Corp. of British Columbia*.[45] The plaintiff had been attacked and shot by car-jackers attempting to steal his vehicle. The court set out a two part test to interpret whether a loss arises from the use or operation of a vehicle: (1) Did the accident result from the ordinary and well-known activities to which automobiles are put?; and (2) If so, is there some nexus or causal relationship (not necessarily a direct or proximate causal relationship) between the loss and the ownership, use or operation of the vehicle, or is the connection merely incidental or fortuitous? The court held that the plaintiff was entitled to coverage, as the plaintiff, when driving the van, was engaged in a well known activity to which automobiles are put and the operation of the van contributed to the injury.[46]

It is worth noting that all provinces and territories offer some type of protection for the victims of accidents involving uninsured or unidentified motorists.[47]

---

[43] The threshold is "death ... permanent serious disfigurement, or permanent serious impairment of an important physical, mental, or psychological function": Ontario *Insurance Act*, R.S.O. 1990, c. I.8, s. 267.5(5).

[44] $15,000 per person and $7,500 for Family Law Act claimants. Saskatchewan's scheme allows motorists to choose between primarily no-fault cover (and limited tort exposure) and a plan providing for greater tort rights and exposure. Saskatchewan *Automobile Accident Insurance Act*, R.S.S. 1978, c. A-35, ss. 41, 104.

[45] [1995] S.C.J. No. 74, [1995] 3 S.C.R. 405 (S.C.C.).

[46] In *Chisholm v. Liberty Mutual Group*, [2002] O.J. No. 3135, [2002] 217 D.L.R. (4th) 145 (Ont. C.A.), the court held that the causation prong of the test needed to be reconsidered in Ontario in light of the statutory change in the definition of accident from one in which the operation or use of the automobile "indirectly or directly" caused an impairment to a more stringent test that omitted the word "indirectly". In *Chisolm*, gun shots were fired directly into the plaintiff's car while he was driving. The court held that the gun shots were not causative of the impairment but rather an intervening act outside of the ordinary course of events. This more restrictive approach was followed in *Martin v. 2064324*, [2013] O.J. No. 172, 2013 ONCA 19 (Ont. C.A.). But the determination will always depend on the specific wording of the legislation. In *Heredi v. Fensom*, [2002] S.C.J. No. 48, [2002] 2 S.C.R. 741 (S.C.C.), the Supreme Court of Canada, in analyzing Saskatchewan legislation, had to determine whether a plaintiff's damages, which were caused when a bus driver's manner of driving caused her crutch to injure her shoulder, were "occasioned by a motor vehicle". The court held that the operation of the vehicle directly caused the injury based on the broad wording in the statute. More recent Supreme Court of Canada decisions have continued to take a relatively restrictive approach to the phrase "use or operation". In *Vytlingam (Litigation Guardian of) v. Farmer*, [2007] S.C.J. No. 46, [2007] 3 S.C.R. 373 (S.C.C.), it was held that an insured vehicle used to transport a boulder that was dropped from an overpass and escaped from the scene afterward did not come within the meaning of the phrase. See also *Herbison v. Lumbermens Mutual Casualty Co.*, [2007] S.C.J. No. 47, [2007] 3 S.C.R. 393 (S.C.C.).

[47] See *e.g.*, Ontario *Insurance Act*, R.S.O. 1990, c. I.8, s. 265. Note that this coverage differs from the optional Underinsured Motorist Coverage, also referred to as the Family Protection Endorsement, which applies when there is a inadequate third party liability coverage. See *e.g.*, Ontario's OPCF (Ontario Policy Change Form) 44R.

This protection may take the form of public or private unsatisfied judgment funds, uninsured automobile coverage in a standard form policy, or a combination of the two.[48] In order to be eligible for unidentified motorist coverage, the claimant must make reasonable efforts to identify the driver and owner of the vehicle. In one case, an insured agreed to allow another driver to move his car off the road but then the driver fled the scene. The insured failed to notice that the other driver had left because he was attending to his wife, who had become hysterical. The court held that it was reasonable for the insured to focus on his wife instead of trying to identify the other driver.[49]

Finally, automobile insurance can also include property coverage for loss or damage to the automobile, including its equipment.[50] Under the standard form policies, the insured is permitted to choose between "collision and upset" coverage, specified perils coverage, comprehensive coverage, and "all perils" coverage.[51] Coverage is usually subject to a deductible, which must be paid each time a claim is made and separately on each insured vehicle.[52] However, there is no deductible where the loss is caused by fire, lightning or theft of the entire vehicle.[53] Further, there is no coverage if the insured operated the vehicle while under the influence of intoxicating substances.[54]

FIDELITY BONDS

Fidelity bonds protect employers from their own employees. Despite the name, these bonds are merely insurance policies — agreements requiring that an insurer compensate an employer for any loss caused by an employee's dishonest or fraudulent conduct.

There are a few fundamental features to the coverage provided by most fidelity bonds. In most cases, coverage depends on the following prerequisites:

- The loss of money, securities or other property;
- The loss resulting from the fraudulent or dishonest acts of an employee, alone or in collusion with others; and
- The fraudulent or dishonest acts that caused the loss were committed with the "manifest intent" to cause the insured to sustain a loss, and to obtain a financial benefit for the employee or for any other person or

---

[48] For example, British Columbia, Manitoba, Saskatchewan and Alberta rely on government-run unsatisfied judgment funds, Yukon Territory relies on uninsured automobile coverage under a standard policy, and Ontario relies on a combination of the two.

[49] *Reid v. Insurance Corp. of British Columbia*, [1994] B.C.J. No. 2172, 26 C.C.L.I. (2d) 256 (B.C.C.A.).

[50] See *e.g.*, Ontario OAP #1, s. 7.

[51] *Ibid.*, s. 7.1.2. Note that even "all perils" coverage includes exclusions, and thus, does not actually cover *all* perils.

[52] *Ibid.*, s. 7.3.

[53] *Ibid.*

[54] *Ibid*, s. 7.2.2.

organization, other than salaries, commissions, fees, bonuses, or other benefits earned in the normal course of employment.

Importantly, the coverage under a fidelity bond is restricted to the insured's loss of property. That is, an insurer is not required to compensate the insured for liability arising out of an employee's fraudulent or dishonest conduct. For instance, in a case where two of a corporation's directors had falsified financial statements, and the shareholders reacted by bringing a class action lawsuit against the company, the court reasoned that the fidelity bond did not respond to the loss.[55]

In addition, fidelity coverage is restricted to the acts of employees. There is no coverage if fraud is perpetrated by the insured's top executives or directors, as these individuals are the "directing minds" of the corporation.[56] If coverage were available for the acts of such individuals, it would undermine the principle that insurance only covers fortuitous losses. In one instance, however, a CEO's fraudulent conduct was covered, as the rest of the corporation's executives had no knowledge of the dishonest behaviour.[57]

As mentioned above, losses are only covered under a fidelity bond if they result from an employee's "dishonest or fraudulent" conduct. While it is clear that mere negligence will not meet this threshold,[58] it is not always clear what conduct will reach the threshold of being "dishonest or fraudulent". In *Sigurdson v. Fidelity Insurance Co.*,[59] the issue was whether a fidelity policy provided coverage for a loss that resulted from two shareholders' alleged misuse of corporate assets prior to a bankruptcy. The plaintiff argued that the shareholders had been treating the corporation's assets as being synonymous with their own. The insurer argued such conduct was not unusual for a closely held corporation, and that there was no moral turpitude in the shareholders' behaviour. The court decided that the shareholders' conduct in intermingling their personal assets with those of the corporation was dishonest and fraudulent.

In addition to being dishonest or fraudulent, actions are only covered if they are carried out by an employee with manifest intent to cause a loss to the insured and to obtain a financial benefit for themselves or someone else. But difficulty arises when an employee's intention is unclear. In *MacNab Auto Sales Ltd. v. Sun Alliance Insurance Co.*,[60] the sales manager believed that, although he was deceiving his employer and extending unauthorized credit to purchasers, some of the funds would eventually flow back to the insured. Although the sales manager's true intentions were unclear, the court reasoned

---

[55] *International Nesmont Industrial Corp. v. Continental Insurance Co. of Canada*, [2002] B.C.J. No. 356, 2002 BCCA 136 (B.C.C.A.).

[56] *Clarkson Co. v. Canadian Indemnity Co.*, [1979] O.J. No. 4299, 101 D.L.R. (3d) 146 (Ont. H.C.J.), affd [1982] O.J. No. 3680, 129 D.L.R. (3d) 511 (Ont. C.A.).

[57] *Tricontinental Investments Co. v. Guarantee Co. of North America*, [1988] O.J. No. 173, 30 C.C.L.I. 33 (Ont. H.C.J.), affd [1991] O.J. No. 3049, 48 C.C.L.I. 1 (Ont. C.A.).

[58] See *e.g.*, *Lynch & Co. v. United States Fidelity & Guaranty Co.*, [1970] O.J. No. 1616, 14 D.L.R. (3d) 294 (Ont. H.C.J.).

[59] [1977] CarswellBC 234 (B.C.C.A.).

[60] [1995] O.J. No. 600 (Ont. Gen. Div.), affd [1998] O.J. No. 743, 1 C.C.L.I. (3d) 301 (Ont. C.A.).

that it was inevitable that the insured would suffer a loss. Moreover, the court determined that this result was or ought to have been apparent at the time when the acts were carried out.

LIABILITY INSURANCE

Lawsuits have the potential to create large unexpected losses, both in terms of the costs of defending the lawsuit and the potential cost of an adverse judgment.[61] Liability insurance allows individuals and businesses to mitigate the effects of such a loss. Here, the discussion will focus on the main categories of liability for which insurance is procured — personal, business, directors and officers, and professional services — and some of the associated legal issues.

Regardless of the type, most liability policies cover only civil liability. That is, they do not provide coverage for criminal liability, as such coverage would pervert the purpose of criminal sanctions.[62] Even beyond criminal conduct, most liability policies exclude acts carried out with an intention to cause injury or damage. Indeed, providing insurance coverage for intentional conduct would go against the fundamental purpose of insurance — which is to address fortuitous losses — and create a moral hazard.[63] Liability policies also tend to exclude liability that arises out of breach of contract, unless liability would exist independently of the contract.[64]

In addition to restricting the types of claims that are covered, insurers place a temporal restriction on liability claims. There are two basic approaches in this regard. Most policies can be classified as either occurrence-based or "claims-made". An occurrence-based policy requires that the underlying loss took place during the time period specified in the policy.[65] A claims-made policy, however, requires that the claim against the insured was brought during the specified

---

[61] An adverse judgment will often also require the losing party to pay a portion of the successful party's legal costs.

[62] Another reason that criminal liability would not accord with the scope of a liability policy is that liability policies provide indemnity for "damages"; criminal sanctions, such as fines or imprisonment would be unlikely to satisfy a policy's definition of "damages".

[63] *Non-Marine Underwriters, Lloyd's of London v. Scalera*, [2000] S.C.J. No. 26, 185 D.L.R. (4th) 1 (S.C.C.). Moreover, most jurisdictions' Insurance Acts provide that a claim for indemnity will be rendered unenforceable where the insured has violated the criminal law and carried out an act with intent to cause loss or damage. See *e.g.*, Ontario *Insurance Act*, R.S.O. 1990, c. I.8, s. 118; Manitoba *Insurance Act*, C.C.S.M. c. I40, s. 92.

[64] *Poplawski v. McGrimmon*, [2010] O.J. No. 4243, 89 C.C.L.I. (4th) 230 (Ont. C.A.). The upshot of the exclusion is that a claim will not be excluded, if it is based in negligence, merely because the plaintiff has also pleaded breach of contract.

[65] Note that, with a CGL (Commercial General Liability) policy for example, the "occurrence" is the property damage or bodily injury, not the event that caused the loss. Thus, a case of sexual abuse might be covered if the injury continued into the policy period, even if the actual abuse took place prior to the policy period: *Chippewas of Nawash First Nations v. Scottish & York Ins. Co.*, [1999] O.J. No. 1596, [1999] I.L.R. I-3738 (Ont. S.C.J.).

policy period.[66] In addition, there are hybrid policies which borrow characteristics from both types.

One important feature of the vast majority[67] of liability policies is the insurer's right and duty to defend the action brought against the insured. This "duty to defend" must be viewed as separate from — and indeed broader than — the insurer's obligation to indemnify the insured.[68] From the point when an insurer is notified of a claim against the insured, the insurer usually has the contractual right to select defence counsel,[69] defend the action and even enter into a settlement on the insured's behalf. In determining whether or not the insurer has a "duty to defend", the analysis is focused strictly on the allegations in the claim. This principle is known as the "pleadings rule". Therefore, while proven facts might be relevant with respect to the insurer's duty to indemnify the insured, they are irrelevant for purposes of the duty to defend.[70]

Policies that address business liability are known as commercial general liability policies (commonly referred to as a "CGL"). These policies often accompany other forms of insurance, such as property coverage, in a composite business policy. Broadly speaking, a CGL provides coverage for bodily injury or property damage caused to third parties as a result of the insured's business operations. While a CGL can take various forms, the Insurance Bureau of Canada has issued a standard form that insurers commonly use.[71]

CGL policies, which are predominantly occurrence based, typically define an "occurrence", in part, as an "accident"[72]. The term "accident" makes it clear that all occurrences must be fortuitous.[73] One question that has arisen in the context of CGL policies is whether a claim involving defective workmanship qualifies as an "accident". In *Canadian Indemnity Co. v. Walkem Machinery & Equipment Ltd.*,[74] the Supreme Court of Canada considered whether the collapse of a crane, which had been negligently repaired by the insured, was an "accident". The insurer had argued that the insured was aware that the crane was in poor condition. The court, however, found that the collapse was an accident because it was not intended by the insured. Similarly, in *Progressive Homes Ltd. v. Lombard General Insurance Co. of*

---

[66] These policies might also require that the bodily injury or property damage took place after a "retroactive date".

[67] Note that Directors' and Officers' Liability policies usually do not require the insurer to defend the claim. Instead, the insurer reimburses the insured for the cost of the defence, and the policy limits usually include the defence costs.

[68] *Nichols v. American Home Assurance Co.*, [1990] S.C.J. No. 33, [1990] 1 S.C.R. 801 (S.C.C.).

[69] *Brockton (Municipality) v. Frank Cowan Co.*, [2002] O.J. No. 20, 57 O.R. (3d) 447 (Ont. C.A.).

[70] That the duty to defend is governed by the pleadings rule and not "underlying facts" has been confirmed by the Supreme Court of Canada. See *Monenco Ltd. v. Commonwealth Insurance Co.*, [2001] S.C.J. No. 50, 204 D.L.R. (4th) 14 (S.C.C.); *Non-Marine Underwriters, Lloyd's of London v. Scalera*, [2000] S.C.J. No. 26, 185 D.L.R. (4th) 1 (S.C.C.).

[71] The latest edition is IBC (Insurance Bureau of Canada) 2100.

[72] See definition of "occurrence" in IBC 2100.

[73] *Fenton v. J. Thorley & Co.*, [1903] A.C. 443 at 448 (H.L.).

[74] [1975] S.C.J. No. 34, [1976] 1 S.C.R. 309 (S.C.C.).

Canada,[75] the Supreme Court of Canada reasoned that water damage caused by faulty workmanship was an accidental occurrence, as the result was neither expected nor intended by the insured. Ultimately, whether damage caused by faulty workmanship will be covered under a CGL will be based on the policy wording and the specific facts.[76]

In addition to lawsuits against the business as an entity, a corporation's directors and officers are also exposed to potential liability. For instance, directors and officers who fail to meet the requisite standard of care[77] might be exposed to claims by the corporation's shareholders or creditors. Accordingly, in order to attract qualified individuals into these positions, corporations need to provide directors and officers with protection against the losses that can flow from these claims. This protection is provided in two ways: indemnification and directors' and officers' policies.

Corporations are permitted, and sometimes mandated,[78] to indemnify their directors and officers against potential claims.[79] In essence, indemnification means that the corporation will compensate the directors and officers for any losses associated with a claim brought against them. Unlike with an insurance policy, though, indemnification is not subject to a limit or deductible.

In order to cover the cost of such indemnification, a corporation might procure a directors' and officers' policy. In addition to compensating a corporation for such indemnification, however, a directors' and officers' policy normally provides coverage for claims against the directors and officers for which the corporation has not provided indemnification. For example, a policy might reimburse the directors and officers where the corporation was bankrupt and unable to provide indemnity. Additionally, a directors' and officers' policy generally provides "entity coverage", which responds to claims made against the corporation itself.[80]

Individuals who are not directors or officers also face potential liability arising out of their personal actions. This liability is addressed in residential insurance policies, which often provide for both property and liability

---

[75] [2010] S.C.J. No. 33, [2010] 2 S.C.R. 245 (S.C.C.).

[76] An opposite result was reached in *Celestica Inc. v. ACE INA Insurance*, [2003] O.J. No. 2820, 50 C.C.L.I. (3d) 190 (Ont. C.A.). In addition to overcoming the hurdle of proving that the event was an "occurrence", damage caused by faulty workmanship might otherwise not be covered on the basis of an exclusion (see *e.g.*, *Bridgewood Building Corp. (Riverfield) v. Lombard General Insurance Co. of Canada*, [2006] O.J. No. 1288, [2006] I.L.R. I-4498 (Ont. C.A.), leave to appeal refused [2006] S.C.C.A. No. 204 (S.C.C.)), a failure to satisfy the definition of "property damage", or wording elsewhere in the policy.

[77] The duty is "to exercise the care, diligence and skill that a reasonably prudent person would exercise in comparable circumstances": *Canada Business Corporations Act*, R.S.C. 1985, c. C-44., s. 122(1) ("CBCA"). There are also provincial business corporation statutes with, for the most part, similar wording. Only the CBCA will be referred to herein.

[78] CBCA, s. 124(5).

[79] CBCA, s. 124(1).

[80] This coverage is normally limited to "securities claims", a phrase that might encompass civil, criminal or administrative proceedings in respect of the purchase or sale of securities.

coverage.[81] The liability coverage comes in two varieties. First, coverage is provided for any liability, due to bodily injury or property damage, that arises out of the insured's[82] personal actions anywhere in the world. The scope of coverage is broad and could include anything from property damage caused by igniting toilet paper on top of a sleeping person[83] to bodily injury resulting from the operation of a motor boat.[84] The second type of coverage is premises liability, which covers liability arising from the ownership, use or occupancy of the household. This coverage would apply to a slip and fall on the insured's property.[85] Most residential liability policies exclude any liability arising out of business activities, as such liability is more properly covered by a CGL.

Finally, liability insurance is available to certain professionals to respond to claims of negligence. This type of insurance is often referred to as errors and omissions ("E&O") coverage. Certain professionals, such as physicians or lawyers, are mandated to carry a certain level of E&O coverage.[86] E&O policies vary significantly, as they are tailored to the needs of the specific profession being insured. Coverage will only apply if the claim arises out of the provision of "professional services", and not an activity which could be performed by a non-professional.[87] Thus, an E&O policy will not respond where a lawyer's guarantee of an investment results in a claim. In that case, the lawyer was not acting in his or her capacity as a lawyer when the guarantee was provided.[88]

PROPERTY INSURANCE

There are various types of policies that address the risk of property loss. Fire insurance policies are the most regulated and uniform across the provinces and territories. Beyond the risk of fire, these policies might also insure against other specified perils, such as hail or theft. On the other hand, "all risks" policies provide for, as the name suggests, broad coverage against all fortuitous property loss, subject to certain exclusions.

---

[81] Although the policies vary, there is a standard IBC policy (IBC Form 1105), much like with the CGL.

[82] Typically, a residential liability policy will insure, while living in the same household, the insured's spouse, any dependants under age 21 and other relatives of the insured or spouse.

[83] *University of Western Ontario v. Yanush*, [1989] O.J. No. 19, [1989] I.L.R. 1-2405 (Ont. H.C.J.).

[84] *Snair v. Halifax Insurance Nationale – Nederlanden North America Corp.*, [1995] N.S.J. No. 424, 31 C.C.L.I. (2d) 279 (N.S.S.C.).

[85] See *e.g.*, *Woodside v. Gibraltar General Insurance Co.*, [1991] O.J. No. 114, 2 C.C.L.I. (2d) 277 (Ont. C.A.).

[86] The Canadian Medical Protective Association ("CMPA") provides insurance to physicians and the Lawyers' Professional Indemnity Company ("LAWPRO") provides insurance to lawyers in Ontario.

[87] *Chemetics International Ltd. v. Commercial Union Assurance Co. of Canada*, [1981] B.C.J. No. 1968, 31 B.C.L.R. 273 (B.C.S.C.), affd [1984] B.C.J. No. 1728, 55 B.C.L.R. 60 (B.C.C.A.).

[88] *Hazelwood v. Travelers Indemnity Co. of Canada*, [1978] B.C.J. No. 963, [1979] 2 W.W.R. 271 (B.C.C.A.).

With the exception of Quebec, all of the provinces and territories have uniform legislation to regulate fire insurance.[89] This legislation sets out statutory conditions and terms that must apply to all contracts of fire insurance.[90] Any attempt by an insurer to alter the application of the statutory conditions will be unenforceable,[91] and courts may rule that an insurer is acting unreasonably if the insurer excludes a loss that would otherwise be covered based on the terms in the statute.[92] Moreover, any policy that contains a limitation of liability clause must have printed or stamped, in red ink and conspicuous type, the words "The policy contains a clause that may limit the amount payable".[93]

All fire insurance policies must insure against fire, lightning and explosion of natural, coal or manufactured gas.[94] Other incidental losses may also be covered, such as wind damage where the structure was made more vulnerable to such damage as a result of a lightning strike.[95] However, this principle has its limits. A court found that coverage did not extend to damage to a shoe store's reputation that was caused by a fire.[96]

There are two approaches that insurers take to provide property insurance that protects against more than fire losses. First, an insurer can specify other perils that are to be covered, such as theft or hail. In this case, any statutory conditions that are limited to fire insurance will not apply in respect of those particular perils. Second, an insurer can issue an "all risks" policy, a type of insurance policy that provides broad coverage for fortuitous property loss. Regardless of which approach is taken, the insurer might wish to incorporate the statutory conditions, which are normally restricted to fire coverage, into the policy as a whole. Generally speaking, insurers are permitted to contractually incorporate the statutory conditions into an "all risks" or "multi-peril" policy, provided that sufficient wording is used.[97]

---

[89] See *Civil Code of Québec*, S.Q. 1991, c. 64, Arts. 2463–2497. Alberta and British Columbia have taken a slightly different approach, as the statutory conditions in those provinces apply to all classes of property insurance, while elsewhere they only apply to fire insurance.

[90] See *e.g.*, Ontario *Insurance Act*, R.S.O. 1990, c. I.8, s. 148; Newfoundland *Fire Insurance Act*, R.S.N.L. 1990, c. F-10, s. 4; Alberta *Insurance Act*, R.S.A. 2000, c. I-3, s. 540 (for all property insurance).

[91] See *e.g.*, Ontario *Insurance Act, ibid.*, s. 148.

[92] See *e.g.*, Alberta *Insurance Act*, R.S.A. 2000, c. I-3 (for all property insurance) s. 545; Ontario *Insurance Act, ibid.*, s. 151.

[93] See *e.g.*, B.C. *Insurance Act*, R.S.B.C. 2012, c. 1, s. 31. An example of such a clause would be a co-insurance clause, which requires that the insured acquire coverage up to a certain proportion of the value of the insured property. The rationale of such a clause is that an insured should not be permitted to undervalue property in order to procure a cheaper policy but still reap the full benefits of insurance proceeds following a loss.

[94] See *e.g.*, Ontario *Insurance Act*, R.S.O. 1990, c. I.8, s. 144(1).

[95] *Roth v. South Easthope Farmers Mutual Fire Insurance Co.*, [1918] O.J. No. 21, 44 O.L.R. 186 (Ont. C.A.).

[96] *Sterling Shoes Alberta Ltd. v. Fire Insurance Co.*, [1970] A.J. No. 162, [1971] 1 W.W.R. 353 (Alta. C.A.).

[97] The wording was insufficient in *Burry v. Co-operators General Insurance Co.*, [2003] N.J. No. 290, 231 Nfld. & P.E.I.R. 356 (N.L.T.D.), affd [2007] N.J. No. 277, 268 Nfld. & P.E.I.R. 257 (N.L.C.A.). In *Walker v. Sovereign General Insurance Co.*, [2011] O.J. No. 4106, 2011 ONCA

Despite the broad nature of "all risks" policies, there are limitations on the coverage provided. Most importantly, the loss must be fortuitous.[98] The insured does not, however, have to prove the precise nature or cause of the loss.[99] In one case, an insured landlord discovered a large amount of soot in his premises at the end of a lease. The court held that the insured did not have to prove the exact nature or cause of the loss. The court was willing to draw the inference that the soot was caused by the tenants burning candles, satisfying the insured's evidentiary burden.[100]

Despite the lack of a standardized policy, there are a variety of exclusions that are common to property insurance policies. Policies commonly exclude the cost of making good faulty or improper workmanship or design, though damage resulting from such workmanship might not be excluded.[101] Moreover, losses resulting from changes in temperature or structural movements (settling, shifting, cracking, *etc.*) are also commonly excluded from coverage.

LIFE INSURANCE

There are several types of life insurance policies. In broad terms, however, life insurance can be divided into individual and group policies. Within these groups, policies can be further subdivided based on the various structures in respect of their value and various options. The only commonality among all life insurance policies is that they are in some way connected to the risk of mortality, a risk that is unique in the insurance world because it is certain to occur, though the timing is unknown.

The main types of individual life insurance policies are known as term, "whole-of-life" and participating. Term insurance provides coverage for a specified period of time and then lapses unless it is renewed. Often, the premium will be increased upon renewal. "Whole-of-life" coverage remains in effect throughout the duration of the insured's life (assuming the policy's conditions are met and premiums are paid) unless the policy is cancelled by the owner. The value of a whole-of-life policy increases over time. This value can be converted to cash, borrowed against, or used to convert the insurance into fully-paid but lower face-value cover. Finally, a participating policy entitles the owner to share

---

597 (Ont. C.A.), the court held that the statutory conditions were incorporated but did not apply to the liability portion of the policy.

[98] The seminal case on this point is *British and Foreign Marine Insurance Co v. Gaunt*, [1921] 2 A.C. 41 (H.L.).

[99] *Capital City Oil Well Servicing Co. Ltd. v. Non Marine Underwriters*, [1959] A.J. No. 44, 27 W.W.R. 241 (Alta T.D.).

[100] *Brennan v. Economical Mutual Insurance Co.*, [2000] O.J. No. 4531, [2001] I.L.R. I-3907 (Ont. S.C.J.).

[101] See *e.g.*, *Simcoe & Erie General Insurance Co. v. Royal Insurance Co. of Canada*, [1982] A.J. No. 722, [1982] 3 W.W.R. 628 (Alta. Q.B.), appeal to Alta. C.A. dismissed without reasons (1983), leave to appeal refused (1983), 31 Alta. L.R. (2d) xl.

in dividends declared by the owner. These dividends may be withdrawn in cash or used to increase the value of the insurance or to reduce premiums.

Group life insurance policies operate on a two-tier arrangement. The insurance contract is between the insurer and another entity, such as an employer, trade union or bar association. Regardless of the type of entity, a group of individuals interacts primarily with the entity as opposed to the insurer. One distinguishing factor with group life insurance policies is that the insurer is less concerned with factors affecting the individuals' insurability, as the individuals with higher risk profiles are thought to be balanced out by those with lower risk profiles. In some cases, an individual's group policy can be converted to an individual policy if the individual ceases to be a member of the group.

Two classes of individuals may be insured under group policies. There are those who are directly connected through, say, employment with the group policyholder. Then there are those who are indirectly connected by being related to or dependent upon someone directly connected. The members of the first category, but not the second, are treated like persons insured under individual life policies in two important respects. They are entitled to designate beneficiaries,[102] and, despite the fact that they are not in a contractual relationship with the insurer, they may enforce the rights given to them in the group policy directly against the insurer in their own names.[103]

With the exception of variable life insurance, where the benefit levels are related to the market value of segregated assets,[104] there is no specified form nor do insurers require government approval of life insurance policies. Similarly, there are no statutory conditions as there are with other classes of insurance. However, each province and territory has legislation with provisions that override any terms in individual policies that are inconsistent or less favourable to insureds than the legislation.[105] The statutes address several issues, including what documents constitute the entire contract,[106] reinstatement after lapse of the policy (the insured is entitled to reinstate within two years with payment of arrears and evidence of insurability)[107] and the processing of claims.[108]

Group life insurance policies are regulated in a slightly different manner from that of individual policies. Due to the unique structure of group policies, the policy form must address the relationship between the stakeholders as well as the rights of the individuals whose lives are insured.[109] The insurer must also

---

[102] See *e.g.*, *Ontario Insurance Act*, R.S.O. 1990, c. I.8, s. 171.

[103] *Ibid.*, s. 201.

[104] See *e.g.*, Ontario *Insurance Act*, R.S.O. 1990, I.8, s. 110.

[105] The *Civil Code of Québec*, S.Q. 1991, c. 64, with respect to its treatment of life insurance, is structured differently than the other Canadian jurisdictions and is arguably more instructive in respect of the contractual relationship between insurer and policyholder. Nevertheless, the effect of the legislation is broadly similar to that of the other provinces.

[106] See *e.g.*, Ontario *Insurance Act*, R.S.O. 1990, I.8, s. 174(2).

[107] See *e.g.*, *ibid.*, s. 189.

[108] See *e.g.*, *ibid*, ss. 203–221.

[109] Legislation requires that the contract include the following information: identification of the group policy-holder, the method of determining the persons whose lives are insured, the amount

deliver a certificate of insurance to the insured, which is to be passed on to the various individuals.[110] The certificate identifies the insurer, the policy, the amount of insurance (or method of determining the amount), and any rights of the insured upon termination.

It is also worth noting that the structure of group life policies significantly impacts on the insured's rights and privileges. For example, although it may require contributions from individuals covered, the insuring entity (the group policyholder) is responsible for paying the premium and has the exclusive right to stop paying, thereby allowing the policy to lapse (following a grace period). The individuals insured cannot step in and pay directly to keep the policy in force. The statutory right to reinstatement applicable to individual insurance does not apply to group insurance.[111] Group insurance may not be voided as against an individual on the grounds of misrepresentation or non-disclosure unless the evidence of insurability is specifically requested by the insurer and, in the absence of fraud, if the insurance has been in effect for less than two years during the lifetime of the individual.[112]

OTHER CLASSES OF INSURANCE

This chapter has not addressed all classes of insurance. While the types of insurance discussed above are the most common, there are several other types of insurance policies. Insurance tends to develop wherever there is a demand to spread the risk of fortuitous loss. Title insurance protects homebuyers against the risk that they have not received their home free of all encumberances and liens. Livestock insurance[113] provides farmers with protection against disease that might affect their animals. Further, the insurance industry is continually responding to new risks with new policies. For example, cyber insurance has developed in response to organizations' concerns about data breaches.

---

of insurance on each person, the grace period for premium payment, and any participation or refund rights of the policyholder. See *e.g.*, Ontario *Insurance Act*, R.S.O. 1990, c. I.8, s. 176.

[110] Ontario *Insurance Act*, R.S.O. 1990, c. I.8, s. 177.

[111] See *ibid.*, s. 189. *Civil Code of Québec*, S.Q. 1991, c. 64, Art. 2524.

[112] *Ibid.*, s. 184. See also *Civil Code of Québec*, S.Q. 1991, c. 64, Arts. 2485-2515.

[113] This type of insurance is really a form of property insurance.

Glossary

The following is a glossary of terms used in insurance and insurance law. Not all of these terms appear elsewhere in this book but where they do, or where there is related material, the relevant page references are provided. Thanks are afforded to Insurance Bureau of Canada for assistance in compiling the glossary.

Absolute liability

Absolute liability is a component of automobile insurance that protects the insured person (the owner or lessee) and others driving the insured vehicle with the permission of the insured person against the financial consequences of being found liable for causing death, injury or property damage to another person. Legislation requires that, if the wrongdoer has violated the terms of the insurance policy, for example, by driving with an expired licence, the insurer must still pay for this liability. This is subject to a limit, usually $200,000, and the requirement that the person in violation reimburse the insurer. The insurer's obligation to pay despite the violation of the policy is referred to as absolute liability. See p. 112 under "Judgment Creditors".

Accident

An accident is an unexpected event which happens by chance and is not expected in the normal course of events and results in harm to people, damage to property or equipment, or a loss of process or productivity. This can include the adverse result of a calculated risk. See p. 69.

Accident Benefits

See **Statutory accident benefits** (coverage).

Accounts Receivable Coverage

This protects a business owner who is unable to collect outstanding balances as a result of lost or damaged account records.

Actual cash value

The actual cash value is usually the cost of replacing the property with something of like kind and quality, minus an allowance for depreciation. See p. 87.

Actuary

An actuary is an employee of an insurance company who analyzes the financial consequences of risk. An actuary uses mathematical models to predict the financial outcomes of uncertain future events. For example, an actuary will use these business models to predict the cost of future natural disasters to ensure that the insurance company has enough reserves to pay resulting claims.

Adjuster
An adjuster is a person who reviews and settles claims on behalf of the insurance company. The adjuster could be an employee of the insurance company or an independent contractor hired by the company. See pp. 46 and 85.

Agent
An agent is someone who solicits business for an insurer, transmits applications for insurance to insurers or who participates in the negotiation or renewal of insurance contracts. Unlike a broker, he or she represents only one company. See p. 45.

All risk policy
An all risk policy covers insured property against loss or damage arising from any cause except loss or damage specifically excluded, deliberately caused by the insured person or that which happens in the ordinary course, such as normal wear and tear. See p. 69.

Application
An application is a form completed by a person seeking to buy insurance. On the basis of the information entered on the form (possibly together with any information from other sources), the insurance company decides whether or not to provide insurance or modify the coverage offered.

Appraisal
A valuation of property made for determining its insurable value or the amount of loss sustained. See p. 89.

Arbitration
An arbitration is an alternative to litigation for resolving a dispute between an insurer and its customer or between insurers. An unbiased person or panel is appointed to review the case and determine responsibility for paying for the loss. See p. 89.

Arson
The willful and malicious burning of property.

Assurance
Same as **Insurance**.

Assured
Same as **Insured** or policyholder.

Assurer
Same as **Insurer** (insurance company).

Authorization
The power or right to act on behalf of another.

Bad faith
Bad faith is conduct by either party to the insurance contract, wherein the other party is deceived or otherwise treated unfairly. Examples are withholding relevant information when the contract of insurance is negotiated (see Chapter 5: Non-Disclosure and Misrepresentation) or the unjustified denial of a claim (see p. 89).

Binder
A temporary or preliminary agreement which provides coverage until a policy can be written or delivered.

Bodily injury
A term, mostly used in automobile insurance, meaning physical injury as a result of a car accident.

Boiler and machinery insurance
Coverage for loss arising out of the operation of pressure, mechanical, and electrical equipment. It commonly includes protection against losses resulting from a breakdown of heating, refrigeration, air conditioning equipment, pressure vessels, boilers, production machinery, electrical apparatus and electronic equipment. It covers loss of the boiler and machinery itself, damage to other property, and business interruption losses.

Bond
A bond issued by an insurance company protects a person (perhaps a corporation), known as an oblige, from loss arising from the acts of another, known as the principal.

Broad coverage
This provides comprehensive insurance coverage for buildings and named perils coverage for contents. See **Comprehensive** and **Named perils coverage** below.

Broker
An insurance broker sells insurance for more than one company. He or she has agreements with several companies and works with these companies to find the best policy for a customer. See p. 46.

Business interruption insurance
When property belonging to a business is damaged or destroyed by an insured peril, business interruption insurance pays fixed costs such as taxes, utilities and other continuing expenses associated with running a business from when the damage occurs until the property is repaired or replaced.

Canadian Loss Experience Automobile Rating (CLEAR)
This is a new method of classifying different models of cars for insurance purposes by using historical data such as theft, collision repair costs and frequency of personal injuries for different models.

Cancellation
During the policy period either the insurer or the customer may terminate coverage according to provisions in the contract or by mutual agreement. See p. 27.

Capacity
The amount of money available to an insurance company, or to the industry as a whole, for underwriting insurance coverage or coverage for specific perils.

Captive insurance company
A company that is owned solely or in large part by one or more non-insurance entities (*e.g.*, a municipality) for the primary purpose of providing insurance coverage to the owner or owners.

Cargo insurance
A type of ocean marine insurance that protects the shipper of the goods against financial loss if the goods are damaged or lost.

Claim
A claim is the assertion of a right to be reimbursed by an insurance company for certain financial losses suffered. There are requirements relating to timing, manner of notice of a claim and proof of a claim. See p. 73.

Co-insurance Clause
A clause in a policy providing that, should the limit on coverage be below a specified percentage of the value of the insured property, the insurer is only liable for a proportion of the loss even in cases of partial damage. See p. 57.

Collision coverage
Collision coverage is an optional category of automobile insurance policy that pays for the cost of repairing the insured vehicle if it is damaged in a collision with another object.

Commercial General Liability Policy (CGL)
The commercial general liability policy is a standard form of liability insurance developed by the insurance industry for use in the business sector. It is usually contained in a broader mercantile policy also covering property loss and business interruption.

Commercial lines
Insurance for businesses, organizations, institutions, governmental agencies, and other commercial establishments and volunteer groups.

Comprehensive insurance
Comprehensive insurance is an optional coverage in auto insurance providing reimbursement for damage to an insured vehicle caused by any perils other than collision or overturning. Examples of perils covered are hail, flood, theft, fire, glass breakage, falling objects, missiles, explosions, earthquakes, windstorms,

vandalism or malicious mischief, riot or civil commotion, and collision with a bird or an animal.

Compulsory insurance
Any form of insurance (usually auto insurance) which is required by law.

Conditions
Conditions are terms of insurance contracts that impose obligations an insured person must satisfy in order to preserve coverage. See p. 58.

Coverage
What the insurance contract covers.

Declarations ("Dec" sheet)
The portion of the contract which contains information such as the name and address of the insured, the property insured, its location and description, the policy period, the amount of insurance coverage, applicable premiums, and supplemental representations by the insured.

Deductible
The deductible is the portion of the loss that, by agreement, is borne by the insured. For example, if there is a deductible of $300 and a loss amounting to $1,000 the insurer would pay $700 (assuming that was within the limits of coverage).

Depreciation
This is the decrease in the value of property over a period of time due to use, wear and tear, and obsolescence. For example, if you paid $500 for a television set five years ago, its current value minus depreciation might be only $125. This will affect the amount of insurance payable if the item is lost or destroyed (see **Actual cash value**) unless there is coverage for replacement cost.

Direct compensation, property damage (Ontario and Quebec)
This covers damage to — or loss of use — of an automobile or its contents, to the extent that someone else was at fault for the accident. It is called direct compensation because, even though someone else caused the damage, the insured person collects from his or her insurer instead of the person who caused the accident.

Direct loss
A direct loss is damage to or loss of the insured property itself. It does not include consequential loss or expenses incurred as an indirect result of the damage, such as the cost of renting replacement items while the originals are repaired.

Direct writer
A direct writer is an insurance company which uses its own sales employees, rather than independent brokers, to write its policies. The term sometimes refers to a company that engages exclusive agents.

Directors and officers liability insurance (D&O)
This is a type of liability insurance that provides coverage for boards, directors and employees of companies. It pays defence costs in the event of lawsuits against the persons insured and damages in the event liability is established for such wrongful acts as errors, omissions, misleading statements, and neglect or breach of duty.

Earthquake insurance
Insurance covering damage caused by an earthquake as defined in the contract.

Effective date
The date on which an insurance policy or bond goes into effect, and from which protection is furnished.

Embezzlement
The fraudulent use of money or property, which has been entrusted to one's care.

Employers' liability insurance
Coverage against common law liability of an employer for accidents to employees, as distinguished from liability imposed by a worker's compensation law.

Endorsement
An endorsement is a modification that is added or attached to an existing policy. See p. 56.

Errors and omissions insurance (E&O, Professional liability insurance or Malpractice Insurance)
This type of insurance protects professionals from the financial consequences of being sued for negligent advice or service.

Estoppel
This is a legal bar to asserting a right owing to the conduct of the person who once held the right. See p. 78*ff.* See also **Waiver**.

Excess Insurance
Excess insurance means insurance which is payable only when loss exceeds a specified amount or when other coverage is exhausted.

Exclusions
Exclusions are events or circumstances described in policies which, if they happen in a way that relates to the loss, result in there being no coverage. See p. 58.

Expiration
The date upon which a policy will end.

Exposure
Exposure is the vulnerability to loss of an insurer (generally) or an insured (usually in respect of liability insurance).

First party
The first party is the person directly protected by the insurance policy. He or she is usually the "policyholder" or "named insured" but there may be other people, named or unnamed, who are covered as well. In contrast a "third party" is someone who may benefit from the insurance but only indirectly. Liability insurance is sometimes called "third party" insurance. This is because, while it directly protects the first party from the consequences of being sued, it indirectly benefits the third party who is the person suing the first party and who, if successful in the suit, will ultimately receive the insurance money.

Floater policy
A floater policy covers the same risk (same property, same perils) at a number of locations. It is used for property frequently moved from one location to another.

Form
An insurance policy itself or riders and endorsements attached to it.

Fortuitous event
An unforeseen accident, *i.e.*, an event neither deliberately caused by the insured nor bound to happen in the ordinary course. See pp. 4 and 69.

Fraud
Fraud involves a deliberate act or omission intended to gain an insurance benefit by deceit. It may include fabricated claims, inflation or padding of genuine claims or false statements on insurance applications. The consequence of fraud is forfeiture of coverage without return of premium and, possibly, criminal prosecution or punitive damages. See p. 75.

Grace period
A period after the premium due date, during which an overdue premium may be paid without penalty. The policy remains in force throughout this period. See p. 26.

Guaranteed replacement cost endorsement (building)
Replacement cost coverage pays for replacement without reduction for depreciation (see **Actual cash value** and **Depreciation**). A guaranteed replacement cost endorsement covers any shortfall in the event that the replacement cost of a building is underestimated.

Hazard
A specific situation that increases the likelihood of a loss arising from a peril, or that may influence the extent of the loss. For example, accident, sickness, fire, flood, liability, burglary, and explosion are perils. Slippery floors, unsanitary conditions, shingled roofs, congested traffic, unguarded premises and un-inspected boilers are also hazards.

Hold-harmless clause/agreement
A clause/agreement written into a contract by which one party agrees to release another party from all legal liability, such as a retailer who agrees to release the manufacturer from legal liability if the product injures someone.

Homeowner insurance
An elective combination of coverages for the risks of owning a home. It may include cover for fire, burglary, vandalism, earthquake, and other perils.

Indemnity
Indemnity is the restoration, but no more than that, of the measurable financial consequences of loss. Restoration may be in whole or in part, by payment, repair, or replacement. See pp. 4, 6, 39, 95, 101.

Indirect or consequential loss (or damage)
Loss resulting from a peril, but not caused directly or immediately by the peril. For example, loss of property due to fire is a direct loss, while the loss of rental income as the result of the fire would be an indirect loss.

Insurance
Insurance is a contract between an insurance company and its customer for a specific period of time. It protects the customer financially against a loss. Insurance is also a mechanism for spreading risk, because it shares the losses of the few among the many. See pp. 1 and 117.

Insurance Bureau of Canada (IBC)
The Insurance Bureau of Canada is the national trade association for the companies that insure the homes, cars and businesses of Canadians. IBC's membership includes the companies that provide more than 90 per cent of the home, car and business insurance sold in Canada.

IBC works on behalf of member companies and their customers to advocate for public policies that create and maintain a healthy insurance marketplace that serves insurers and consumers. IBC facilitates communications, seeks consensus and, when possible, undertakes solutions to common insurance concerns.

Insurance policy
A policy is a document setting out the terms of the contract of insurance. It is usual for a policy to be issued but, for most forms of insurance, is not a requirement. See p. 53.

Insured
The person (or persons) whose risk of financial loss from an insured peril is protected by the policy (sometimes called the policyholder or assured).

Insurer
The insurance company; sometimes called the assurer.

Liability
This is a legally enforceable financial obligation. Liability insurance pays for the damages or losses of others for which you are legally responsible. See p. 91.

Liability limits
The amount or amounts beyond which an insurance company does not protect you on a particular policy. For example, where there is a liability limit on an auto insurance policy of $1 million, any amount of a judgment in excess of $1 million, is the responsibility of the insured.

Lloyd's
This term is used to describe a group or group of individuals, known as syndicates (not insurance companies), that assume liability through an underwriter. Each individual assumes a portion of the insurance assumed by the underwriter.

Loss of use insurance
Extra coverage you purchase to compensate you for the loss of use of property, if it cannot be used because of a loss covered by the policy. This is most common in auto insurance. Loss of use insurance will have your insurance company pay for the use of a rental car while yours is being repaired.

Material misrepresentation
Where a policyholder or applicant makes a false statement of material (important) fact on the application, he or she is guilty of a material misrepresentation which may result in loss of coverage. See Chapter 5.

Mediation
Mediation is a process of dispute resolution wherein a neutral third party seeks to facilitate a settlement. Unlike arbitrators, mediators generally have no authority to impose a settlement. See p. 90.

Moral hazard
An attitude that increases the probability of loss from a peril. The attitude of, "It's insured; so why worry?" is an example of a moral hazard. See p. 5.

Mortgage clause
This is a term in a policy protecting the interests of a mortgage holder wherein the insurer agrees to notify it of changes in the policy and that its right to be indemnified in the event of loss of or damage to the insured property is unaffected by acts or omissions of the insured. See p. 109.

Mutual insurance company
Mutual insurance companies are home, car and business insurance companies without stockholders. The owners are the policyholders. It is the policyholders (the owners) who elect the directors of the company. Each policyholder is allowed one vote. See p. 119.

Named insured
The person in whose name the policy is issued, the policyholder, is often referred to as a "named insured". Technically, he or she would be the first party to the contract, the second party being the insurance company that issues the policy.

Named perils coverage
This covers only those perils, such as fire and theft, that are specifically named or included in the home insurance policy.

No-fault
This is a form of automobile insurance that provides some compensation for personal injury and death arising out of a motor vehicle accident. Payments are made without regard to the negligence of anyone directly involved in the accident. However, some forms of fault are relevant. For example, a drunk driver will be disqualified from some benefits. Moreover, a driver responsible for an accident will likely experience an increase in future premiums.

Occurrence
An occurrence is an event that results in an insured loss. In some lines of insurance, such as liability, it is not necessarily an accident that is sudden or unexpected. An occurrence can result from continuous or repeated exposure, leading to bodily injury or property damage that is neither expected nor intended by the insured.

Optional coverage
In automobile insurance, optional coverage is a commonly used term for insurance that is not required by law, *e.g.*, coverage for fire, theft or comprehensive claims.

For home insurance, optional coverage is that which is not normally included in standard home insurance policies but which can be purchased separately; *e.g.*, coverage for damage from earthquakes, furnace oil spills and sewer back-up.

Package policy
This is a combination of the coverages normally contained in separate policies in one contract with one premium.

Peril
This is the cause of loss or damage. A homeowner's policy, for example, insures against perils like windstorms, fire and theft.

Personal articles floater
Provides all risk coverage, subject to reasonable exclusions, for valuable items such as furs, jewellery, cameras, silverware, *etc*. The items are generally listed by description and value. Note: this is different from a personal effects floater.

Personal effects/property floater
This covers personal property, anywhere in the world. Typically, it is issued in one of two forms, all risk (or broad) form or specified perils form.

Personal lines insurance
Home or auto insurance for individuals, rather than commercial lines insurance for businesses.

Personal property
Home insurance covers the contents of a home and other personal property that the named insured and members of the household own, wear or use (including clothing, cameras, furniture, *etc.*) while on the premises. It may even cover personal property of others (excluding roomers or boarders who are not related to the insured) that is not otherwise insured. There will normally be cover for personal property while it is temporarily away from the home anywhere in the world. Personal property not normally kept at home is not covered. Personal property in a warehouse is usually covered against theft without time limit; but other perils may not be covered, or may be covered only up to 30 days.

Physical damage coverage
The physical damage section of an automobile policy provides cover for damage to the insured vehicle. It may cover all perils, collision or upset, all perils other than collision or upset (comprehensive) or specified perils.

Policy limit
The maximum amount a policy will pay, either overall or under a particular coverage.

Pool
This is an organization of insurers or reinsurers through which particular types of risk are underwritten with premiums, losses and expenses shared in agreed ratios.

Premium
The premium is the sum of money paid by the insured in return for the insurer's acceptance of the risk covered by the contract. See pp. 25 and 41.

Private passenger vehicle
A private passenger vehicle is a vehicle not used as a commercial vehicle. For example, if a small van is used as a family vehicle, it is considered a private passenger vehicle. However, if this same van is used as a full-time delivery vehicle, it is considered a commercial vehicle.

Product recall insurance
Designed for manufacturers, this optional coverage insures against the unexpected cost of recalling a product from the market due to: faulty design, errors in manufacturing, or intentional tampering, not caused or known by the insured, that may cause harm to your customers.

Professional liability insurance
See **Errors and omissions insurance**.

Proof of loss
Proof of loss is a formal statement by the insured when making a claim to the insurance company regarding the loss. The purpose of the proof of loss is to give the insurance company information about the loss to enable it to determine its liability under the policy. See p. 74.

Property and casualty insurance
This is the branch of the insurance industry that covers home, car and business insurance (the other branch of the industry is life and health insurance).

Property and Casualty Insurance Compensation Corporation (PACICC)
In the unlikely event of the collapse of a home, car or business insurance company in Canada, the industry-funded, non-profit PACICC will respond to claims of policyholders under most policies issued by home, car and business insurance companies. This protection is extended automatically to eligible policies.

Quote
An estimate of the cost of insurance, based on information you have supplied to the insurance company.

Rate
Commonly confused with the premium. The rate is the amount that insurance companies are allowed by government to charge.

Reinsurance
The purchase of insurance by an insurance company from another insurance company (reinsurer) to provide it protection against large losses on cases it has already insured.

Replacement cost
The cost of replacing property without deduction for depreciation. See also **Actual cash value**. See p. 86.

Residual market
A system through which insurance is made available to buyers that represent unusually high risks. This is sometimes referred to as the "Facility Association".

Rider
A rider is an amendment to the policy used to add or delete coverage. See also **Endorsement**.

Risk management
Risk management ensures that an organization has identified and understands the risks to which it is exposed and has created and implemented an effective plan to prevent losses or reduce their impact if a loss occurs. A risk management plan includes strategies and techniques for recognizing and confronting these

threats. Risk management may be as uncomplicated as asking and answering three basic questions:

1. What can go wrong?
2. What can be done to prevent the harm from occurring and, if it does occur, to respond to it?
3. If something happens, how will the loss be compensated?

Salvage
On paying for a total loss of property, an insurance company is entitled to what remains of, or what is recovered of the property. This is a right of salvage. See pp. 17, 73 and 95.

Second party
The insurance company that issues the policy is considered the second party of the two parties needed to form a legal contract. The first party is the policyholder.

Statutory accident benefits (Ontario)
This component of auto insurance provides benefits to insured persons injured in motor vehicle accidents regardless of cause. This includes medical and care benefits and income replacement benefits.

Subrogation
An insurer may recover some or all of its costs incurred in settling a claim by suing others responsible for the loss. The insurer is able to do this because it is subrogated to the rights of its customer. See p. 96*ff*.

Surety
This is an agreement to assume the obligation to pay the debt or answer the default of another.

Terrorism exclusion
This is a clause excluding damage caused by terrorism from cover. A common definition of terrorism is: ideologically motivated unlawful act or acts, including but not limited to the use of violence or force or threat of violence or force, committed by or on behalf of any group(s), organization(s) or government(s) for the purpose of influencing any government and/or instilling fear in the public or a section of the public.

Third party
A third party is anyone who is not a party to an insurance contract. In some circumstances a third party may benefit from an insurance contract indirectly. See Chapter 15.

Total loss
A total loss of property occurs where it can be said there is nothing left of value. The most common example is complete destruction of the property or its disappearance. The term is sometimes (inaccurately) used to mean a loss requiring the maximum amount a policy will pay.

Underwriter
The term underwriter is used in several ways. It may refer to an employee of an insurance company who examines applications and decides whether or not the company should accept them based on the risk presented. It may refer to the insurer itself or to a person accepting responsibility for insurance on behalf of a syndicate that agrees to cover all or part of a particular risk. See pp. 29 and 119. See also **Lloyd's**.

Underwriting profit or loss
This is the amount of money which an insurance company gains or loses as a result of its insurance operations. It excludes investment transactions and federal income taxes.

Uninsured/underinsured motorist coverage
A form of insurance that pays for bodily injury or property damage caused by the owner or operator of an uninsured or inadequately insured automobile.

Valuable papers insurance
Insurance that protects a business' valuable documents, such as architectural drawings, law libraries, medical reference books, *etc.*

Valuation
See appraisal.

Valued Policy
A valued policy contains an agreed value on insured policy. In the event of total loss insurance is based on the agreed value regardless of actual current market value. See p. 86.

Waiver
Intentionally giving up a right. A waiver can also be a document or a clause in a document that states that rights are being given up or waived. See p. 78*ff.* See also **Estoppel**.

Warranty
A warranty is a term in an insurance contract wherein a party, usually the insured, undertakes to do or refrain from doing something in order to maintain coverage. A warranty is similar to a condition but must be strictly, as opposed to substantially, complied with. See p. 58.

Writing off
When insured property is lost or totally destroyed in that sense that it would cost more to repair it than replace it, it is written off by the insurer. See p. 95.

Index